UNACCOMPANIE

CRITICAL PERSPECTIVES ON YOUTH

General Editors: Amy L. Best, Lorena Garcia, and Jessica K. Taft

Unaccompanied

The Plight of Immigrant Youth at the Border

Emily Ruehs-Navarro

NEW YORK UNIVERSITY PRESS

New York

NEW YORK UNIVERSITY PRESS
New York
www.nyupress.org

References to Internet websites (URLs) were accurate at the time of writing. Neither the author nor New York University Press is responsible for URLs that may have expired or changed since the manuscript was prepared.

Library of Congress Cataloging-in-Publication Data
Names: Ruehs-Navarro, Emily, author.
Title: Unaccompanied : the plight of immigrant youth at the border / Emily Ruehs-Navarro.
Description: New York, N.Y. : NYU Press, 2022. | Series: Critical perspectives on youth | Includes bibliographical references and index.
Identifiers: LCCN 2021012500 | ISBN 9781479821099 (hardback) | ISBN 9781479838615 (paperback) | ISBN 9781479806423 (ebook) | ISBN 9781479838493 (ebook other)
Subjects: LCSH: Children of immigrants—Education—United States. | Border security—United States. | Child welfare—United States. | Neoliberalism—United States.
Classification: LCC LC3746 .R84 2022 | DDC 371.826/912—dc23
LC record available at https://lccn.loc.gov/2021012500

New York University Press books are printed on acid-free paper, and their binding materials are chosen for strength and durability. We strive to use environmentally responsible suppliers and materials to the greatest extent possible in publishing our books.

Manufactured in the United States of America

10 9 8 7 6 5 4 3 2 1
Also available as an ebook

For Silvia. May every day be a little brighter and better than the day before.

For Sofia. May you always approach the world with compassion and wonder.

CONTENTS

ABBREVIATIONS

CBP—Customs and Border Protection

DHS—Department of Homeland Security

ICE—Immigration and Customs Enforcement

INS—Immigration and Naturalization Service

IRB—Institutional Review Board

ORR—Office of Refugee Resettlement

SIJS—Special Immigrant Juvenile Status

TVPRA—Trafficking Victims Protection Reauthorization Act

UNHCR—United Nations High Commissioner for Refugees

Introduction

Para mí hasta ahorita, no es una vida que ha sido normal. Es
como un trauma que uno tiene para acordarse toda la vida.

(For me, up until this point, life has not been normal. It is
like a trauma that you will remember the rest of your life.)
—Nicolas, age eighteen

There were two primary reasons why Nicolas decided at age sixteen to
leave his small town in the Amazonian region of Ecuador. The first: "*La
vida es medio dura allá*" (Life is pretty hard there). Nicolas had left school
to work on a cacao farm in order to support his mother and younger
brother. He felt trapped by the work, not making as much as he wanted
and seeing few opportunities to move ahead in life. His father already
lived in the United States, so Nicolas anticipated that reunification would
provide better economic opportunity. The second reason: Nicolas was
terrified. His family had inadvertently become the target of a criminal
network. His uncle had disappeared during his own migration to the
United States, and his family wanted answers. Although he had been gone
for nearly a decade, a *curandero* (a healer believed to possess clairvoyant
abilities) had told the family that he was still alive, enslaved in Mexico.
The family continued their desperate search. They could not find him in
any registries, there was no documentation of his death, but there was
also no documentation that he was still alive. The police could not—or
would not—help the family. And then, the threats started. The family
had looked where they were not welcome, and a group of men attacked
them on motorcycles, leaving them injured but alive. The men warned
Nicolas's family that someone would be coming to kill them.

Nicolas left Ecuador soon after. He anticipated that migrating to the
United States would help him to alleviate some of this horror. What he
learned, however, is that trauma, unlike people, is not contained by bor-

ders. For Nicolas, the trauma of his life is knowing the exact locations of every country between Ecuador and the United States, because when he was sixteen, he traveled them all with a group of strangers, by car and by foot, with terror as his most faithful companion. Trauma is being placed in a prison when he crossed the border to the United States—a place so cold and accusing that he began to believe that he deserved to be there. Trauma is reuniting with a father whom he did not know, the dashing of hopes that he would be able to bond with the stranger whom he was supposed to love. Trauma is the ever-looming threat of a failed court case and deportation back to the original fear.

Nicolas feels very alone in his experiences of fear, flight, and trauma as an adolescent. *No es una vida que ha sido normal.* This is not a normal life. In reality, however, he is not alone. Young people have been crossing international borders by themselves for as long as the United States has taken these records. In recent decades, the United States has built an entire infrastructure around these youth with the hopes of supporting youth into their transition to American life and in their fight for legal belonging. In this book, I explore the intersections between this system of humanitarian assistance and youths' histories. I show that the adult professionals who intend to help youth do so within the restraints of a system that works at the crossroads of border security, racialized child welfare, and neoliberal humanitarianism. Wittingly or unwittingly, these professionals often find themselves complicit in practices that further harm immigrant youth. Yet, despite these structural limitations, youth in this research are never passive: as they navigate the humanitarian systems in the United States, they make individual decisions to work with, against, or around the services they encounter.

Landscapes of Aid for Immigrant Youth

Over the past decade, the number of youth migrating alone to the United States has increased significantly. While youth migrate by themselves from across the globe, the majority of these young people come from Mexico and the Northern Triangle region of El Salvador, Guatemala, and Honduras. In 2014, the number of youth from the Northern Triangle region skyrocketed, placing these young people into the national spotlight. Only five years prior, in Fiscal Year (FY) 2009, the United States recorded just

3,304 youth from this region, while in FY 2014, there were 51,705 youth detained at the border. By FY 2019, Customs and Border Protection recorded 62,748 apprehensions from the Northern Triangle and an additional 10,487 youth detained from Mexico.[1] These waves were dominated by teen boys, although girls have made up between a quarter and a third of the youth, over the last several years, and children under the age of twelve make up between 10 and 20 percent of those apprehended.

The increase in youth migration corresponds with an overall increase in migration from this region. An extensive study conducted by the United Nations World Food Programme points to intersecting environmental, economic, and social shocks that contribute to migration decisions.[2] In particular, the report reveals that droughts starting in 2014 have significantly increased the level of food insecurity and unemployment in the region, creating states of emergency for households. The report further points to sustained violence, particularly in El Salvador, which saw a dramatic increase in homicides in 2014.[3] In fact, a report by the United Nations High Commissioner for Refugees (UNHCR) on 404 children suggests that 58 percent of child migrants were "forcibly displaced because they suffered or faced harms that indicated a potential or actual need for international protection."[4] In the same study, 48 percent of children interviewed discussed violence by armed criminal actors in their communities. This violence has deep roots in the United States' intervention in the region.[5]

Within these larger migratory trends, youth migration is also linked to several additional push and pull factors. In some cases, youth migrate to reunify with family members who are residing in the United States. US laws have systematically separated families across borders, and youths' solitary migration is often the result of these separations. Youth may also make decisions to emigrate based on violence within the home; in the UNHCR study, 21 percent of the youth interviewed reported home violence as a push factor in their migration. Notably, while there exists a common refrain in American media that increased child migration during the Obama administration was due to the perception of lax immigration policies, only one child in the study reported this to be the case.[6]

There are a variety of ways that youth embark alone on international migration, dependent often on their financial resources. Youth with the fewest resources available may make the journey across Mexico riding the tops of trains.[7] Youth with more resources may journey through Mexico on buses with fake documents or even by planes with human smugglers.[8] Once at the US-Mexico border, youth may cross alone or with a smuggler, hiding in trucks or crossing the Rio Grande on rafts, and walking the desert by foot. The commonality in these experiences lies in youths' vulnerability in clandestine, international crossings. While all migrants are susceptible to violence and exploitation, these risks are even greater for young people.[9]

Upon arrival to the United States, there have historically been three possible outcomes. The first is that the young person enters into the country undetected by border control and becomes a member of US society. While some organizations reach out to these youth, they often remain hidden, sometimes forming their own support groups.[10] The second possibility is that the young person is apprehended by border enforcement and is subjected to "voluntary return." This is the case for most Mexican children, who are typically deported within hours of apprehension.[11] However, many of these children will often return immediately with another attempt to cross into the United States; one report found that 15 percent of Mexican children in detention have been apprehended at least six times.[12] Finally, as stipulated in the Trafficking Victims Protection Reauthorization Act (TVRPA), youth from non-contiguous countries and Mexican youth who appear to have a viable claim to asylum are legally permitted to argue their case in immigration court.[13] These youth are held in detention by Customs and Border Protection (CBP) for up to seventy-two hours before being transferred into a shelter system run by the Office of Refugee Resettlement (ORR).[14] Youth are simultaneously placed in deportation proceedings.

The ORR is required to place children in the "least restrictive setting that is in the best interests of the child."[15] On the basis of an assessment of psychological health, behavioral concerns, and criminal history, youth are detained in shelters that vary in degree of security, therapeutic treatment, and concerns for "tender-age" or pregnant teenagers.[16] Youth may have their first court date while in this shelter and are often brought to court by the shelter facility staff. In the fiscal year 2018, the average length of stay in these state-sponsored shelters was sixty days.[17]

Youth are released from these shelters once government workers find appropriate placements for them with family or friends or in the foster care system. These placement decisions are made by government-contracted social workers who put possible sponsors through an arduous process to ensure the safest possible placement for the youth. Historically, the government did not contact youth once they were released from the ORR facilities. However, the ORR changed this policy recently to provide postrelease services to youth who raised concerns. In 2018, just under 29 percent of youth received these services.[18] As of August 2015, the ORR also began issuing well-being calls to youth within thirty to thirty-seven days of release. They report that in the first quarter of fiscal year 2016, workers reached 87 percent of youth and 90 percent of their sponsors.[19] These calls raised relatively few issues, with only 5 percent being referred to assistance for legal and educational needs and only 0.1 percent needing to be reported to state child protective services or law enforcement. Further, only 0.5 percent of well-being checks found that the child no longer lived with the sponsor.[20]

Since youth have historically been released into communities with no further government support, some activists have argued that there needs to be more assistance upon release.[21] Over the past decade and a half, individual organizations have stepped up to fill the gap. In 2003, the Young Center for Immigrant Children's Rights was the first program to provide volunteer child advocates for youth who raised specific concerns regarding complicated legal cases or barriers in community resettlement. The advocates often meet with youth while they are detained in ORR shelters and then follow the youth upon release, helping them to gain access to legal assistance, education, and other resources. In theory, the volunteer advocate is the only individual who will remain with the child throughout his or her entire case. However, in practice, this has proven more difficult for advocates on the ground.[22]

Once released to families, sponsors, or foster parents, youth continue to fight their deportation proceedings in court. While youth are not guaranteed access to an attorney, the government provides lists of pro-bono and low-cost attorneys in their areas, and some of these attorneys provide case screenings after group hearings. There are several relief options for unaccompanied youth, although the most common are asylum, Special Immigrant Juvenile Status (SIJS), T Visas, and U Visas. First, asylum is based on the claim that an individual either has no country or is unable to return to his or her country because of a fear of persecution due to membership in certain groups. Approval of asylum applications varies drastically by region. For example, in the San Francisco office, which covers the Pacific Northwest, 86 percent of unaccompanied youth asylum cases are approved. In comparison, only 15 percent are approved in the Chicago office, which covers fifteen midwestern states.[23] The fear of gang persecution is often the most relevant asylum claim; however, it was historically a difficult claim to win, and more recently, the Trump administration has more aggressively blocked these claims.[24] Second, SIJS is granted if a child is unable to return to his or her home country due to abandonment, abuse, or neglect by one or both parents. Youth who have legal counsel are often eligible for SIJS, but most children lack this legal counsel.[25] T Visas are granted in the case of human trafficking and other crimes, although these cases may be difficult to identify. Finally, a U Visa is available for immigrants who have been victims of a crime and are able to provide the authorities with helpful information regarding criminal activity for investigation. In addition, children may be granted prosecutorial discretion, which does not provide a pathway to legal residency but administratively closes the removal proceedings. The Obama administration also granted parole to youth who did not qualify for refugee status, allowing them to continue to live and work temporarily in the United States. However, the Trump administration reversed this policy.[26]

Human rights groups have presented numerous concerns about the immigration process and children's access to these options. While many unaccompanied youth may be eligible recipients of these programs, their lack of legal representation often inhibits this process. Other issues raised by human rights groups include the lack of a best-interest standard, inadequate protections, inappropriate service-delivery models, and lack of reintegration support.[27] Further, youth are often in need of wide-reaching community support in order to navigate the legal system. Support from educators, community social workers, counselors, and other community members is essential in youths' ability to fully integrate into their communities, both legally and socially.

When youth such as Nicolas leave their homes and journey to the United States, they enter into the borderlands, a space that is not just geographical but also ideological. Chicana cultural theorist Gloria Anzaldúa suggests that borders exist to create dichotomies of belonging. Crossing into the United States does not mean that youth belong; rather, youth remain on the edges of American institutions and in a perpetual borderland. Yet, there are many structures that are set up explicitly to help youths' integration into the country. When youth reside on the borders of families, the field of family reunification (as an extension of the child shelter/detention system) is meant to help youth find adults who will become their guardians. When youth exist on the border of the state, the field of legal aid works to help youth find legal status. When youth exist on the border between adolescence and adulthood, the field of immigrant student outreach works to integrate youth into the education system and away from labor. The fields of family reunification, legal aid, and immigrant student outreach compose the landscape of aid for immigrant youth.

Many individuals throughout these fields work diligently to provide youth with heartfelt assistance and support. However, despite their best intentions, the apparatus of aid was built upon well-established institutions and ideologies that have a strong influence on how work with unaccompanied immigrant youth is carried out. Workers must contend with a long history of border enforcement and the confluence of immigration enforcement and the criminal justice system. They work within the same racialized and classed ideologies about youth that have created the child welfare system, relying on middle-class and American ideals of childhood and adulthood. And, they operate under the particular logics of neoliberal humanitarianism, which guide how youth are constructed as children and victims. I argue that because the landscape of aid for unaccompanied youth was built upon these histories, many workers find themselves complicit in a range of practices that further harm youth and their communities: surveilling families, ignoring trauma, reifying cultural and racial hierarchies, enforcing harmful dichotomies between childhood and adulthood, and criminalizing migrants. The work of helping unaccompanied youth is filled with paradoxes and ethical dilemmas that enact further harm on youth and pull well-meaning professionals into questionable practices. In the following section, I further explore the histories and logics that underpin this system.

Histories and Logics of Aid for Immigrant Youth

Border Enforcement and Crimmigration

As immigrants, unaccompanied youth today enter the United States amidst a long and contentious history of immigration policy and border enforcement. Questions about who can enter the country and who can access citizenship have dominated American politics for much of its history. These questions have often been answered on the basis of race, nationality, gender, and the ever-changing supply and demand of foreign labor.[28] From the Chinese Exclusion Act, which limited Chinese immigration and increased a demand for smuggled Chinese workers,[29] to the Bracero period, which brought in Mexican workers under abusive conditions, the demand for labor has always been matched by xenophobic policies that have restricted the rights of migrants in the country.

The current state of immigration politics can be traced back to the mid-1980s, when there was renewed attention to the perceived dysfunction of the US-Mexico border. Sociologist Douglas Massey and his colleagues explain that the 1986 Immigration Reform and Control Act "transformed what had been a well-functioning, predictable system into a noisy, clunking, dysfunctional machine that generated a host of unanticipated outcomes that were in neither country's interests."[30] A flurry of federal, state, and local policies followed, responding to the public's fear by increasing funding for border control and effectively militarizing the region. Policies such as the 1990 Immigration Reform Act, Operation Blockade in El Paso in 1993, and Operation Safeguard in Tucson in 1994 all worked with a prevention-through-deterrence strategy. In 1994, Operation Gatekeeper increased the number of border patrol agents, erected further barriers, and introduced more technology, such as sensors and biometric-data collection, to deter migrants from established crossing routes in California. In response, migrants and smugglers simply moved their routes to more desolate locations.[31] In 1996, President Clinton signed the Illegal Immigration Reform and Immigrant Responsibility Act, which, once again, tightened barriers at the border, advanced border technology, and increased criminal and civil penalties for illegal entry.[32]

The terror attacks of September 11, 2001, marked yet another era for the United States. While the previous decades had been preoccupied with security, in this era, the threat of terrorism became one of the primary justifications for securing the border with even greater zeal. Whereas the border was seen as a place of chaos and disorder prior to 9/11, it was now viewed as "a conduit for weapons of mass destruction and terrorists."[33] Immigrants themselves quickly became conflated with terrorists.[34] This belief has manifested in the acute militarization of the region and increased scrutiny of and racist attitudes towards immigrants.[35] Indeed, immigration politics became so intertwined with national security interests that the Homeland Security Act of 2002 reorganized immigration agencies, disbanding the Immigration and Naturalization Service and placing Customs and Border Protection (CBP) and Immigration and Customs Enforcement (ICE) under the purview of the Department of Homeland Security (DHS). The militarization of the border region continued to intensify, and in 2004 Congress passed the Defense Authorization Act, which provided funding, when needed, for the National Guard to assist at the border in the event of "a threat of aggression against the United States."[36] Operation Streamline, in 2005, enacted a zero-tolerance policy, criminalizing undocumented crossing and turning undocumented immigrants over to marshals instead of to immigration court or back to Mexico.[37] Just a year later, Congress authorized further construction of a border wall with the Secure Fence Act of 2006.[38]

Despite the increasing resources allocated by the federal government, individual states also continued to flex their muscles at the border with increasing force in the mid-2000s. For example, with Operation Jump Start in 2006, President Bush deployed over six thousand National Guard members to the border.[39] At the same time, Texas's Operation Linebacker directed $6 million in state resources to border counties for extra "manpower, specialized equipment and planning resources," as well as funds to "train local volunteers and strengthen community awareness and involvement in border protection."[40] In the following year, the governor of Texas issued Operation Rio Grande, stating, "The state will not wait for Washington to take all the necessary actions. What we can do, we will. Starting now."[41]

Increased border security has come hand in hand with increased deportation and the criminalization of migrants. Over the past three decades, multiple policies have been implemented that have increased the number of deportable crimes and reclassified undocumented entry into the United States as a misdemeanor and reentry as a felony.[42] At the same time, the United States has entered into an era of mass incarceration, raising concerns about the overpopulation in the prison system. Sociologist Patricia Macías-Rojas argues that in response to this, the government implemented the Criminal Alien Program, which focused on deportation of so-called criminal aliens.[43] This created the rise of "crimmigration," in which criminal law and immigrant law became inexorably linked. These policies are also gendered. Sociologists Tanya Golash-Boza and Pierrette Hondagneu-Sotelo refer to modern deportation policies as a "gendered racial removal program."[44] While historically many deportation policies were aimed at women in order to deter family settlement, the focus has shifted over the last few decades. They argue that the criminalization of Black and Latino men in US society—along with male unemployment and the War on Terror—has resulted in a deportation regime that targets working-class Latino men.

Today, the public continues to view the border as a dangerous and porous region, guided by the belief that incoming migrants threaten both the economic system and national security. Former president Donald Trump campaigned on the promise to build "an impenetrable physical wall on the southern border, on day one," stating clearly on his website, "Mexico will pay for the wall."[45] Trump fulfilled his promises to crack down on undocumented immigration with multiple changes in immigration policies. Among these changes, Trump signed an executive order with the purpose of "enhancing public safety" that threatened to restrict funding to sanctuary cities—jurisdictions whose law enforcement officials do not readily cooperate with federal immigration enforcement.[46] His administration launched a new office through Immigration and Customs Enforcement called the Victims of Immigration Crime Engagement Office, which explicitly serves "crime victims and their families who have been affected by crimes committed by individuals with a nexus to immigration," and, among other objectives, provides lists of crimes committed by undocumented immigrants.[47] His administration engaged in horrific tactics such as separating children from their parents in order to deter undocumented immigrants from entering the country. He increasingly threatened to ramp up deportations, through initiatives such as the ICE raid on poultry farms in Mississippi in mid-2019, in which nearly seven hundred community members were arrested. And, the administration has sought to prosecute parents of unaccompanied youth for having colluded with criminal smuggling organizations.[48]

The thread throughout the history of the border is the constant fear that surrounds the politics of immigration. Migrant bodies have been viewed as diseased, a menace to the biological integrity of the country, and a threat to national fertility rates.[49] Migrant cultures are blamed for corroding American values and morality.[50] The undocumented are believed to "diminish the value of citizenship," drive down wages, and hurt the economy.[51] Indeed, the very existence of undocumented immigrants is seen as a social problem.[52] Anthropologist Leo Chavez calls the accumulation of these discourses regarding Mexican and Central American immigrants the "Latino Threat Narrative," and provides numerous examples of the way discourse is framed by this threat narrative, using themes of invasion, loss of control, and the *Reconquista*—an allusion to the original founding of the US-Mexico border and the belief that Mexicans are attempting to reestablish sovereignty in these territories.[53] Anthropologist Gilberto Rosas refers to this as a "dark fantasy"—a nightmare that legitimizes warfare on the border.[54]

The securitization history has significantly influenced how young migrants are treated in the United States today. In her seminal work, cultural theorist Gloria Anzaldúa suggested that the borderlands operate to distinguish those who belong from those who do not, those who are safe from those who are dangerous.[55] Youth migrants must constantly struggle with their position in these dichotomies. They are burdened by the history of fear mongering of brown-skinned migrants, and they must contend with the relentless criminalization of their very existence.

Racialized Child Welfare and the Office of Refugee Resettlement

Response to youth migrants is also mediated through the lens of childhood. In the United States, there is a persistent belief that children are particularly vulnerable and deserving of protection.[56] These beliefs come from a relatively recent shift in modern society's views about children. Through changes brought about by modernism in America over the last century, many children are now freed from the burdens of labor and have access to full-time education.[57] Indeed, in only the last century and a half, children have transformed from "useful" workers to emotionally "priceless" members of families.[58] Connected to these shifting beliefs, a system of child welfare has emerged in order to protect children from the burdens of adulthood and the violence of adults. Yet, beliefs about child welfare have not been granted equally to all children. In fact, the modern system of child protection has been sullied by racism, classism, and a suspicion of independent teenagers, even as it has evolved to protect these children and youth.

Law scholar John E. B. Myers suggests that there have been three eras of child protection in modern American history.[59] First, from colonial times to the late 1800s, he notes, there was no organized protection for the rights of children, although there were some criminal prosecutions against adults who abused children. This changed in 1874, with the advent of the New York Society for the Prevention of Cruelty to Children, which was a private organization seeking to reduce harm against the young. That year marked a shift in child protection, and in this second era, private organizations became the primary guardians of children's rights. While the government created the Children's Bureau in 1912, this did not specifically work against child maltreatment. In the 1960s, there was a renewed interest in children's rights, largely led by a physician movement against child abuse. In this third era, the federal and state governments moved to form new legislation and government services for children. These changes included amendments to the Social Security Act in 1962 to fund welfare services and the Child Abuse Prevention and Treatment Act of 1974. Since the 1960s, there has been considerable progress in working against child sex abuse and protecting the rights of foster children.

However, throughout these eras, child protection often intersected with race, class, and nationality and has been a form of control and domination over families. In some cases, organizations have denied services to children on the basis of the child's social location. For example, Black children were explicitly excluded from some of the original legislation designed to protect children, such as laws involving the foster care system.[60] Just as frequently, child protection has been used to control poor children and children of color. There are numerous historical and contemporary examples of the control of populations and families under the guise of child rescue. Criminologist Anthony Platt suggests that movements to "save" children in the early 1900s operated out of a middle- and upper-class desire to create social control around perceived delinquents.[61] These movements effectively worked to target poor children, especially in cities, and enforced the dependency of children on families and away from perceived "deviant" institutions such as dance halls and saloons. These "child savers" typically relied on feminized values of home and family to judge whether a family was fulfilling its obligation to the children—values based on criteria that few poor families could meet.

During this same period, religious-based organizations that were purported to save children targeted immigrant youth from cities to place them with adoptive families in rural areas, sending them on "orphan trains." While the explicit purpose of these organizations was to save indigent youth, critics argued that a lack of oversight meant that families often used these children as slave laborers and that the movement was more focused on ridding urban areas of undesirable elements.[62] Additionally, race has always been intertwined in the ways these movements have been carried out. In her book *The Great Arizona Orphan Abduction*, historian Linda Gordon follows the story of a Catholic organization that worked to send orphans to Catholic families.[63] One such group of Irish orphans was sent to Mexican families in Arizona. This led to an uproar in the community, where white community members led a vigilante attack to "free" the orphans from their new Mexican families.

Child welfare measures have also been used in nation-building projects. Native American boarding schools in the late 1800s and early 1900s were constructed with the explicit intention to acculturate Native American youth with white American values and beliefs. Run by educators and reformers, these schools often claimed to save children from broken homes. Simultaneously, the schools claimed to provide opportunities to children through assimilation into white society and the removal of Native culture. However, between the abuse of children in the schools, the deliberate erasure of culture, and the intentional separation of children and parents, the legacy of these schools has been disastrous for Native communities.[64] Similarly, Operation Pedro Pan, which was a partnership between the State Department and the Catholic Welfare Bureau of Miami, was meant explicitly to protect the children of Cuban families who expressed fears about indoctrination under the new Castro government. However, the removal and fostering of over fourteen thousand

Cuban children was just as much about Cold War foreign policy and efforts to undermine the new communist regime.[65]

More recently, evangelical movements have centered international adoption as an act of faith and a way to evangelize to communities around the world. Journalist Katherine Joyce argues that this mandate has created a cycle in which children in crisis due to war, famine, or other tragedy have been publicized to American evangelicals, which has then created pressure on the countries in question to put children up for adoption.[66] This demand for children has resulted in fraud and abuse, leading to the objectification of poor countries and children and the institutionalization of kidnapping.[67] Indeed, while modern adoption often claims to respond to human needs through American altruism, anthropologist Eleana Kim argues that transracial adoptions are political and gendered processes that are "implicated in the United States' imperialist, capitalist modernity and indeed its foundational or constitutive projects of racial formation and 'nation-building.'"[68]

Today's response to unaccompanied immigrant youth is grounded in this convoluted relationship among child protection, the control of communities, and American hegemony. Unaccompanied immigrant youths' relationship to government policies that treat them explicitly as children began at the turn of the last century, with the Immigration Act of February 20, 1907. This act instructed border officials to hold unaccompanied children under the age of sixteen for "special inquiry," admitting them only in the case "(1) that they are strong and healthy, (2) that while abroad they have not been the objects of public charity, (3) that they are going to close relatives who are able and willing to support and properly care for them, (4) that it is the intention of such relatives to send them to school until they are 16, and (5) that they will not be put at work unsuited to their years." This act was explicitly aimed not to help migrant children but rather to ensure that they did not become public charges of the federal government.

Awareness of and activism for unaccompanied migrant youth increased in the 1980s, with the confluence of several events. First, the numbers of youth arriving alone to the US-Mexico border began to increase, coinciding with increasing conflict in Central America.[69] Second, the US system of immigrant detention was quickly expanding and becoming privatized, with the Corrections Corporation of America initiating its first governmental contract to open an immigrant detention facility and policies from the Reagan administration increasing the length and frequency of immigrant detention.[70] Finally, a 1984 rule barred the release of unaccompanied children in detention, except to a parent or legal guardian, thus lengthening the detention for many youth.

These factors raised alarms for activists, who noted that there was no distinction between children and adult migrants in these detention centers. In 1985, the Center for Human Rights & Constitutional Law and the National Center for Youth Law filed a lawsuit for the plaintiff, fifteen-year-old Jenny Flores, whose experience in adult detention included frequent strip searches.[71] After a decade of lawsuits against the government regarding the treatment of unaccompanied youth, the *Flores* settlement agreement of 1997 explicitly laid out national standards for the detention, treatment, and release of youth.[72] This case mandated basic protections for minors and dictated the responsibilities of the US Immigration and Naturalization Service (INS) concerning future influxes of unaccompanied youth. It created new guidelines regarding the detention of youth, mandating in particular that youth be placed in the "least restrictive setting" appropriate for their needs.

However, within a few years, human rights groups started to highlight new concerns regarding the conflict of interest that existed, as INS remained responsible for both the legal prosecution and the protection of unaccompanied youth.[73] To resolve this tension, the Homeland Security Act of 2002 divided responsibility for unaccompanied youth between the Department of Homeland Security and the Office of Refugee Resettlement. With this reorganization, the ORR was made responsible for the care and reunification of unaccompanied youth while DHS remained in charge of the prosecution of the youth. However, attorney and advocate Aryah Somers suggests that there remains an imbalance between the role of DHS and that of ORR, as the needs of DHS are consistently viewed as more important than the role of ORR.[74] Several years after this separation, the Trafficking Victims Protection Reauthorization Act of 2008 further increased the protections for immigrant minors, out of concerns that youth were not being adequately screened for trafficking issues or repatriated with the appropriate resources. The TVPRA required that all youth from noncontiguous countries be transferred to custody and placed in removal proceedings while youth from

Mexico and Canada be provided with a screening before their immediate transfer to their home country. The combination of these legislative interventions created the current Office of Refugee Resettlement Unaccompanied Minors Division, which has quietly processed these youth through a system of immigration detention for the past decade, using the logics of child welfare while at the same time acting as an arm of the same government that works for the quick removal of the children.

Neoliberal Humanitarianism

The United States government and media have frequently framed youths' migration to the border as not just an issue of child welfare but a humanitarian crisis. The Obama administration declared the increased numbers of youth in 2014 a humanitarian emergency, and the Trump administration frequently referred to migrant youths' experiences as a "humanitarian crisis" in his push to build a border wall (although his administration has also frequently referred to youth as criminals and invaders).[75] So, in addition to ideologies of border securitization and racialized child welfare, when youth arrive to the United States unaccompanied, they enter into a wide humanitarian net.

While definitions of humanitarianism vary, general agreement centers on the alleviation of human suffering as the primary goal. In their book on humanitarianism, Michael Barnett and Thomas G. Weiss suggest that humanitarianism is an "act motivated by an altruistic desire to provide life-saving relief; to honor the principles of humanity, neutrality, impartiality, and independence; and to do more good than harm."[76] Anthropologists Peter Redfield and Erica Bornstein argue that humanitarianism's primary tendency and motivation is to ease physical and emotional suffering and respond to basic human needs.[77] However, as these and other scholars have noted, American humanitarianism has several distinct features: it is neoliberal, ahistorical, and frequently coopted.

The particular brand of humanitarianism that today's unaccompanied youth encounter is framed by the current neoliberal economy. Tracing its origin to the rejection of the welfare state and the global economic turns of the 1980s led by the likes of Margaret Thatcher and Ronald Reagan, neoliberalism relies on a belief that liberating the economy will increase human well-being.[78] Political scientists Manfred B. Steger and Ravi K. Roy argue that there are three dimensions of neoliberalism: "(1) an ideology; (2) a mode of governance; (3) a policy package."[79] As an ideology, neoliberalism is a discourse of consumerism and free market. As a mode of governance, neoliberalism celebrates self-regulation and elevates business models over the public good. And, as a policy package, neoliberalism implements deregulation, liberalization of trade, and privatization. Neoliberalism is a powerful economic and political force; indeed, social-worker scholars Susan Braedley and Meg Luxton argue that "neoliberalism is no longer an alternative to hegemonic political thought as it was in the mid-twentieth century. It *is* hegemonic political thought."[80] In addition, the implementation and effects of neoliberal policy are deeply racialized and gendered.[81]

Neoliberal practices, particularly aspects such as privatization and self-regulation, have deeply influenced humanitarian responses to migrants. For example, immigrant-rights groups have raised concern over the increase of for-profit, private detention facilities, including facilities that purportedly house and care for youth.[82] Even nonprofit organizations find that the care of unaccompanied youth can be economically advantageous, as the government has handed out billions in grants for nonprofits that hold migrant children.[83] As a result, voluntary organizations and those explicitly dedicated to charity and immigrant rights have found themselves roped into participating in the immigrant market. Sociologist Imogen Tyler and colleagues have suggested that groups who intend to support immigrant youth have found themselves inexorably linked to other government projects. "One of the risks for migrant support groups in an era marked by the rise of mandatory partnership working is that they become entangled within the very governmental systems of immigration and border control which they ostensibly contest."[84] Similarly, in their study on groups who work to combat "*notario* fraud" (when an individual impersonates an immigration attorney), sociologists Jaime Longazel and Benjamin Fleury-Steiner demonstrate that even pro-immigrant groups become easily subsumed by the neoliberal ideologies of personal responsibility.[85] What these studies suggest is that humanitarian responses towards immigrant youth are always situated in this broader economic and political context, where market forces are prioritized over the public good and where individual responsibility reigns.

American humanitarianism is also decidedly ahistorical. Humanitarianism as a practice exists as a response to a supposedly "sudden, unexpected, and morally compelling" tragedy.[86] A compelling humanitarian crisis cannot implicate the United States in global wrongdoing. A compelling humanitarian subject must exist outside historical memory and political conversation.[87] American humanitarianism insists on framing human tragedies outside of the messiness of global politics. This is not to say that most humanitarian crises are actually sudden and unexpected. It is the humanitarian response, alone, that presents crises in a political vacuum. In the case of unaccompanied youth, Latina/o studies theorist David Hernández argues that unaccompanied immigrant youth today are not ahistorical at all but rather the inevitable result of a long history of government misdeeds; yet, framing the presence of these youth as a humanitarian crisis helps to obscure this history.[88]

Although ahistorical, humanitarian subjects must simultaneously rely on racialized, colonialist, and gendered scripts in order to further gain legitimacy.[89] For example, in their study of LGBTQ asylum seekers, sociologist Lionel Cantú Jr. and his colleagues show that the asylum seekers must often rely on stories that frame their home cultures as deficient and backwards while furthering a narrative of the United States as a progressive haven.[90] These stories help to legitimize the hegemony of the United States. Similarly, women make particularly compelling humanitarian subjects, especially when they can be homogenized and demobilized. Gender theorist Chandra Talpade Mohanty shows how the idea of the "third world woman" is created out of an "ahistorical, universal unity between women based on a generalized notion of their subordination."[91] In this sense, the oppressed woman as a subject of humanitarian aid is a Western creation that works to uphold beliefs in American superiority.

Children are also useful figures in creating an ahistorical humanitarian discourse. Anthropologist Liisa Malkki suggests that youth symbolize several important ideals in modern humanitarianism, including being the "embodiment of basic human goodness," "sufferers," and "seers of truth."[92] These perceptions make it easy both to sentimentalize children and to turn them into symbols. Malkki suggests that viewing children as symbols robs them of their agency and truth-telling abilities. So while children are seen as bearers of truth, they are also seen as untrustworthy in their memories and are thus "denied existence as complex social beings who know the world and represent themselves."[93] This, in turn, creates what anthropologist Didier Fassin calls "fragile and ambiguous" mobilizations that do more to exalt the suffering of others than to call the world to action.[94] In the same vein, sociologist Jessica Taft argues that girls, in particular, can be invoked as desirable figures for empowerment, as they embody symbols of hope and harmlessness, which ultimately renders them powerless.[95] Indeed, the movement to help girls around the world uses colonialist scripts, erases structural inequalities, and relies on girls' personal responsibility for themselves and their communities.

Finally, humanitarianism is frequently disrupted and coopted. Despite the effort to keep humanitarianism ahistorical and humanitarian subjects apolitical, the paradox is that humanitarian efforts often become political acts. Many humanitarian groups working on immigration issues have faced increasing pressure and scrutiny from private citizens and government entities alike, who argue that the humanitarian work defies federal and state policies. In extreme cases, humanitarian actions at the border have been criminalized.[96] For example, in early 2019, four activists were convicted of abandonment of property and harboring an illegal alien in their efforts to leave water and seek safety for migrants.[97]

However, disrupting humanitarian efforts is not always this obvious. In fact, theorists have recently demonstrated that humanitarian efforts can be coopted by securitizing forces who use humanitarianism as a mere guise for warfare.[98] This process has been seen clearly on the US-Mexico border. In his insightful study of this region, sociologist Timothy Dunn explains that the Low Intensity Conflict doctrine at the US border between 1978 and 1992 included the use of private humanitarian aid to assist in military and policing projects.[99] In another example, the 1998 Border Safety Initiative was a partnership between the United States and Mexico to warn migrants of the dangers along the border; however, the underlying purpose of this campaign was to reduce migration, not to protect migrants. This ideological initiative continues to this day, with both governments reminding potential migrants through a multitude of public service announcements such as "No Mas Cruces en Las Fronteras" (No More Crosses on the Border) and warning specifically of the risks of "falling under the prey of smugglers."[100] Such campaigns do nothing to address the causes of migration; rather, they frame human movement as the problem and ignore the danger that is often the impetus for these very journeys. Similarly, the narrative of border enforcement demonstrates the cooptation of humanitarianism. Discourse on border crossings often suggests that human smugglers are criminals, migrants are victims, and border enforcement acts as the hero, rescuing these migrants.[101] The Trump administration was adept at this cooptation, in its narrative that building a wall is a humanitarian action. Ultimately, this cooptation of humanitarianism creates a policy of contingent care, where aid is provided only as it helps to buttress existing power structures.[102]

Intersectional Identities of Youth and Their Families

The Social Construction of Childhood

Youth arrive to the United States at the complex juncture of these three histories. Their experiences are further complicated by the shifting meanings of childhood, intersections of inequality, and realities of transnational lives. Throughout this work, I use the word "youth" to denote a social category. In legal discourse, the term "minor" is more often employed as a legal status, but I avoid this language, as it does not capture the entirety of the social relations that make this life stage. I also tend to avoid "child," as it connotes a stage that lacks agency, and that connotation does a disservice to the young people I study, who are decidedly agentic, regardless of their age. I also do not make a distinction that is often made to separate child (typically under thirteen) and teenager (typically thirteen to eighteen) because although these distinctions matter very much in public discourse, the young people in my study often transgressed these categories in their everyday lives. "Youth" as a term better encompasses the agentic experiences of young people who cross international borders alone.

Part of the issue in defining this language is that child and adolescent, as categories, are often shifting and historically fluid. The meaning of childhood has changed throughout history and is dependent on the cultural, social, and economic relations of the time. In his classic work, French historian Phillipe Aries argued that childhood is socially constructed and that the very concept of childhood must be produced by a society in order to recognizably differentiate this category from adulthood. Childhood, he argues, was discovered in modernity.[103] Since this assertion, multiple social scientists have tracked the ways in which childhood has been constructed throughout history. Sociologist Nanette J. Davis documents the changing beliefs around childhood, from conceptions of children as "incomplete" and "inherently polluted" in the 1500s to sentimentalized portraits around the industrial period. Over the centuries, children's individuality, their relation to family, their access to education, beliefs about their holiness or sinfulness, views on child sexuality, and ideologies around child protection shifted frequently, and were both a product of the time and also a product of the individual child's social relations. That is, rich children and poor children have always experienced childhood in very different ways. Davis explains that in the preindustrial period, wealthy children had access to "elaborate and intensive" education, while working-class children labored for the wealthy families, and children from so-called pagan countries were sold as slaves. By the industrialization period, wealthy children continued to access high-quality boarding schools, and working-class children shifted from family-related labor to work in mines and factories. Davis argues that although oppression characterized much of the history of childhood, children and youth have also consistently found ways to exert agency and freedom.

In addition to being historically structured, childhood as a category is also culturally contingent. Anthropologists have noted the wide range of beliefs and experiences of childhood across cultures. David F. Lancey, for example, tracks hundreds of cases of child-rearing practices across the globe, giving credence to the claim that childhood is understood in very different terms across cultures.[104] He provides evidence that while much of the Western world today exalts the innocence of children, this is not a universal belief. While children in some cultures are the center of the family, other cultures view children as property to be used by parents or a temporary drain on a family's resources. Education, which is highly institutionalized in some cultures, is seen in others as a natural byproduct of observation that need not be formalized. Beliefs about physical punishment vary tremendously, particularly in terms of the psychological damage that physical punishment causes—or the deficiencies caused by its absence. While some cultures work to protect children, others view children as natural survivors and childhood adversity as a necessary step in developing human competency.

Of course, these variations in childhood are impacted by an increasingly global world. So while local communities shape childhood practices, international organizations increasingly exert influence on children's lives. International law has begun to standardize global norms surrounding childhood. Most prominently, the United Nation's Convention on the Rights of the Child shapes an increasingly universal view of childhood. Such conventions work to create a global reality regarding the personhood of children and the rights of children within the family. They create international understandings of the obligation of the state, which is constructed as a benevolent protector of children's rights. Yet, the decidedly Western nature of these conventions is sometimes met with resistance at the local level.[105]

These global contradictions play out in the lives of migrant youth. Youth discover that as they cross borders, they also cross ideologies about childhood. Furthermore, the act of crossing borders itself affects the lived experience of childhood, although this impact is nuanced. Some scholars suggest that immigrant youth enter into adulthood more quickly than their native-born peers due to responsibilities that arise from transnational lives, such as translating for parents in adult situations. In this sense, immigration itself acts as a mechanism of transition into adulthood.[106] Other scholarship suggests the opposite: transition into adulthood can be delayed for immigrant youth. Especially for youth who are undocumented, legal status often affects youths' ability to reach milestones associated with adulthood, such as the completion of their education and the commencement of full-time work.[107]

Intersections of Inequality

Every youth migrant experiences life stages as they are mediated by the historical moment, their (fluid) cultural contexts, and the realities of transnational lives. Additionally, their experiences are further complicated by the layers of inequalities within their identities. Indeed, each individual has numerous, sometimes shifting identities that create multiplicative experiences of oppression and privilege.[108] Emerging work has begun to reveal the nuances of these intersections for migrant youth, although there is still much to uncover. For example, anthropologist Greta Uehling explores how race and nationality influence the United

States' response to children.[109] She explains that the smuggling of Latin American children has garnered less public sympathy and institutional response in comparison to child smuggling by "snakeheads" in Asia, due to racialized conceptualizations of human trafficking. Anthropologist Lauren Heidbrink unveils the ways in which indigeneity shapes the migration and deportation of youth from Guatemala.[110] Class, too, is an important social location. Sociologists Alejandro Portes and Alejandro Rivas demonstrate how children of immigrants experience vastly different worlds when their parents are high-human-capital migrants versus manual workers, especially as these categories intersect with race.[111]

Gender is a particularly important intersection in the experiences of unaccompanied youth. Broadly speaking, the understanding of migration as it intersects with gender is relatively new, with the focus on women as migrants occurring only in the last few decades.[112] Men and women experience vastly different impetuses for migration, migratory paths, and settlement outcomes. Women's lives are more often marred by sexual and gendered violence, before, during, and after the actual migration.[113] Gendered arrangements in the family may shift upon migration, led either by the separation of family members or the demands of new settlement, which may allow women to work out of the home.[114] Even perceptions of migrants are colored by gender, with women confronting stereotypes of hyperfertility and anchor babies while Latino immigrant men often face stereotypes of violence and gangs.[115] Centering girlhood, ethnic studies scholar Lilia Soto shows how girls' relation to migration differs from boys'. Girls, she suggests, are taught to be dependent on adults, instead of networks, and are thus more likely to be excluded from independent migration.[116] Whereas immigration acts as a rite of passage for boys, it does not seem to hold the same cultural significance for girls. Boys, on the other hand, use migration to become adults and men.[117]

Youth migration decisions are often dependent on age, with primary school–aged children more often migrating in response to violence and educational barriers, while secondary school–aged children tend to migrate for economic reasons.[118] The work of sociologist Rubén G. Rumbaut further explores how migrant youth experience varied outcomes in acculturation measures such as education and occupational attainment, depending on their age at arrival. Children who migrate in early childhood (the 1.75 generation) may have more of a connection to the receiving country, whereas those who migrate towards the end of adolescence (the 1.25 generation) have fewer connections to the receiving institutions and culture.[119] Furthermore, once in the United States, youth face more concrete *beliefs* about their life stage (despite their varied experiences). Adolescents, in particular, find that their age category is met with suspicion. Anthropologist Liisa Malkki explains, "When children are referred to as 'teens' or 'teenagers,' their moral authority as innocents is attenuated. The temporal progression built into the category of 'children' is also a moral progression: it is easiest to attribute to children a pure innocent presociality when they are youngest."[120] The image of immigrant teenagers complicates this narrative further, by placing together both teenage-threat and immigrant-threat narratives. For example, researchers in the past have suggested that immigration itself is a risk category for teen rebellion, thus creating new categories of suspicion.[121]

Transnational Families

These intersections of oppression and privilege exist not just for youth but for their families as well. The literature on immigrant youth often assumes that children are inexorably linked *with* their parents. The legal designation of "unaccompanied" supposes that youth exist *without* parents. Yet, the reality of unaccompanied youth and their relationship to parents (and parental figures) is much more complicated than either of these conceptualizations suggests. Youths' decisions to migrate, experiences while migrating, and lives in the United States upon arrival are often linked in complicated ways to adults. As anthropologist Lauren Heidbrink states, "The term *separated child* more accurately reflects the contingent and temporary nature of separation."[122] Further, as borderland subjects, youth are, in fact, required to connect themselves to parental figures in ways that often contradict the nuanced realities of their lives. So, whether youth have left parents, have been pushed to immigrate by parents, hope to reunite with parents, or have no legal guardians and must be placed with other adult caregivers, adults are important figures in this story.

Much of the literature on transnational families explores the dynamics that arise when parents migrate and leave their children behind[123] or when parents are forcibly removed from the country.[124] Not surprisingly, transnational lives exert tremendous pressure on the family system and children's outcomes.[125] Family separation is correlated with increased depressive symptoms among children[126] and poorer school performance relative to children who are not separated from their families.[127] Children may struggle to maintain emotional connections with parents who have left,[128] and they may find it difficult to connect with their parents when and if they are reunited.[129] Many transnational parents work hard to mitigate these risks, although the parents' gender mediates their responses. Mothers who migrate and leave children behind might exert tremendous effort in maintaining emotional ties across borders, even while they redefine good motherhood.[130] Fathers often lean on their financial giving as an essential element of maintaining the family ties.[131] Even children influence the dynamics of the transnational families, exerting some power in the decision making of their parents.[132] Indeed, all members of transnational families must engage in a "reciprocal, though uneven, exchange of caregiving."[133] However, the power experienced by these families is limited. As sociologist Leisy Abrego makes abundantly clear in her research, the traumas experienced by transnational families are not located in the dysfunction of the family but rather in government policies that exert immense harm.[134]

This analysis of immigrant youth and their families points to the intersections of structures that impact youth migrants. But, youth have always exerted agency over structures as well. Books such as Jessica K. Taft's *Rebel Girls: Youth Activism and Social Change across the Americas* have been important in changing the traditional understanding of youth culture to one that is active instead of solely acted upon.[135] Other scholars have pointed to immigrant youths' participation in protests, their strategies in building and navigating identities, and their ability to push against structural forces on the border.[136] This literature shows how to balance an analysis of youth agency *and* structure, in order to provide a full picture of youths' experiences. By focusing on structure, we see limitations in youths' options; yet, by focusing on youth agency, we see the ways in which youth can exert power in their own lives. In this way, agency and structure are always intertwined. This balance avoids problematizing youth as a category and places the onus for social problems on society at large.

The Study

My research is located where unaccompanied migrant youth arrive: at the intersection of border security, racialized child welfare, and neoliberal humanitarianism. It is at this juncture that youth navigate their lives. In order to understand youths' journey in the United States, I employed multiple qualitative methods: I interviewed fifteen youth and sixty-seven professionals who worked with unaccompanied youth in various capacities. I volunteered as an advocate for unaccompanied youth in order to keep an autoethnographic account of the work. Finally, I reviewed government documents and conducted a qualitative analysis of news reports on unaccompanied youth from 2014. This mixed-method study was fraught with difficulties: my access to youth was stymied by a blanket research ban by the Office of Refugee Resettlement, and I placed additional limits on myself due to ethical concerns about the vulnerability of youth participants. A full account of the research ban and the resulting dilemmas can be found in Appendix A.

Interviews with Professionals

First, I interviewed sixty-seven professionals from a wide range of careers who worked with youth. My plan in this research was originally to conduct an institutional analysis within youth shelters/detention facilities. However, these youth shelters all exist under the auspices of the Office of Refugee Resettlement, which at the time had a strict ban on all researchers. Because of this, I was unable to do official research in the shelters or to work in any official capacity with nonprofit organizations. Instead, I contacted professionals as individuals, rather than speaking with them as representatives of their organizations.

Without being able to go directly through organizations, I located individuals using a range of methods. First, I used existing networks from my own advocacy work and my former employment to identify possible participants. I also contacted other participants through blind emails, calls, and social media outreach. I relied on both the US government websites, which list their contractors and pro-bono attorneys, and newspaper articles that highlighted migrant programs that serve unaccompanied youth in various communities. I also focused my email campaigns on areas that received high numbers of migrant youth, sending blind emails out to schools and social services in those communities. Jumping off from these contacts, I proceeded with a snowball sampling method described by Jon Lofland and colleagues.[137] The snowball sampling technique proved useful in identifying pockets of people in various locations across the United States. Because of the interdependence of many of these workers, I could often rely on an attorney to introduce me to a schoolteacher who could then introduce me to a counselor in the area, providing data on how these networks functioned in numerous locations.

However, participants varied in their willingness to speak with me, depending on their occupation. Attorneys and other legal workers were most responsive to my requests, as they often felt comfortable with their ability to abide by confidentiality standards while speaking with me. Educators were slightly more difficult to access; school administrators often acted as gatekeepers and rarely gave me information about employees who might work with immigrant youth. However, when I was able to contact a teacher or school worker directly, these individuals were often eager to share information with me. Professionals working for nonprofits and government organizations were the most difficult to connect with. No organization agreed to work with me due to the ORR research ban, so I had to contact individuals outside of their professional environment. I was unable to find individual contact information for most workers on their organizations' websites, so I relied on social media searches to find workers. For example, I used LinkedIn and searched for the phrase "unaccompanied minor" and then reached out to everyone whose profile came up and whose job title was linked to my research. While this process produced multiple hits, it was still limited. The organizations for which many of these professionals worked had strict confidentiality agreements, and current employees often felt that they should not speak to researchers.

The professional interviews include eighteen attorneys and legal service providers, fourteen government workers helping to reunite youth with sponsors, six government facility workers, seventeen educators, and twelve other social workers, community members, and activists who worked with unaccompanied youth. (See Appendix B for the complete list of these participants.) Only eleven of these participants were men; the remaining fifty-six were women. The fact that women compose much of the system is an important piece of the story. The racial and ethnic makeup of the participants varied, although the majority were white and a little over a third identified as Latinx.

These professionals worked in states across the country. My data is thus not a portrait of a single institution but a diagram of the entire landscape: a vast network that youth traverse. I picture my data on a map of the United States, with a pin in the different locations a youth might travel. On this network map, there is a pin for a case worker in a shelter that receives youth who have been recently detained. Another pin is a worker who places the youth in a home several states away. There might be a cluster of pins where the youth is placed, for the counselors, social workers, attorneys, and teachers with whom the youth may or may not connect. Another pin may be a postrelease case worker who lives hours away and attempts to keep track of the youth from a distance. These pins may be connected—but they also may not. This is not a precise data set because the landscape is not precise. It is expansive and includes multiple institutions and people that are simultaneously insular and yet interdependent. My data set is, indeed, indicative of how youth may actually experience the United States.[138]

I followed semistructured interview guides, created specifically for attorneys, educators, social workers, and shelter workers, adjusting the questions as necessary to the specific participant. While each interview guide had a set of questions tailored specifically to the participants' expertise, all of the interview guides shared general themes. Specifically, I asked all participants about the networking they did with other professionals, the most and least successful cases they had experienced (and how they defined that), the difficulties of building rapport and interpreting truth with youth, and the impact of trauma on youths' experiences. Finally, I asked all participants to discuss the different barriers faced by youth with different social locations, asking specifically about gender, ability, language, and criminal history.

With only rare exceptions, the individuals I interviewed conceived their role to be one of protection and advocacy, and their relationships to American institutions were often fraught with tension. Many had strong political views and some—though not all—had nuanced critiques of the US immigration system. During interviews, these participants would talk about issues such as white privilege, global inequality, and the need for activism. There were only a small number who did not employ this progressive rhetoric; these individuals felt that the system was working smoothly and the rights of immigrant youth were being protected. It is possible that the data set is skewed, in this sense. The individuals who spoke to me often did so because they felt that they needed to go public with what they perceived as unjust treatment of immigrant youth.

Interviews with Unaccompanied Immigrant Youth

In addition to the interviews with the professionals, I collected fifteen interviews with unaccompanied youth, ranging from ages seventeen to twenty-four at the time of the interview. There were three young women, and the rest were young men. They came from Mexico, El Salvador, Guatemala, Honduras, and Ecuador. The youth had all participated in an unauthorized crossing, without legal guardians, and while under the age of eighteen since 2003, the year in which the Office of Refugee Resettlement began to care for immigrant children in federal custody.

My access to youth was limited in ways that I had not anticipated at the outset of this research. Because my original intention was to conduct an ethnographic account of a government facility, I expected to collect years of observations and dozens of interviews. With the research ban by the Office of Refugee Resettlement, this original plan was completely obstructed. While the Office of Refugee Resettlement does allow limited contact with youth by the media, organizations had the discretion to permit or deny these interviews, and despite my efforts, I never successfully connected with youth through these institutionalized means. Instead, as with my data with professionals, I was able to recruit youth participants almost entirely through informal means.

My recruitment of youth participants occurred in two waves. In 2011, I conducted a preliminary study of unaccompanied youth, and I used entirely informal recruitment. I found youth through my own connections in my community. I cold called churches and community organizations, I used my own networks in immigrant communities, and I recruited at workplaces that hired immigrant youth. In a short period of time, I was able to collect eighteen interviews, although only eight of those interviews are used in the current research. (The other ten did not fit into the narrow age and date range I used for this study, as most had migrated prior to 2003.) I did a second wave of youth interviews in 2016, attempting to locate unaccompanied youth through more formalized methods. I attempted to go through nonprofit organizations or utilize the networks of professionals, although this rarely produced the necessary contacts. The vast majority of the professionals whom I interviewed felt uncomfortable or restricted in giving me information about the youth that they worked with.[139] Those who did help make connections were teachers, attorneys, and workers in a community organization who were not restricted by government oversight.

In the interviews with youth, I used a semistructured interview guide, but followed it loosely to allow the youth to control the interview. I focused on questions about the youth's childhood, their decision making in coming to the United States, their experience in migration, and their experience once they arrived to the country. My preference was to ask several general questions and allow youth to talk without interruption. When youth fell silent or finished their stories, I would retrace their steps with follow-up questions. I embraced the methodology of *testimonios*, not just to obtain information but to collect critical knowledge from individual experience, allowing participants to assert themselves as subjects in the process.[140]

Youth as a category are considered vulnerable in research, and this particular population of youth is even more vulnerable due to past traumas. I took this into account as I created my research process and was sure to place youths' agency and safety at the forefront (sometimes to the detriment of my research). First, I paid special attention to ensuring that there was no coercion during the recruitment process and when gaining consent for the interview. In order to do so, I allowed community members to reach out to youth first and direct them to me (rather than me contacting youth directly). When youth contacted me, usually by phone, I would explain the research and then request that they talk to a trusted adult before consenting. Further, I had a designated research advocate, whose information I provided to youth, if they wanted to ask someone else about their participation. These multiple steps did help to ensure that youth were in the driver's seat with their decision to participate, but it also meant that many possible connections did not result in an interview. When youth did complete the recruitment process, I was sure to receive full consent regarding the themes of the interview. Psychologists Ann T. Chu and Anne P. DePrince suggest that when teenagers are told in advance that an interview might involve discussing their traumatic experiences, their decision to participate does not decrease and, in fact, they report after the interview that there was an overall "positive cost-benefit ratio" to their participation.[141]

Second, I utilized trauma-informed techniques during the interviews.[142] Psychologists know that interviews with young people who have experienced traumatic events require special attention to the interpersonal communication between the researcher and the youth participant. Trauma manifests differently among different people; for example, girls often display more overt symptoms of traumatic stress than do boys, and young children are more vulnerable to traumatic events than older children and adolescents. While crying or angry outbursts may indicate stress, teens, in particular, may actually exhibit stress by "shutting down" or becoming "uncommunicative."[143] The American Psychological Association encourages adults to listen for words that may signify distress; while teens may not communicate distress using the language of trauma, words such as "worried" or "angry" may be stand-ins for significant distress, as may negative self-directed language.[144] In working with unaccompanied immigrant youth, in particular, researchers might look for unusual behavior in their conversations with youth, as trauma can present in ways that appear emotionally "inappropriate"; laughing, for example, may be a sign that the teen is struggling to communicate or understand a traumatic event.[145] For this reason, I worked to be highly attuned to the various ways that my participants signaled levels of distress during the interview.

I also worked to implement trauma-informed responses when my participants signaled distress during the interview. Once again, this meant using a high level of introspection and putting youths' well-being before the interview goals.[146] In particular, I allowed youth participants to lead discussions of trauma, creating interview questions that were broad enough to allow participants to make a decision to talk—or not talk—about traumatic events.[147] However, I did not avoid these topics, if youth directed the interview in that direction. Anthropologist Janice M. Morse and her colleagues suggest that signs of emotional distress should not be a cue to stop the interview immediately but rather should be a signal to initiative a conversation in which the participant may decide whether to stop; these researchers suggest that having the interviewer make the decision may actually be more harmful to the research participant.[148]

Autoethnography

From 2015 to 2019, I volunteered as a child advocate through the Young Center for Immigrant Children's Rights. While I was not able to collect ethnographic data of this work due to limitations of the ORR, confidentiality agreements with the Young Center, and IRB limits, these experiences within ORR shelters and at immigration court have significantly informed my research. I have maintained autoethnographic notes of this time, focusing on my own work processing cases, but not on the cases themselves. I use this experience to triangulate my findings, to provide overall insight into the systems that aid immigrant youth, and to reflect not on the youth I worked with but rather on my own work, decision making, and emotional reactions.

As a volunteer child advocate, I received an informative two-day training with the Young Center and started my advocacy work as soon as my background check and fingerprints cleared. My job was to visit the youth detained in a shelter on a weekly basis, advocating for the child if any problems arose in the shelter, in the court, or upon release. All of the youth who receive a child advocate have been flagged as being at high risk for reasons ranging from mental health problems to difficult family-placement issues. During my visits, I tried to gain information that would help the case and determine the best interests of the youth, be it a specific type of placement in the United States or return to the home country. I maintained contact with an attorney to discuss concerns that arose. If necessary, I served on a Best Interest Determination Panel, to provide recommendations to the state regarding the youth's future placement options. When the young person was released from the shelter, I would follow up by phone to make sure that they were connected with appropriate services in their area.[149]

I have worked on multiple cases of youth residing in four government shelters. I have attended court hearings, contributed to one Best Interest Determination Panel, and visited shelters every week with crafts, games, nail polish, and, in one case, a clandestine cake, to entertain the youth and win their trust. I have also remained active as a member of the Young Center, receiving additional trainings and attending events that allowed me to interact with and learn from fellow advocates.

When reflecting on my experience as an advocate, I use not the stories of the people I encounter but rather the stories of myself as one of the professionals in the immigrant system. Following the advice of ethnographer Heewon Chang, I treated my autoethnography as any ethnography, collecting weekly field notes and self-observations about my feelings and positionality. Chang suggests that "like ethnographers, autoethnographers are expected to treat their autobiographical data with critical, analytical, and interpretive eyes to detect cultural undertones of what is recalled, observed, and told to them."[150] In conjunction with these notes, I had the rare opportunity to be interviewed by researcher Lina M. Caswell about my experience as a child advocate. This interview has been shared with me, and I have analyzed it along with my other interviews as a reflection of my own thought process and experience.

Document Analysis

Finally, I conducted extensive media and document analyses. I systematically collected online media sources in 2014 to understand the political climate in which youth arrived. I also reviewed multiple documents from the Office of Refugee Resettlement and Customs and Border Enforcement, among others. Finally, in the summer of 2019, I worked with a student research team to collect documents from school districts across the country, regarding their treatment of unaccompanied immigrant youth.

Organization of the Book

Throughout this book I explore how the histories of border enforcement, racialized child welfare, and neoliberal humanitarianism create conflicting ideologies in which professionals who work with unaccompanied youth must operate. Each chapter explores a different field of support for immigrant youth in order to analyze the tensions present as professionals and youth work together in each arena.

With a focus on family reunification, chapter 1 explores the dynamics between youth and the adults who care for them. This chapter opens with several stories of youth and their process in deciding to migrate. I use these stories to highlight the differing levels of agency and dependency that youth have with their family members. I then argue that the system of family reunification—an extension of the child welfare system—is often blind to the varied and nuanced family dynamics of the youth. Because of this, youth and their sponsors are often forced to perform particular family dynamics and are rarely provided services that are appropriate to their individual needs.

Chapter 2 focuses on the legal system. Instead of analyzing the laws themselves, I look at how attorneys work with youth to build stories—I call these "borderland legends"—that help youth gain legal relief. A borderland legend is a life history that is used as a productive humanitarian narrative in order for youth to gain legal relief. The process of creating the legend is one in which attorneys must identify stories that exist within frameworks of cultural deficiencies and individual (as opposed to structural) suffering. They must teach youth the language of trauma, abuse, and neglect, and they must coach youth in appropriate affect before a judge. This process reflects neoliberal humanitarian values and consistently works to support American hegemony.

The educational system is the final institution that youth must enter, and in chapter 3, I explore the barriers and opportunities in this system. Unlike the system of legal aid and family reunification, the education system was not built specifically to aid immigrants. However, the influence of education on youths' experience is notable, especially as the education system can often bridge gaps between youth, attorneys, and families. However, education is not immune to some of the same pitfalls of racialized child welfare, neoliberal humanitarianism, and border securitization. In fact, education itself can be used to enforce and exacerbate the tensions present in the other fields, particularly as it often exists in opposition to the labor market. In this chapter, I analyze the role of the education system, both looking at the ways in which it can provide an important lifeline in youths' lives and also providing a critical lens through which to view practices by some schools that further exacerbate the problems youth face in their lives.

In chapter 4, I take a broader view of the landscape of aid as a whole by looking at some of the overarching patterns and tensions that arise throughout the three fields discussed in the other chapters. I explore several major paradoxes that youth must contend with as they navigate their lives in the United States. First, I explore the ways in which all of these fields criminalize youth while simultaneously expecting youth to enact innocence. Second, I explore the ways in which youth must prove their dependency as youth while also being required to act agentically and independently. Finally, I explore the tension present in a system that is based on underlying trauma and that also assumes youth have overcome that trauma.

In chapter 5, I look at the experiences of the workers in the system. Because family reunification, legal aid, and immigrant student outreach are fraught with conflict and tension, I find that workers must employ a variety of methods in order to fulfill their own goals for youth. I show how workers face strain with their roles in their organizations and how they work with both legitimized and illegitimate means to help young people. I also unveil the ways that both workers and youth create new pathways, outside of institutionalized aid. Finally, I explore the deeper underlying tensions that workers must contend with, as they work alongside and sometimes with an immigration system they abhor.

To conclude the book, I grapple with the types of solutions we might implement to disrupt the systemic oppression of immigrants and young people. I wrestle with the embeddedness of this oppression but also explore practical ways that practitioners might reduce suffering in the present moment.

1

Leaving and Finding Home

El lugar donde yo crecí, prácticamente, solo es de pandillas, de mareros. Yo crecí en medio de todas esas personas. Yo veía lo que pasaba y todo. Cada vez que pasaba algo malo, yo veía todo eso. Yo crecí en medio de toda la delincuencia que ellos hacían.

(In the place where I grew up, it is basically just gangs and thugs. I grew up in the middle of those people, and I saw everything that happened. Every time that something bad happened, I saw all of that. I grew up in the middle of all of the delinquency.)
—Angelica, who migrated from El Salvador at age sixteen

Eighteen-year-old Angelica does not mince words when she is asked to give an account of her life growing up in El Salvador. Angelica does not express anger in this accounting, and she opens up with this history with a matter-of-fact air that reveals the tenacity that she relied on to get through the violence she has experienced in her lifetime. She continues: "They were always doing drugs, and they would kill people—they would kill each other! They were always watching, so you couldn't enter another neighborhood. If they didn't know you, the gang would kill you." For Angelica, death was always only a few streets away.

The gang violence that Angelica confronted in her everyday life had a long history. A vicious civil war had embroiled the country throughout the 1980s, and the United States had put its finger on the scale, supporting a president known for his human rights abuses by providing millions of dollars of assistance in the form of army training, arms, and aircraft.[1] With the chaos of this war, over a sixth of the population fled the country, many ending up in large cities throughout the United States. Youth in these cities faced a wide range of discrimination and violence, and in response, many joined or formed local street gangs. However, with the passage of the Illegal Immigration Reform and Immigrant Responsibility Act of 1996, these young people faced mandatory deportation, and the United States quickly removed tens of thousands of young people back to El Salvador. Between these young people's existing gang ties, the easy access to weapons supplied by the United States, and continued paramilitary activity in their communities of arrival, the gangs that started in the United States soon became transnational, and cities such as Angelica's became deadly.[2]

In the 2010s, Angelica's city had only gotten worse. The gang in her neighborhood slowly encroached upon her family's property, and by the time Angelica was a young teenager, her family had lost control of their own home. "The gang had basically seized my parents' house," Angelica explained. "They are always in the entry, watching. As it is today, the gangs use it as a guard house." The situation had gotten so tense that it resulted in a confrontation between the police and the gang just in front of the house. "There were shots and everything. My family hid inside, terrified."

Angelica gives her mother the credit for her own safety: her mother raised her in the sanctuary of the church, keeping Angelica busy and providing her a foundation of hope that she could stand on. Angelica described her father as a man with a temper, a womanizer who spent much of the family's money on other women. Yet, he treated Angelica well, and she expressed a deep love for him. Angelica was happy in her parents' home, but she explained that for years she wanted something more. Plus, as she got older, she became more and more afraid of the dangers in her neighborhood: the gangs who stood outside her classroom when she finished the school day, the gangs she confronted on her walk home from church, and the gangs who kept her crouched below the window on a weekday night.

Angelica's parents did not want her to leave El Salvador. While they understood that her future was limited in her native city, they felt devastated by the thought of her migrating alone. She talked to them frequently about her desire to go; they thought she was crazy. When her boyfriend left and migrated to the United States, Angelica's desire to leave became even stronger. Eventually, a day came when she learned that some trusted acquaintances were heading north. Angelica convinced her parents that this was her time, too, and they agreed to help fund her migration. Her boyfriend also agreed to send money for the trip. This final decision happened within the span of a week. She learned of the migration of these acquaintances only days before they left on a Monday morning. She woke up while it was still dark—4:00 in the morning, she remembers. Her mother got up with her to make breakfast. The smell of her last home-cooked meal filled the air, and she recalled her father, slumped in a corner, pleading with her to stay. He begged her: "You have everything you need here. Don't go, *m'ija*. Don't go." Her mother remained at the stove, back turned, refusing eye contact. She looked at her daughter only once, to give her a plate of *huevos picados*.

Angelica's voice became shaky as she recalled this morning to me, and she let escape a wail at the memory of her father in the chair and her mother stirring food on the stove. Despite her father's pleas and her mother's silence, Angelica did not waver. She had a deep sense that she must leave that particular Monday morning—or never. She recalled that her mother's grief spilled out in anger, and she pushed Angelica out the door with a choked, "Go already! I won't detain you and take your time any longer." Angelica refused to look back at her house as she got into her father's car. She wept silently, tears running down her cheeks, her sobs locked in her throat, as the car drove slowly away from their home, through their *colonia*, and to the meeting place of the travel group. When the group saw the pain on her face, they told her she did not have to leave with them, but she insisted. "My only goal was to not go back," she told me.

Angelica's story of departure has both parallels to and differences from the story of Cynthia, a young woman from Guatemala who fled from her home at age fourteen. Cynthia's life was not touched by the intense local violence that Angelica experienced, but it was shaped by her identity as a young, indigenous woman in a poor, rural community. Born in the 1990s, Cynthia came of age in a country undergoing significant changes. In 1996, a thirty-six-year civil war ended with the signing of a peace accord, although political instability and violence continued. The new president, Alvaro Arzú, rushed in neoliberal reforms, including the privatization of utilities, trade liberalization, and reduced regulation. Although many hoped this would stimulate economic growth, it resulted in furthering economic inequality and increasing poverty among poor, indigenous communities, including Cynthia's.[3]

Like Angelica, Cynthia was the individual who initiated migration, but her reasons were very different. Cynthia was not afraid of violence in her community, which was small and relatively peaceful by her account. However, unlike Angelica, Cynthia had no refuge in her home. She had been abandoned by her father, neglected by an alcoholic mother, and her rural community offered her little support and future opportunity. Having raised herself and her younger siblings, Cynthia was accustomed to acting as an adult. When she made the choice to leave, she told her mother, who agreed to the plan as Cynthia promised to send money home. However, she purposefully withheld the plan from her grandparents, who had threatened to lock her in a room if she ever tried to leave. In fact, Cynthia's departure was carried out in secret, in the darkness of night, so she would not be stopped by her grandparents. Her migration was also not paid for by family members. Instead, she was contracted to work off her migration debt but out of sheer luck managed to escape this fate.

While both Cynthia and Angelica clearly initiated their own migration, they had very different experiences in doing so. Some of these differences are related to age, life stage, and family relations. Angelica had a loving family whom she had to convince to let her leave. Her departure was a distinct marker in her life, as she made the decision independently, and it served as a transitional moment into adulthood. Although she did not plan to move in with her boyfriend when she arrived to the United States, the presence of her boyfriend made the transnational move part of a journey in leaving her childhood home to explore the possibilities of an adult life. Cynthia left to flee an abusive family, and she largely found her own way north. The distinction between childhood and adulthood was not as clear in her life, as she had been largely independent even as a very young child, so migration did not change her own perception of herself in terms of her independence.

Class certainly played a role in these differing experiences. Cynthia, who came from an extremely impoverished family in an indigenous community, had no family resources to rely on, even if her mother had desired to help. Indeed, it was only with the promise of remittances that her mother supported Cynthia's migration. Angelica, on the other hand, was able to use her family's resources to fund her trip to the United States. Her decision to leave was based not on an ability to send money home but rather on a desire to escape violence and increase her own future opportunities. The resources based on class and family also impacted the relative safety of the girls on their journeys north. Cynthia's lack of resources and lack of family support also meant that she had fewer opportunities to find a safe way to travel. While many migrants are able to rely on trusted networks to connect with a smuggler, Cynthia relied only on rumors and loose connections.[4] While she was able to quickly locate a smuggler, she did not have the benefit of relying on the smuggler's reputation among close friends and family members. Finally, the two girls' stories diverge along racial lines, as well. As an indigenous young woman, Cynthia spoke Q'eqchi as her first language, and she had only a basic command of Spanish when she initiated her migration. This created further vulnerabilities, as she was often confused during her migration when the primary language spoken by the smugglers was Spanish, and she rarely had a full understanding of what was happening around her.

While Angelica and Cynthia came from very different family backgrounds, they shared the common experience of being largely in control of their final decision to migrate, despite being discouraged to do so by their family members. Their experiences varied in this sense from that of young people, such as Carlos, whose parents encouraged migration. Carlos grew up with both parents in a southern state in Mexico. Migration to the United States was always part of Carlos's life. Brothers, uncles, neighbors, and friends had been traveling to and from the United States for as long as he could remember. Like small towns throughout Mexico, his town was intimately connected to the United States. Due to a wide range of push and pull factors, including the influence of NAFTA on Mexican agriculture, the lack of local job opportunities, and increasing unemployment in Mexico after the US 2008 recession, labor migration of Mexicans to the United States has become essential for the stability of both economies.[5] Towns such as Carlos's often rely heavily on remittances from migrants for their own economic base.

Carlos describes seeing his older brother migrate when Carlos was just ten years old. He asked his parents if he could go too, but they told him he was too young. Instead, Carlos remained in Mexico several more years, working in agriculture with his father. Once he turned fifteen, Carlos still had a strong desire to migrate and, by that age, his father supported and encouraged the decision, although his mother remained ambivalent. Carlos described a conversation in which his father said that it was Carlos's decision to migrate but that he needed to be brave. Carlos's father then arranged for a coyote. In Carlos's description, there is no clear individual who initiated migration. Carlos himself surely wanted to migrate and discussed this with his parents at a young age. But his immigration was not initiated until his father also agreed and provided the support for him to leave. Further, since Carlos's parents remained in Mexico, he knew that his migration also entailed an obligation to send remittances to them. There was an unspoken contract that Carlos's migration was meant to enable him to work and support his family.

It is clear that Carlos's family came to a mutual decision about his migration, through both gendered and classed logics. While the stories of Cynthia and Angelica reveal that a girl's migration may be contested by the family, Carlos received encouragement from his father to migrate, once he reached a certain age. This encouragement was imbued with masculine ideals, such as responsibility, bravery, and duty. As multiple scholars have shown, migration often acts as a rite of passage for young men.[6] It serves as a way for adolescent boys to distinguish themselves as adults. Further, since Carlos's mother was excluded from the final decision to migrate, and as Carlos was following an older brother, it is clear that migration was a masculine endeavor in his family. Carlos's brother also provided a migratory model for Carlos to imitate, having already established a family dynamic of migration. Finally, with the family's financial needs, Carlos's parents also depended on Carlos to use migration to support the family. Carlos's solitary migration was thus a mutual decision based on financial need and gendered values.

Like Mexico, Guatemala, and El Salvador, Honduras faces many of the same problems of poverty and violence. It has been labeled one of the most violent countries in the world, with the murder rate at 86.5 per 100,000 people in 2011.[7] Political unrest has haunted the government since the 1970s, when the relatively peaceful country found itself embroiled in Cold War conflict. The United States worked to squash community agitation in the country, training more than a thousand Honduran citizens. The United States also supplied Honduras with millions of dollars in assistance for its help in US interventions in neighboring countries. As in El Salvador, many immigrants who left Honduras during this time ended up in violent neighborhoods in the United States, where youth formed gangs as a mechanism of protection. These youth were deported in the 1990s back to Honduras, where they were able to organize and access weapons left over from the US military involvement, contributing to the violence experienced in the country today. In addition to the violence and political unrest, poverty has remained an important issue for everyday Hondurans. Since 1990 various presidents have implemented structural adjustments through the IMF and USAID, but these programs have burdened the country with debt, created an ongoing budget crisis, undermined critical programs that maintained political stability, worsened existing environmental issues, and increased poverty and unemployment.[8]

Mariana grew up in the middle of a large city in Honduras. She lived with her mother, and she described being very happy with her life. Her mother provided her a loving household, her father provided the necessary financial support through remittances he sent from the States, and she had close friends whom she loved. However, as she entered her teen years, some members of the Mara Salvatrucha gang began to follow her every time she left the house. On her walks to school, as she carried groceries home from the store, and as she left church with her friends, young men would follow her on their motorcycles, yelling pickup lines laced with threats. One day, this harassment escalated, when one of the gang members got off his motorcycle, pushed Mariana against a wall, and shoved a loaded gun into her stomach, whispering threats of violence into her ear if she did not become his girlfriend. Immediately after this assault, Mariana called her father in the United States. Although they did not have a close relationship, she asked if he would fund her migration north. Her mother did not like the idea of Mariana migrating, but she ultimately told her daughter that it was her decision alone to make. So, with her mother's reluctant support and her father's financial assistance, Mariana was able to leave Honduras at age sixteen, using a Nicaraguan coyote whom she trusted due to his reputation with other family members and friends.

Edwin grew up in rural Honduras, and although he did not report direct experience with community violence, his family was deeply burdened by the economic problems of their country. Edwin had been raised by a grandmother after his father had migrated to the United

States when Edwin was a young boy. By age thirteen, Edwin was no longer in school but had started to work to help his grandmother. Edwin describes coming home from his construction job one day, sweaty, tired, and filthy. He lay down in a hammock to take a nap in the shade and was approached by his grandmother: "Hey, your dad says to get ready. He says that you're leaving, that he has money for the coyotes to bring you." Edwin was ecstatic at this news, saying, "Oh my God! This is my time! I'm going to go there!" Edwin's grandmother, however, was not excited and begged Edwin to stay. Nevertheless, Edwin had dreams of reuniting with his father, learning English, going to school, and ultimately working hard enough to buy his grandmother some land and a house. The words that Edwin used to describe the migration decision suggest that he was a largely passive recipient of the decision. Within days, Edwin was placed in the hands of a coyote, whose job it was to bring Edwin to his father.

Although both Mariana and Edwin were from Honduras and ended up reunifying with fathers in the United States, their stories are distinct in important ways. Mariana's migration was initiated due to gendered violence, and her goal for migration was to start a safer life with a better future. This migration was largely initiated out of her own will. With her father's remittances, Mariana's family did not have a financial need for her to work or send remittances herself; indeed, Mariana was still in school in Honduras and continued school when she arrived to the United States. Further, reunification with her father was merely a side note in migration and in no way a driving factor. On the other hand, Edwin describes a much more impoverished upbringing, where he had left school at a young age to help support the family financially. His father initiated Edwin's migration to allow Edwin educational opportunities in the United States but also with the hope that Edwin would help in sending remittances to his grandmother. Edwin also articulated that he was excited to be reunified with his father. While his grandmother had been Edwin's caregiver for many years, Edwin expressed a keen interest in being with his father again. However, his grandmother's presence as well as her discouragement regarding Edwin's migration suggest, again, that extended family exerts an important influence in migration decisions. Finally, the idea that Edwin was told to migrate allowed him to maintain an identity as a child since there was still an adult making a migration decision based on what his father perceived to be in his best interests. Edwin's father would receive him, so the decision was to send Edwin between one adult (the grandmother) to another (the father), whereas Mariana actively decided to switch from one household to another. Finally, rural and urban living, and the intersection of gender, impacted Edwin's and Mariana's premigratory educational experiences. Although Edwin's family valued education, they did not have the resources and the educational infrastructure in their small community to support Edwin in these endeavors past early childhood. In her urban center, Mariana was able to continue her education until she migrated. This difference reflects the intersection of gender, rurality, and class in Honduras, in which girls, middle- and upper-class children, and those living in urban areas are more likely to complete their education than poor and rural families, especially boys. In fact, only half of boys from poor families in rural areas complete primary school, compared to nearly all children from wealthy families.[9]

The reasons why youth leave and the ways in which youth depart from their homes are very diverse.[10] These stories demonstrate a wide range of family dynamics that frame migration: Angelica left a loving home out of her own free will in order to escape violence and pursue a better life through education. Cynthia escaped an abusive household with no money to her name, and no plan for her future. Carlos came to a mutual decision with his parents about his migration, with the sole intention of finding work and supporting his family. Mariana's decision to leave had little to do with a desire to reunify with her father, whom she barely knew, but was instead prompted by community violence. And Edwin was sent for, with the purpose of reunification with his father and the idea of starting his education. Each of these stories was made possible by the specific economic and political climate of the respective countries. These diverse stories are imbued with classed and gendered logics and respond to family dynamics, work opportunities, and community violence. They demonstrate a wide array of possibilities in terms of youth independence and parental responsibility. And, the youth articulated a wide range of goals for their migration, including seeking safety, reaching a better life and educational opportunities, and working to support a family. These stories clearly demonstrate diverse needs upon arrival. However, at the point when youth are detained in the United States, the government begins a process that flattens these diverse realities and requires very clear relationships between parents and children. Indeed, the complexity of these youths' experiences all but disappears as they enter into social agencies that are required to address these youth with a one-size-fits-all solution to their futures.

The Family Reunification Process

The next part of every single story described in this chapter was the same: Angelica, Cynthia, Carlos, Edwin, and Mariana were all apprehended by border enforcement upon entering the United States. After they were detained at the border for seventy-two hours, they were sent to long-term government shelters for minors, where their detainment continued while their legal cases were processed. One of the most immediately important staff members in these shelters is a family reunification caseworker. This social worker's job is to find a family placement for youth outside of the shelter. In order of preference, placements might happen with parents, other family members (such as adult siblings or an uncle), friends of the family, or foster care. In rare situations, older youth might be sent to independent-living transitional facilities.

The determination for sponsorship is conducted by case managers through interviews with the youth and then verification of the sponsor's identity and relationship to the child through documentation and fingerprinting. All adults residing in the household must have their identity proven, fingerprints taken, and background checked. Case managers then conduct assessments regarding the suitability of the home, the motivation of the sponsor, and any factors that might put the young person at risk. Potential sponsors must also attend orientations regarding their responsibilities to the released child. The adult who is tasked with the responsibility to take care of the youth must sign an official "Sponsor Care Agreement," which outlines thirteen basic responsibilities. These include providing for the basic "physical and mental well-being" of the youth, ensuring that the young person attends immigration proceedings, and becoming the legal guardian of the youth.

The Trafficking Victims Protection Reauthorization Act of 2008 requires further scrutiny of sponsors for cases that raise red flags. These "red flags" include suspicions of trafficking, children with disabilities, victims of physical or sexual abuse, and concern that the "child's sponsor clearly presents a risk of abuse, maltreatment, exploitation or trafficking." In these situations, a home study is required, in which a social worker goes to the home to conduct in-person interviews and evaluate home conditions. This report is considered a "collaborative psychoeducational process" in which the caseworker both evaluates the sponsor and provides resources for areas of possible concern. If a sponsor or an adult member of the household fails to pass a background check, he or she is further evaluated according to the severity of the offense, the time that has passed, and the evidence of rehabilitation. A denial of release to a particular sponsor will occur on the basis of several conditions, including convictions related to child abuse, convictions in the past five years related to physical assault or drug use, or convictions related to trafficking in persons. Upon release, some families that raised concerns receive additional services and support. Case managers are also required to provide a thirty-day well-being follow-up call. The success of this call closes the government's intervention in the case.

Many of the case managers whom I spoke with described the requirements of family reunification as a swinging pendulum. Even those who had worked in the system for a relatively short amount of time felt that they were dealing with a constantly changing target in regard to the rules that they followed and the goals they were supposed to meet. They constantly dealt with public and political pressures between two seemingly opposing goals: on one end, they felt that they needed to process youth and their families as quickly as possible, so as to avoid youths' long-term stays in the centers. The negative outcomes of long-term detention are well known by child advocates, and even in shelters that fully abided by the established standards for education, homelike environments, and child-appropriate practices, advocates of youth felt strongly that the stays should be limited—if not altogether abolished.[11] On the other hand, following highly publicized cases of abusive guardians, workers also found that they faced pressure to slow the screening of potential sponsors in order to avoid dangerous or inappropriate placements. Professionals frequently cited a case in Ohio, in which six Guatemalan youth were released on separate occasions to the same sponsor, who was actually a labor trafficker and forced the boys to work at an egg farm under horrendous conditions.[12] Indeed, this very case was often cited as a rationalization for the strict processes that case managers must go through to approve families—an onerous process that often increases children's stay in detention.

Although this is certainly a difficult tension, it is also a somewhat false dichotomy, which pits two aspects of child welfare against one another, assuming that long-term detention is necessary for safe placements. Indeed, many of the requirements that might delay a release under the guise of protection are, in reality, inappropriate or particularly onerous for transnational families.[13] For example, when a social worker asks for a birth certificate, this might not be a document that a family from a rural area possesses. Mercedes, a case worker who primarily worked in family reunification decisions, described at length the difficulties of getting some of this documentation for youth from rural communities. She told one story in which she attempted to obtain a youth's birth certificate from a mother who lived in a rural area in Guatemala. The mother spoke an indigenous language that was used only in that region, making translation virtually impossible. Further, when Mercedes was finally able to communicate that the mother needed to fax a copy of the daughter's birth certificate, the mother did not understand what a fax was—much less know where to access one. Mercedes laughed as she explained that she advised the mother to go ask young people or educated people in the community what a fax was. The situation was eventually resolved after the mother traveled a significant distance to a university, where she was able to send the birth certificate. Although these situations were less common when families lived in urban areas, they were significant barriers for rural families or families who spoke lesser-known languages. This could delay reunification cases for months, thus extending the youth's stay in the government shelter.

Once identities have been established, case managers must begin to dig into the monotony of everyday life, a process that creates new kinds of barriers for immigrant households. Nicki, who conducts home studies for cases that have raised red flags, explained that she follows a checklist, looking at everything from income to the physical household. She explained, "There is the description of the sponsor's home and of their community. I have to see every room in the home and make sure that there is nothing of concern in the home, including smoke detectors, and that the minor has a room of his/her own. And I have to be shown that room." As Nicki rattled off the checklist, I was struck by the requirement that the young person have their own room. I asked several other professionals about this requirement and received several different interpretations. Most loosely, some felt that they could pass the case if the young person just had their own bed or was sharing a room with a sibling. Others agreed with and followed the stricter interpretation. While rooms and beds are objective measures, they are steeped in assumptions about class and culture. The requirement ignores, first, the realities of income and space, especially for poor families living in expensive, metropolitan areas. Further, it is rooted in an American standard of privacy that was only accessible to the average American teen after World War II and has been driven by consumption practices and beliefs about private space being a tool in teen maturation.[14] In short, this "objective" standard is full of class and culture biases.

The more subjective areas of the evaluation include understandings of relationships and motivation. Nicki discussed how she must "read between the lines" in her interviews to determine whether she believes the sponsors will truly "step up to the plate" to parent the youth. Ashley, another worker who evaluates the "red flag" cases, explained that she looks at the discipline techniques a parent might use: "How do you discipline your kids? What would be appropriate discipline for this child? What are your rules going to be in your home?" If parenting techniques are not deemed suitable, Ashley provides education to shape parenting practices to align with American standards of discipline. Nicki does the same: "I try to have a discussion about the parent, about what their parenting style is like and their discipline and how they might imagine parenting, you know, whether it is an adolescent that they don't know very well or a younger child. So what their discipline style might be like, as well." In this way, parents find that they must defend their parenting, even when there is no explicit reason for that parenting to be in question.

Parents who are undocumented also face a different set of barriers in proving their ability to care for their own children. Being undocumented does not preclude a parent from reunification with his or her child. However, it does create tensions that appear to case managers as red flags. For example, youth are often afraid of discussing their parents with social workers in the shelter, if they know their parents to be undocumented. Undocumented parents might also decide to not come forward. This was the case for Edwin, from Honduras, whose father had sent for him. Although Edwin's father lived in the United States and had made the decision for Edwin to migrate, he did not come forward to have Edwin released from the ORR shelter. Instead, a family friend who was documented completed the sponsorship process, and once Edwin had been released to him, he promptly turned Edwin over to his father. This issue may also occur when case managers attempt to contact family members in the home country in order to ask about the sponsor: these family members are also wary of providing information if they know that the potential sponsor is undocumented.

This fear is not unfounded. In a 2017 executive order titled "Border Security and Immigration Enforcement Improvements," President Trump called for the prosecution of any parent who "facilitates the illegal smuggling or trafficking of an alien child" through the placement of the parent in removal proceedings or other criminal prosecution.[15] In practice, this policy can be applied to any parent whose child has come to the United States alone, with the help of a coyote. The implementation of this specific policy confirmed the suspicions that already existed around the cooperation between ORR and DHS. Parents feel that they must stay in hiding, and they may avoid communicating with their detained children out of fear of prosecution.

In addition, undocumented status can also influence the mundane course of everyday life. Family reunification worker Mercedes explained that a particularly frustrating aspect of undocumented status is having what is called a "transportation plan" in place. Sponsors must prove that they are able to transport their children safely and legally. Undocumented sponsors who drive without a license must set up an alternative plan for their children. This frustrated Mercedes tremendously. She commented that she knew that in an emergency, the licenseless parent would surely drive a car. But instead, she must ask for a specific transportation plan: "I feel so stupid asking for that. The sponsor was like, 'well he's going to school by bus, and we live in a little city, so we can use public transport if I can't drive my kid.' And I was like, yeah, okay." For undocumented parents who live in rural communities, the transportation plan can be much more difficult.

One of the most paradoxical aspects of the work of family reunification was that case managers had to help parents and sponsors create a deportation plan. This plan ensured that undocumented sponsors had alternative arrangements in place, in the case of their own deportation. The irony of the situation here is that the US government carries out multiple, contradictory roles in relation to these transnational families. Under the guise of ensuring children's well-being, government agencies must ask for parents' contingency plans if that same government rips the household apart again.

Finding Families

The lived realities of poor, undocumented, and transnational families may impede the release of a young person from a shelter. However, even beyond this issue, I argue that there is a more fundamental problem with how the ORR understands the needs of youth and their sponsors and transnational families. Generally, the family reunification workers with whom I spoke felt positive about the youths' futures with the sponsors who had been approved by the ORR. These social workers felt that they had followed the rules and had adequately prepared youth and families for reunification. Further, the ORR currently conducts thirty-day follow-up calls to determine whether these placements are adequate. According to the ORR website, 90 percent of parents and sponsors were reached in this thirty-day follow-up, and of these, only 5 percent reported problems that required interventions.[16] However, on the basis of my interviews with both youth and professionals, I argue that these numbers do not reflect the actual lives of youth, perhaps because thirty days is very little time in which to measure the success of a placement. In my findings, of the seven youth I interviewed who had been given a placement from the government, only two had remained with those placements while minors. Additionally, community professionals had numerous stories of working with youth who quickly left the placement they received from ORR.

Although my data is not quantitatively meaningful, it does reflect an overlooked reality in many youths' lives. First, many youth who live transnational lives experience a distinct fracturing in their relationship to their families. The stresses of migration rupture family ties before, during, and after the migration of a family member. These stresses are felt by all family members, and include the guilt experienced by parents (mothers, in particular) who are not physically present, the trauma and anger experienced by children who wish to be in the presence of their parents, and the burdens borne by extended family members who take on caregiving activities when parents are separated from children. Some transnational families find that it is impossible to experience the traditional sense of family when legal institutions prevent physical closeness.[17] Second, as I explored at the beginning of the chapter, the youth in this system come from a wide array of family arrangements and maintain varying degrees of independence and dependence in relation to their family members. The expectations of life in the United States also varied tremendously, with youth such as Angelica hoping to pursue an education, while youth such as Carlos imagined working full-time. This reality creates another significant disconnect between the expectations and the rules of the ORR and the actualities of these youths' lives. In particular, there is a distinct failure to recognize life processes that vary from traditional notions of American adolescence as well as nontraditional relationships between the adults and youth in a household. Thus, while sponsors in government placements might have the correct number of smoke detectors in their household or be able to articulate discipline standards in accordance with American values, the ORR requirements often fail to meet the needs of the youth in much more fundamental ways and do not provide the structural supports that correspond to the realities in these families.

Sponsors: Foster Care without the Check

There is an implicit assumption that every nonparent sponsor assigned by the ORR will act as a parent to the youth placed in their care. They must be willing to sign youth up for school and accompany youth to court. Additionally, they agree to become the youth's legal guardian as soon as possible. Family reunification workers are often very skeptical of these placements and work hard to ensure that the sponsors are willing to take on the parenting role. Maribel, a family reunification worker, explained that she would often "test" sponsors to see if they were willing to go above and beyond by making themselves available to her when needed. She explained that she expected these sponsors to support the youth beyond providing just a shelter and food.

Is this person going to give the kid what he needs: food, clothing? And is he going to do it further than when the kid turns eighteen? Is he still going to check up on him? Is he still going to make sure that he goes to school? Is he going to make sure that he enrolls in college and keeps up with his immigration case? Things like that. And the working thing . . . I wonder if the sponsor is going to continue to push education on this kid or just kind of give in to that: "Ok, just start working. That's what you came for."

Taylor, another worker with family reunification, looked explicitly at sponsors' emotional capacity to handle the trauma that youth faced: "What we always look for is sponsors who are very aware. They are aware that a minor has been through this journey, that a minor has experienced sexual abuse or has reported some kind of abuse. They are aware that that is something I should pay attention to, something I should stay on top of, something that I am responsible for." And Brenda tried to ensure that sponsors would provide significant financial assistance:

A lot of the youth and their families acquire a debt for the journey, and I ask: Is the minor going to be responsible for paying that? If they say yes, that is kind of a red flag. Then I ask, "So, is he going to be responsible to pay it off right away? Or, is it going to be something that, once the minor can legally work and has graduated high school . . ." Although we know that in many cases they are not going to do that, especially older kids. . . . But I inquire about sponsors' long-term commitment, especially if this is a kid who is seventeen. I say, "Well, even though your legal responsibility is going to end when he turns eighteen, you understand that the kid is going to need help beyond the age of seventeen."

These quotations demonstrate that the expectations for the role of the nonparent sponsor are high. Sponsors—who may be family, friends, or other community members—essentially agree to take on the role of foster parents. Yet, they are entirely distinct from foster parents in some important ways. As Layla, an educator whom I interviewed, wryly stated, sponsorship is "foster care without the check." Indeed, this is a racialized foster system, in which predominantly Latinx families are charged with providing foster care without the financial support that other foster families would have. Because these sponsors are part of the networks of the immigrant youth, they too often are undocumented and have limited resources. This means that, even when sponsors have the intention of meeting the expectations of ORR, they do not always have the ability to do so.

Angelica's story provides a clear example of this discrepancy. Through the ORR, Angelica had been placed with an uncle whom she did not know, in a suburb of Houston. She did not talk a lot about this uncle, other than explaining that he lived with his wife and daughter, and that she felt uncomfortable living with someone who was virtually a stranger to her. Angelica said she put up with only two weeks there before she sought out someone else whom she knew who would take her in. These were family friends who lived in a town nearby who went to a church that she wanted to be a part of. Angelica told her uncle that she would move in with them instead, so that she could go to the church. The uncle agreed to the move. This new family provided a stable home for Angelica for several months, and they helped her to register for school. However, she soon became unsettled there as well. She explained to me that it can be difficult, as someone raised in a different country, to get along with people here. Angelica felt uncomfortable sleeping in a makeshift bed in the corner of the daughter's bedroom. Plus, the family often wanted Angelica to do the cooking and cleaning for the household. Angelica explained that she was trying to go to school and keep up with the family's chores, and she often was unable to get enough sleep. Further, the family did not provide Angelica her own food, so Angelica was forced to buy this on her own. Angelica's boyfriend—who had immigrated to the States a year and a half before her—began helping her pay for food. Soon, Angelica made the decision to leave this family and move in with her boyfriend. She explained that he had always supported her and her desire to finish her education. Although she still had to work several hours a week to help pay for expenses, her boyfriend was fully supportive of her education, and he paid for the bulk of food and rent so that she could finish high school.

In Angelica's story, it is clear that the government-appointed sponsor, although related, was simply not a viable option for Angelica. Presumably, Angelica and her uncle jumped through the hoops of the ORR as it was the quickest way for her to be released from the shelter. However, despite government policies regarding sponsors' obligations to the youth, this uncle did not seem concerned about letting Angelica leave. His sense of obligation, at least according to the story Angelica told, was minimal. The second family had not agreed to any governmental requirements, but did provide some support, such as helping Angelica pursue school. However, it was clear that Angelica was required to earn her very meager keep in this household, which made Angelica uncomfortable. She felt conflicted that she was both a dependent of the household and also essentially an employee.

Angelica finally landed in a safe home with her long-term boyfriend. This became the first house in which Angelica felt welcomed, supported, and, indeed, loved. It was also a placement that was strictly forbidden by the Office of Refugee Resettlement, since Angelica was a minor. Living with her boyfriend, who could not become a legal guardian, meant that Angelica was not eligible to pursue Special Immigrant Juvenile Status. Further, the social workers I spoke with would sometimes actively avoid placing a young person in the same community as their romantic interest. Occasionally, these preferences were based on concerns about abusive behaviors by the partner. However, this was also a very gendered practice, driven both by subjective beliefs around girls' sexual agency and the cultural realities of laws around statutory rape.[18] Social workers expressed concerns that young women would be taken advantage of by their partners and that young men would get into legal trouble for engaging in sexual relations with a partner who was under the age of legal consent. "This actually happens," Samantha, an attorney, would explain to her youth clients. "We actually see people who are arrested, go to jail, and then they get deported, because they had sex." These concerns meant that ORR workers would very actively avoid placements that might facilitate romantic connections.[19]

Like Angelica, Marco also received a placement that failed to meet the expectations set by the ORR. Marco immigrated from Guatemala at age sixteen to pursue educational dreams, which he could not afford in Guatemala. He was apprehended at the border and then detained in a shelter for four months, since the workers had a difficult time finding a sponsor for him. His family first found a cousin who initially came forward as a potential sponsor. However, the cousin was honest with the family reunification worker about his financial limitations and was unable to support Marco. Eventually Marco's family found a friend who, in Marco's words, agreed to help Marco "get out." The friend went through the approval process, and Marco was eventually released to him. This friend was working as a farmworker in Florida for an employer who provided both a salary and a place to live. However, the friend was undocumented, and not long after Marco arrived, he lost his job—and, as a result, his home. Marco found himself out of a home as well. The sponsor was willing to find another home with Marco, but since the new living situation would no longer be attached to an employer, the sponsor would need to pay rent. Because of this, he stipulated that Marco would have to work in order to help cover expenses. Marco decided to pursue other options. Through a local church, Marco connected with an older man who agreed to take him in. This placement finally met Marco's needs. Marco lived with the older man and continued to pursue his education. He said that he felt like an adopted son.

Many professionals told similar stories of youths' precariousness in their households. Paul worked for a school district that enrolled many unaccompanied youth, and he reported that it was not uncommon to hear stories such as these. He explained that cases of extreme neglect and abuse were rare, but it was more common for youth to be with sponsors who were struggling financially and who would eventually ask the young person to leave. Amanda, who worked in the same school district, agreed: "Sponsors don't get any kind of compensation, so taking on another person sometimes puts on a lot of strain, and we see those kids, you know, more often needing to pay rent, or not feeling well inside the home. Actually being put out of the home." Amanda went on to explain that sponsors often found the demands such as accompanying youth to required doctor appointments or court dates particularly burdensome, since they would have to take time off from their own jobs.

These types of stories do not coincide with the reports from the family reunification workers. From ORR's perspective, sponsors have been thoroughly vetted to be able to take on the emotional and financial role of parents. Yet from the perspective of community members, this is not the case. The disconnect here seems to be not in the family reunification worker's inability to follow the ORR protocol around sponsors but rather in the lack of support upon youths' release and the narrow expectations of what youths' lives might look like upon release. Although thorough, the vetting process for sponsors does not align with the actual needs of youth.

Romanticized Family Reunifications

While ORR case managers often felt confident about sponsor placement decisions, they were even more optimistic about family reunification between parents and their children. Reunification worker Lindsey commented that it was the best part of her job: "My favorite part is working with the [parent] sponsors, being able to facilitate that reunification. It is a beautiful thing, being able to see a child and a mother, for example, and how they interact after being separated for so long."

Yet, these sentiments fail to acknowledge the depth of harm and trauma exerted by government policies that tear families apart. Researchers have already established that even placements with parents are complicated, after years of family separation. Family reunification is often highly anticipated but leaves many teens disillusioned and alienated.[20] This is especially true of older teens and in cases in which the parents have started new families.[21] When I spoke with research participants who saw the aftermath of this reunification, these realities were clear in my research as well. Susana, an attorney, explained, "A lot of people really romanticize the reunification process. This kid made it here, and now he's going to be together with his mom or uncle or whoever. And that situation, at first, seems really exciting. But then all of these issues start coming up."

Four of my research participants were reunited with parents immediately: Nicolas, Javier, Mariana, and Edwin (although Edwin had been placed with a friend but quickly reunified with his father). However, Nicolas was the only one to remain living with that parent at the time of our interview (less than a year after his arrival to the United States). He reported that he felt comfortable in his dad's house, although he did not feel as though he knew his father very well. The other three participants did not remain with their parents while minors. This speaks to the legal violence produced through government policies that make it impossible for fractured families to function once again as a traditional family.[22] Once they are torn apart, it is difficult for families to be put back together again. Although families are often at the mercy of government policies, the resulting emotional pain is frequently directed inward, toward other family members. In her research on transnational families, sociologist Leisy Abrego shows that children may harbor resentment towards their parents who have been separated from them, particularly towards their mothers, due to cultural expectations around mothering. Furthermore, the legal status of family members residing in the United States can result in lengthy separation, where contact is limited to phone calls that are unsatisfying to the family members. The emotional toll that lengthy separations have is tremendous, and children who do not have any physical contact with their parents fare much worse than those who are visited by parents, even if infrequently. Uncertainty also plagues separations, when neither parents nor children know when or if reunification is possible. This means that trust becomes ever more fragile and, if reunification happens, it is difficult to restore once more.

Javier was generally reticent when he discussed his migration with me. I asked him questions, such as why he immigrated, and he would respond, "It is really difficult to explain. It is hard to explain." However, when I asked what happened when he was placed with his family and why he did not stay with them, he quickly and easily articulated the details:

> Because I haven't known them since I was a boy. I haven't seen them. Or rather, we talk, but it's on the phone, and I don't know if it is really them or if they are other people, like friends. That's why when I arrived, I saw them, and I started thinking, "Let's see if they are really my parents or not." I have younger sisters that are from here, two of them. But I don't get along with them either because I feel like they bother me, that's why. And, I would fight with my dad every day. There are times that he would tell me things, and I would get angry . . . and that's why I went to live with my uncle because I don't know if my relationship [with my dad] will ever work.

Javier moved in with an uncle who, according to Javier, treated him like his own son. I asked what the difference was, and Javier explained that he did not fight with his uncle and his uncle gave him advice. Javier said that his father would give him advice too, but this advice would make him angry. For example, his father would tell him not to do drugs. But,

Javier insisted that he would never do drugs; he had been straitlaced since he was a kid. Javier expressed deep resentment towards his father, who knew so little about Javier that he failed to understand what Javier believed was an essential part of his nature. Javier's difficulties living with his family stemmed both from his anger that his father did not understand him and the difficulties of entering a "blended" family, with some of his sibling born in the United States. Just as other youth shared, Javier found the cultural difference with his siblings, paired with his own alienation from his parents, too much to bear.

Edwin shared a similar experience with Javier. ORR did not release Edwin to his father but to a family friend; however, when this man picked him up from the airport, he told Edwin that he would be living with his father after all. As discussed at the beginning of this chapter, the purpose of Edwin's immigration was to reunify with his father. However, Edwin did not remain with his father either. When I spoke with him, at age seventeen, Edwin was living on his own, attending high school in a Chicago suburb, and working as a bus boy. He explained that his father had a new family, and so Edwin had left the household. Like Javier, Edwin experienced a profound sense of alienation from both his father and also his American half-siblings. In addition, although he had lived with his grandmother in his home country, Edwin had been largely independent as a child. He had been working to feed his family from a young age, and he was comfortable continuing to live in this independent way in the United States. Edwin explained that he no longer needed his father or his father's advice: "I don't want his advice anymore. I can live my own life." Unique to Edwin's situation was the fact that Edwin was able to manage work full-time and attend high school while living independently. This was not without significant barriers, of course, but Edwin felt more at ease balancing these demands by himself than he did living with his father.

Mariana's reunification with her father had far worse consequences than these examples. Mariana, who had immigrated to flee gender-based gang violence, was placed with her father and his new wife in Houston, once she was released from the government shelter. However, within weeks she knew that this new situation was not going to work. She described her father as a jealous man who would not let her leave the house, who demanded the passwords to her social media accounts, and who insulted her. This culminated one night when she woke up to find him on top of her, touching her, drunk and mumbling that she looked like her mother. Only a few nights later, he arrived to the house intoxicated again, and began hitting his wife. Mariana's step-sister called the police, and within two months, her father had been deported.

While her father's deportation relieved the violence in the household, Mariana soon discovered that with him away, she was no longer welcome. As with other youth in this study, Mariana's ability to integrate into a blended family proved difficult, and her belonging in this family was contingent upon her father's presence. The family wanted her to pay rent, which she could not afford as she wanted to finish high school. Mariana was fortunate to have a supportive school system, and when she told her school counselor what had happened, the counselor worked to help find Mariana housing. She lived in a shelter for a short time before the counselor located an unofficial American foster family in the community. This family has provided Mariana tremendous support, and she remains with them to this day.

The ORR has strict mechanisms in place to avoid placing youth in abusive situations. However, in this case, these mechanisms failed, leaving Mariana vulnerable to violence and, ultimately, trapped in a household that did not support her goals and growth. The school system proved to be Mariana's lifeline, finding her supportive community members who could provide the financial support and caring environment that she wanted. In Mariana's situation, a positive placement was one in which she did not have to work; she was happy to focus on advancing her educational goals.

The professionals working in communities with youth—particularly educators and attorneys—often witnessed first-hand the difficulties that youth and their families faced as they navigated their newly reunified family dynamics. The issues presented in the three cases above, particularly resentment and feelings of disconnection with blended families, came up in multiple interviews with professionals. Emmanuel, a counselor, talked about working with youth on becoming part of the family system again. He noted that in addition to the feelings of abandonment, youth might also resent the traditional parent-child relationship that parents hope to establish upon reunification.

There is a lot of disconnection, and there is a lot of hurt feelings from the youth that their parents or their relatives kind of left them in their native country on their own. [. . .] There is a lack of connection, lack of trust, a lack of relationship. So when family members have certain expectations of them—like, oh you've got to behave in this manner—the youth, not only do they have trauma, but they already have their way of living. . . . It is difficult to listen to [their parents] when there is no trust or relationship.

Emmanuel noted that youth were often resistant to the idea of having to live under the authority of parents for the first time in their memories. They had already established themselves in independent ways, and moving in with parents was a significant emotional challenge due both to their independent sense of self and also expectations and resentments that have been harbored.

These conflicts are often overlooked by the family reunification process. While advocates for immigrant youth are often concerned about the tension between long detention stays and thorough vetting of families, I argue that this is not the only tension that should be considered. Instead, my concern resides with the inadequate understanding of the realities of reunified lives. The emphasis on rigid roles for adults and children in the family—such as concerns over discipline techniques— ignores the reality that youth might not fit into these traditional roles with their parents. The romanticization of reunification overlooks the very real barriers that many of these families will encounter. Reunified youth may not have a strong connection to their families; they may feel confused by new expectations to live as dependents; and they may feel angry about the changes that their parents have undergone. Additionally, although some youth hope to pursue education alone, many will have both the desire and the need to work, no matter whom they are placed with. Blindly assuming that all youth will be able to fall into the "typical" American adolescence in relation to their parents fails to see the realities of the immigrant families.

I do not believe that more screening or vetting would assist in creating better placement outcomes for youth. Instead, just as nonparent sponsors need support, families also could benefit from additional resources to navigate these tensions. While case managers were tasked with documenting legal relationships, teaching discipline techniques, and testing potential sponsors for the level of their commitment, youth would be better served by postrelease and community-based support that could aid in repairing fractured families and supporting the economic needs of sponsors.

2

Legends for the State

I met with Lavonne in her private law office, located in a small midwestern city. Her office is a refurbished townhouse, and I sat in what
clearly used to be a living room, watching a large grandfather clock
tick past my scheduled meeting time. Multiple social workers had
suggested that I speak with Lavonne, as her legal work with unaccompanied youth was legendary in her community. When she finally
emerged from her office, a half-hour late, Lavonne was scolding a
middle-aged Latino man, in her accented Spanish. She towered over
him in both stature and energy. When she saw me, she quickly shooed
the man away before ushering me into her office. Lavonne was not
short for words; she spoke loudly and quickly and needed no questions from me to start talking. She had been taking pro bono cases for
unaccompanied youth for over a decade, but she did not just accept
any case that passed through her office. She liked the meaty cases, she
explained: young children, dramatic situations, interesting legal questions. She wielded her compassion like a machete, charging forward
with the youth she took under her wing, cutting away the legal barriers in front of them. Lavonne was impatient, and, as she put it, she
had a sharp "bullshit radar" for both her clients and the judges who
heard their cases. She knew how to play the game. She was not intimi-
dated by judges, and she recognized exactly what would and would
not move them to support her case. In explaining her experience with
asylum cases, she complained, "You got to have a dead relative . . .
can't be injured, got to be dead. Mother's lost an eye, they darn near
killed her, but apparently darn near ain't good enough."

My meeting with Jennifer could not have been more different from
my meeting with Lavonne. Jennifer had only recently passed her boards
when we met in the rented office building of her legal aid clinic. Her bare
office was organized and meticulously maintained. She spoke slowly,
quietly weighing her words with misty eyes as she spoke about the youth

clients she had worked with over the past year. She explained that she had not been familiar with the unaccompanied youth population when she started law school, but "upon meeting my first little client for the first time, my heart just opened wide up!" She was moved by clients who had humble beginnings and big dreams, something she related to from her own story. She explained that the judges she worked with were "hit and miss" when it came to sympathy for immigrants. They preferred that she present cases in which youth were impressive, eloquent, with a strong command of English and a clear path to legal relief.

Lavonne and Jennifer were dissimilar in personality, experience, and their approach to their youth clients. Yet, they both acted as important gatekeepers in the legal system. Youth who wish to stay in the United States must find a pathway to legal relief, and attorneys are essential in this process.[1] When youth meet with attorneys, they must explain their story in a way that the attorney deems workable—that is, the attorney must see a way in which that story can be massaged into a legal claim. In this way, the telling of a story is the currency of the legal system, and young people who wish to remain in the United States must, above all, be able to communicate a good story about their lives. They must first convince an attorney that their case has merit, and then, along with that attorney, they must construct a specific narrative—what I call a border-land legend—that tells the story of their life in such a way that it can be traded for benefits in the United States.

Stories are powerful tools. Stories give oppressed people and communities the ability to self-define, make political alliances, advance their needs, create communities, legitimize experiences of marginalized groups, and contribute to peace making and peace building.[2] Stories, when given the authentic voice of the oppressed, are potent tools that dismantle power structures. But, stories are also tools to maintain power. "Storytelling often represents the most ideological moments," explains sociologist Eduardo Bonilla-Silva, in his work on color-blind racism.[3] Stories can help to frame the world we live in while also obscuring the complex and sometimes hidden nature of that world. In this way, storytelling can also promote the status quo, obscure inequalities, stir up national panics, or rationalize inadequate responses to injustices.

Storytelling by humanitarian subjects has a particular function. Humanitarian storytelling is used to reveal past suffering with the purpose of legitimizing that suffering as psychological trauma. This trauma, in turn, provides humanitarian subjects the ability to receive aid. Humanitarian victims who can master these "confessional technologies" are more able to access benefits and safety.[4] Anthropologist Erica Caple James calls these "technologies of trauma," which are the means by which a humanitarian subject can be granted legitimacy as a sufferer.[5] In this rests a strange irony: suffering—the language of the humanitarian subject and story—is privileged, and those who can best tell their story receive more rights from government entities than those whose stories and suffering are not legitimized.[6]

In this sense borderland legends are, in the most practical way, currency to be exchanged for legal relief, a testimony to be handed to a judge in hopes of US residency. They are also currency exchanged among professionals, the media, and politicians. These legends become fodder in political debates about the United States' response to youth, and they are passed among stakeholders as justification for immigration reform. Simultaneously, they are used to rationalize the inclusion of some youth and to justify the exclusion of others in the United States' system of aid. Borderland legends follow a political strategy that places some immigrants on a national pedestal to serve as exemplars of "good" immigrants, and those who "deserve" help from the US government—at the expense of others. This is a strategy that has been used frequently in immigration debates. As sociologist Roberto G. Gonzales shows, young activists and politicians who fought for the DREAM Act did so in the early years by emphasizing the innocence of young migrants: "They were framed as clean-cut, college-bound youngsters who spoke fluent and largely unaccented English."[7] While the strategy was politically advantageous in its work of humanizing young migrants, it created further divisions between the so-called innocent youth and their "criminal" parents. This strategy privileges the few at the expense of the larger immigrant community. Similarly, as I explore in this chapter, not every story can become a borderland legend. As in all humanitarian realities, access to resources or legal relief is granted through the performance of suffering and moral legitimacy.[8] Indeed, these borderland legends have a specific shape that fits neatly into legal categories and, as such, excludes many youth from the promises of the American dream.

The Shape of the Borderland Legend: Cynthia's Story

Borderland legends are productive narratives that present very specific storylines regarding youths' past and present. A borderland legend begins with strong characters, children whose origins in poverty and violence do not dim their internal lights. We root for these characters, and feel deeply that they are innocent and deserving. The rising action of the legend occurs when youth make the extraordinary decision to rely on their own strength and resilience to flee this dangerous beginning. The harrowing quest follows, where despite their great vulnerability, youth traverse international borders, escaping, if not unscathed, still relatively whole in body and spirit. The falling action is the arrival: the warm welcome into the generous country that opens its arms to the refuse of the world. And then, the resolution: youth find a loving home, they receive help and education, and we watch them walk into the bright horizons of their American dreams.

I am not immune to borderland legendry with its miraculous, yet utterly predictable, story arc. Whether through my personal contacts, the youth I advocate for, or the participants who share their stories for interviews, I find myself filled with admiration as I hear these accounts. One of the first borderland legends I encountered came from Cynthia, who was both a personal contact and also volunteered to talk with me when she heard about my research. As discussed briefly in the previous chapter, Cynthia fled a perfect storm of legend making: poverty, neglect, and patriarchal oppression. She was a desperately poor indigenous girl in rural Central America. Her father was gone and her mother neglected to care for her, frequently disappearing on drunken binges, leaving Cynthia in charge of younger siblings for days on end. Going on just ten years of age, Cynthia would stop her infant brother's crying with water and coffee—the only sustenance that was available while her mother was gone. Cynthia laughed bitterly as she told me this; her own infant was in her arms, drinking a bottle of formula. But Cynthia did not hate her mother. She explained, "When she wasn't drunk like that, she would help me and all that. She was good. But when she would leave, she would leave for weeks. She wouldn't come back, and I would have to look for her because she would leave us with nothing." Cynthia began working, washing clothes to buy shoes for her brother: *"Era como mi hijo"* (He was like my son). But life did not get better: as rumors swelled about her mother's licentious money making, Cynthia, too, became an object of ridicule. "*Puta!*" (Whore!), people would yell at her as she walked down the streets. Cynthia described being suicidal at this point, unable to cope with the hardship around her. So, she began weighing her options: she considered going to the capital to find better work and send money to her siblings. Instead, she heard a rumor that a man was taking women and girls north. He would find them work in the United States, and they could pay him through that work. Cynthia did not hesitate.

At the point when I was listening to Cynthia's story during our full interview, I had known Cynthia for years and had put together bits and pieces of her life through multiple conversations. But I was struck by this moment, this rumor of a man who would bring her to the United States. I stopped her midstory, a bit shocked: "Did you trust him?" I asked. Cynthia reflected on this question: "In those times, I didn't know evil. As they say, I was really ignorant. I didn't know anything about life. For me, everything was normal. Oh, they just want to help. But I didn't know what was happening. Now I realize: Oh wow. That happened. Well, knowing what I know now, I wouldn't have come. With how much they kill, they rape and they do all of those things . . ." Cynthia's story continued. She decided to trust this man and leave. She described her leaving as an escape. Her mother wanted her to migrate north, but her grandparents were not convinced. They believed she was just looking for men, and, regardless, immigrating was not a woman's role. The day that her grandparents threatened to lock her in the house so she could not leave, Cynthia escaped at midnight into the mountains. She met up with a woman from the community who was also going with the man, and they began their journey.

It was difficult to follow Cynthia's recollections of this journey because it was difficult for her to understand everything. She spoke Q'eqchi, and her Spanish at the time was limited, so she could only grasp pieces of the conversations around her. The man brought them to Mexico, where Cynthia believed that he sold them to police—or other coyotes, she was not sure. She believed they were sold again, probably to new coyotes. They traveled between houses, and Cynthia explained that the coyotes would call the girls into separate rooms by themselves; the girls would always come out of the rooms crying. Cynthia thought to herself, "I don't know. Maybe they don't have money or something happened." One night, the men called her into the room. The woman from Cynthia's community exclaimed, "What are you going to say to her? She is my daughter. I have to go with." The men decided to take another girl that night instead.

Eventually they arrived to the US border, where they were apprehended the first time they crossed. Cynthia told the border agents who caught her that she was from Mexico, and they sent her back across the border. She and the group tried to cross again the next night, and they were apprehended again. In the third crossing and third apprehension, in which Cynthia was stuffed in a trunk with four other migrants, the truth came out: she was a fourteen-year-old from Guatemala, and this fact qualified her to fight for her right to stay in the United States and argue her case in immigration court.

It is hard to say how Cynthia's story would have played out had she been eighteen. At fourteen years old, Cynthia was separated from the rest of the group and put in a cell for minors. She never saw the group again. I felt extremely grateful as she explained this. I asked if she ever paid the coyote who brought her from Guatemala: "No, because we all got separated. I don't know anything about him now. I don't know if he exists or if he is alive. Nothing. . . . And thank God I don't know because imagine the debt I would have on top of it all. Because he paid a lot of money." My stomach turned as I listened to this. I felt tense just knowing the what-ifs.

Cynthia's story arc had a happy ending, like all good borderland legends. She was transferred to a small, homelike shelter run by the US government, where she felt loved and cared for. She believed that she was gifted, for a moment in time, the childhood that she never had. She received clothes, the staff took care of her when she was sick, and she was taught daily lessons in English and other subjects. She remembered, in particular, that a staff member named Don Victor would make pancakes for breakfast. Cynthia reflected on this time as some of her happiest days. After her detainment in the shelter, Cynthia was transferred to a foster home in a small midwestern city. Her foster mother was loving but very religious and very strict. School was terribly difficult, and Cynthia cried often in the bathroom, but she moved forward with significant help from her foster family, social workers, and volunteer advocates. She dug deep into her reservoirs of tenacity and resilience and pushed forward.

The short story from there: Cynthia graduated high school and got her license as a certified nurse's assistant. She was able to receive immigration relief, although she could not remember what kind. I asked if it is was the Special Immigrant Juvenile Status, and she said that sounded right. She had a baby, got married, bought a house, and had another baby. She and her young family adopted a tiny Chihuahua. This was, indeed, a happy ending.

Yet, during our interview, I asked Cynthia if she was happy. She gave me a tired smile. She responded that she wished she could do things differently. She got pregnant too early and married too fast. Work was exhausting, and she and her husband (who was also an unaccompanied youth migrant) worked opposite shifts to save on childcare. She battled with intense guilt associated with her abandonment of her younger siblings, although her own children had helped to assuage this pain. She was able to visit her home country a few years ago and was entirely disillusioned. She had planned to stay for a month but lasted only a week before purchasing a return flight back to the United States. Both she and her son had gotten sick, and she was overwhelmed caring for him without her partner's support. Her mother had continued drinking, her younger sister had married, and her brother, whom she had left at age two, no longer recognized her. Cynthia felt that her life had been split in half, and she could not salvage what she had lost. In the end, this was a bittersweet legend.

In reality, this legend existed only as it was carefully constructed. Cynthia herself had learned to tell her story, emphasizing certain elements while deemphasizing others, placing events in chronological order, centering our desires as the listeners instead of her preferred memories as the protagonist. In fact, in this iteration, Cynthia was no longer the narrator: I was now the author, further interpreting Cynthia's words. In fact, this story exists outside of Cynthia now. I have decontextualized her, torn her out of her indigeneity and away from the global processes that have shaped her life. The story fails to mention why Cynthia's community was so impoverished in the first place. It ignores the international complicity in human smuggling, including the role of US immigration law. Her community members have been turned into one-dimensional villains, void of the complexities of social ties that surely existed. Even her mother—whose role in Cynthia's life was important in Cynthia's access to legal relief—has been taken out of her historical context. In this narrative, she is only a failed mother and immoral woman. I have not explored the historically situated and deeply gendered violences that surely shaped her own life, creating intergenerational traumas that Cynthia now bears.[9] Finally, the indignities and violences in Cynthia's life are located only in her past and the journey north. This telling whitewashes the humiliations and hostilities she experienced in immigration detention and as she navigated her life in the United States. In such tellings, the United States is always a benevolent force, with the power to rescue, and it remains free of the implications that it can also cause tremendous harm. In this legend, we have smoothed the rough edges and blurred the lines, and so despite its utter improbability, Cynthia can be used as an exemplar of a borderland legend. This is the process of legend making.

Legend Making

Cynthia's story is true, yes, but it was also created, molded, and shaped by multiple adults who worked with her. Cynthia represents a privileged segment of youth migrants in that sense; youth are not guaranteed access to attorneys, so those who do get this access have either the money, the institutionalized connections, or a superhuman storytelling ability that can draw in compassionate adults from the beginning. Because Cynthia was connected to a foster care program, she was automatically connected with attorneys who would work with her. From that point, it was the job of the attorney, and to some extent advocates, social workers, and counselors, to sift through her history in order to uncover traumatic events that align with specific requirements in immigration law. For the vast majority of unaccompanied youth, the relief options available will be either a Special Immigrant Juvenile Status (SIJS; based on abuse or neglect by a family member) or asylum (based on a well-founded fear of persecution based on membership in a social group). There is a three-step process of turning their complex and contextualized histories into borderland legends: revealing stories, teaching trauma, and coaching affect.

Revealing Stories

The first step in creating a borderland legend is to reveal what already exists but is not always centered in youths' telling of their lives. Attorneys must mine youths' histories to identify specific events that can be narrated into legal categories. However, the types of events that are suitable for relief are often narrow in scope, shaping youth into victims of very specific trauma. These narratives often explicitly ignore global systems of inequality, and instead privilege individual stories of Latin American inferiority.

When a young person first sits in front of an attorney and is asked to tell their story, the first narrative that comes out is not always a useful narrative. In Cynthia's telling of her story, her first narrative of her migration might be that she wanted a better future, to get an education, to find a job, and to pursue her American dream. This narrative might not have centered her negligent mother or the harsh treatment she received in her community. But without those details, the story of a young girl wanting a better future is not an acceptable narrative. An attorney must brush past those facts and ask Cynthia to dig into the traumas in her life. The attorney will ask about violence in her past, about her relationship to her absent father, the abuse she experienced by her alcoholic mother, or the threats directed at her by her grandparents. These were perhaps not the memories or facts that Cynthia would choose to center, as they represented only a fraction of her history, and certainly not the fraction that demonstrated Cynthia's unique resilience. Centering these stories in the court, versus the story of a young woman pursuing a better future, required Cynthia to redefine herself as a victim of an abusive family rather than a strong young woman with a dream of changing her life.

Getting to the core of the "important" narratives can be a very difficult and sometimes heart-wrenching task. Even some of the most violent experiences or intense fears in youths' lives do not always make the cut in the correct legal narrative. This in turn requires attorneys to dismiss some details that youth might want to discuss while probing for other, more useful horrors. Jacqueline, an attorney, explained this difficulty: "Some kids will say, the first thing they want to tell you is: 'Yeah, I've been recruited by a gang.' And you're like: 'What happened?' And the details come out and they're not really strong, and you're like, 'Well, tell me about your home life. What was life like in your house?'" Gang recruitment can be a terrifying and violent experience for many young people, and it is often the experience that is the final impetus for migration. Yet, gang recruitment rarely counts in court. While there are active campaigns to change the practice, gang-related asylum cases are difficult to win.[10] So, when a young person reveals to Jacqueline the horrors of this experience, she must tell them that it was not enough and not sufficient for the law. The attorney's job is certainly not to act as a therapist, but the requirement of the job flies in the face of trauma-informed practices, which center choice and emphasize the importance of being seen and heard in the processing of trauma.[11]

Jacqueline continued:

> It comes out that they've been abused by an uncle for three years straight and raped multiple times. And you're like, oh my God, that is so much stronger. And they don't necessarily—of course they don't know asylum law. They don't know what is important and what isn't. . . . The fear is much more of the gangs, whereas the stronger asylum claim they may have is maybe based on something happening in the home. They don't really think about it that way. That's not why they came to the US. Sometimes I think it is all part and parcel of the same thing.

Jacqueline rightfully saw youths' lives as a culmination of multiple, overlapping violences that arose from intersecting systems of power.[12] Yet, the story she had to create privileged certain types of violence and ignored what often was most salient in youths' lives. Indeed, Jacqueline had to pinpoint an individually experienced violence (family trauma) outside of the structures that created it. This individual violence is "clean" in that it does not have to incriminate global systems and can be framed entirely as a problem within a failed family. On the other hand, community violence (which may actually contribute to family violence) and gang violence (which is often more salient in the youth's decision to migrate) are based on a historical system of global oppression that often implicates the United States in a country's instability.[13]

In a similar way, attorneys must sometimes reshape stories that actually reflect global inequality into stories that demonstrate family dysfunction and parental negligence. Problems in the family often arise because of multiple factors, such as access to employment and economic stability.[14] Yet, the telling of these stories locates family problems in bad parenting and a deficient culture, not the complex structures operating around the families. Susana, an attorney, discussed this process when explaining a case she built around child neglect: "Especially with kids who have been neglected, a lot of kids don't want to say anything bad about their parents, and I can kind of tell. I try to explain again, like, 'Hey, I'm not saying that this was bad or good or anything, but this is what neglect is in this country.' I explain it, like, 'In this country, kids have to go to school. They can't decide when they're ten that they are going to work the fields.' Sometimes it works, sometimes it doesn't." In building this case, Susana framed the child labor as the core example of the family's neglect. In reality, the International Labour Organization estimates that, as of 2012, 16.7 percent of children globally were employed and 10.6 percent of global children were employed illegally, according to ILO standards.[15] Scholars have proposed multiple reasons for the existence of child labor, focusing specifically on how poverty drives the need for children's employment and how there is a demand for this work, based on the belief that children are more suited for certain tasks than adults.[16] Further, global demand for products by the Global North, foreign investment, increasing natural disasters, and socioeconomic shocks further incentivize child labor in the Global South.[17] However, as an attorney, Susana had to convince youth that their own childhood labor was a result of neglectful decisions made by the parents—not a result of economic constraints. This coaching effectively shifts the blame for a child's life from the structural to the individual, releasing global inequality and poverty of any wrongdoing and implicating parents for irresponsible parenting.

The stories that attorneys must reveal are always true. Youth do experience abuse in their families and children do work in the fields at a young age. But the way these stories are told and the details that are centered explicitly fail to tell the whole, global story. They fail to center the truths youth would like to tell about their lives, and instead force attorneys to lead children through a psychologically painful experiment in which they must find the "right" trauma. These stories also fail to implicate world systems, instead privileging horrors that arise within families and between individuals.

Teaching Trauma

Once attorneys identify a story as a valid option for legal relief, they must then help their youth clients to frame these stories through the specific medicalized language of trauma and abuse. In a study on Southeast Asian refugees, anthropologist Aihwa Ong explored the rise of immigrant psychology, which medicalizes refugees' emotional well-being into categories that fit into Western constructions of health. Ong explores the emergence of Southeast Asian Mental Health, which includes a heavy reliance on posttraumatic stress disorder and depression to define the experience of refugees' mental health without contextualizing that experience within the traumas of war and political repression. Instead, doctors "cram the riot of [patients'] suffering into little boxes on the psychiatrists' charts."[18] Context and complexity are replaced by an acculturation process wherein medical labels become a tool of cultural belonging. Ong suggests that these medical interventions are about health but also about "shaping the social needs, rights and norms deemed appropriate for members of a modern civil society."[19] Refugee medicine, she argues, is a "mix of good intentions, desire to control 'diseased' and 'deviant' populations, and the exigencies of limited resources."[20]

Similarly, when working with unaccompanied youth, attorneys and other professionals find that it is their job to teach youth to label events in their lives using the language of trauma and abuse. These labels function for the same trifold purpose of help, control, and resource allocation. Ricki, a social worker, told several stories about the process of reaching shared meaning around trauma. He explained, "Trauma is a huge part [of the youths' lives]. . . . Once they are able to understand. Because it is a trauma for us. For them, it is normal. It is everyday living. Waking up and having to do things they were doing or experiencing the things they were experiencing was a part of life. It only becomes a trauma when we help them understand that that was a very traumatic experience." For Ricki, events "become" trauma when labeled as such. The experiences of violence and suffering exist but cannot be overcome until they are named with this language. We see here, just as Ong posits, that the medicalizing language is meant to ease suffering but also to govern youths' lives. That is, the process of medicalizing youths' emotional experiences allows professionals to understand youths' lives through a Western lens and then respond accordingly. Youths' experiences can then be fixed through therapy and medications. And, in their legal cases, youths' suffering can be appropriately categorized for their integration into the state.

The concepts of abuse and neglect are especially useful labels that can be employed to make youths' stories legible to the court. Abuse and neglect have culturally contingent meanings, so attorneys must actively define and teach youth about neglect and abuse, defining the boundaries of appropriate family behavior according to US standards. In doing so, attorneys pathologize families in order to create productive narratives. Attorney Nancy explains, "Every kid I meet has anxiety and depression and PTSD, definitely, but I think a lot of the cultural norms make kids matter-of-factly tell you things: 'Oh no, I was never abused.' And then I would say, 'Has anyone ever hit you with a belt or have you ever had to sleep outside?' And they would say, 'Oh yes, whenever my Dad got drunk, he would hit me with his belt.'" Here, Nancy did two things. First, she engaged in the medicalization process. "PTSD, definitely," she stated. She wielded the power of labeling her clients with a psychological disorder that she was not actually qualified to diagnose. Second, she acted as a memory guide, walking youth through their family histories and pointing out incidents that can be labeled as abuse or neglect. She did so not to assist in psychological healing around these experiences but rather to train youth to use this language themselves when they tell their stories.

Teaching the language of abuse is explicitly meant to help youth access the Special Immigrant Juvenile Status (based on abandonment, abuse, or neglect by a parent). Implicitly, the language of abuse becomes a force to govern youth migrants' bodies and families. The language of abuse and neglect negates complex and gray realities of family life, and in doing so, creates heart-wrenching dilemmas for youth who must position their desire for immigration relief against their loyalties to their families. Testifying before a judge for SIJS often requires youth to reframe their own childhoods in order to make clear dichotomies of good and bad parenting. As attorney Linda explained, "It is a tough situation, having a kid who adores his mother say, 'This is how my mother punished me, and I think this is abuse.' . . . Because many of them won't say a bad word against their mother." According to attorney Lavonne,

> Sometimes the way a child might feel about their parents can interfere with how they convey what has actually happened to them. We've had cases where the child has been brutalized. Brutalized. I'm talking about being hit with vines, lemon tree branches, forced to kneel in the sun naked. I mean, things that would make anybody say, "Uh uh. That is out of bounds." But to them, they have normalized it. So when you are talking to them about what has happened to them, they cannot articulate that their parent has done wrong. They will put the blame on themselves. They will say things like, "Well, I hadn't done my homework," or "I hadn't done what she asked me to," or "he was drunk." They are unable to articulate, like, "I didn't want that abuse to happen to me." And they won't testify, they refuse to testify negatively if it implicates their parents.

For some youth, pursuing SIJS means making a morally complicated decision regarding the telling of their family history. Their testimonies must center the worst of their parents' behaviors while ignoring the love and affection that may have existed simultaneously and, indeed, may be more salient in youths' memories and self-concepts. Both Linda and Lavonne lamented that youth might prefer to shape their histories with loyalty to their parents than to shape productive narratives that center abuse.

Using the language of abuse and neglect is also often replete with cultural judgments. Attorney Jacqueline discussed a commonly communicated view on the nature of abuse in other countries: "It has been interesting how, especially in cases of the child experiencing abuse in the home, they don't think about it in terms of criminal behavior or 'I'm afraid to go back.' They don't. I don't know if it kind of extends from the whole way the country views it: issues in the home stay inside the home." In this comment, Jacqueline placed child abuse within a framework of a deficient culture. She followed a script that understands child abuse as a problem unique to a country with values that apparently differ greatly from American values. She implicitly suggested that American culture, in contrast, has widespread cultural agreement on the meaning of child abuse and discipline as well as culturally open conversations around family behavior.

The use of abuse and neglect for the purpose of pursuing SIJS implies that youth should be separated from the abusive or neglectful parent. Indeed, unlike with other relief options, a young person who pursues SIJS agrees that he or she cannot sponsor parents to come to the United States. Yet, attorneys pointed out that even when a young person decides to frame their childhood through a lens of abuse, this does not mean that the child is, should be, or wants to be estranged from their parents. This is evident in Susana's description of a situation in which she was preparing an SIJS application for a young man based on father abandonment, only to discover later that the youth was living with the father. This living arrangement meant that the abuse claim was invalidated. In Susana's estimation, the child was not lying on purpose but was trying to supply Susana with the information that she wanted.

Linda explained a similar situation in which a young person did not want to testify against her parents—indeed, they were still in contact with one another and openly discussed the implications of an SIJS claim: "The parent will tell them, look, you need to improve your life. *Seguir adelante*. You want to go forward. So this is your way to go forward. And eventually they come to the conclusion that they do want to apply [for SIJS]." In this situation, the youth must rationalize two opposing realities: one in which a childhood with their parents was unhappy and abusive and the second in which these same parents are willing to put their own reputations on the line for the child's success.

Coaching Affect

Once a productive story is revealed and once it is labeled with the language of trauma and abuse, youth must engage in performing the emotions of the borderland legend. The final job of the attorney, therefore, is to help youth present emotions that can be fully read by the public and, most importantly, by the judge. The problem, of course, is that emotional presentations vary by individual and are also influenced by outside factors. For many youth, the sheer repetition of their story may work to distance them from their feelings. As attorney Linda explained, youth often reveal their histories to multiple adults, including border control agents, shelter staff, advocates, and counselors. Linda worried that this repetition may dilute the story's emotional quality or, on the other hand, make the storytelling so painful that youth are no longer able to do it for her.

> Remember, these kids have been telling their story multiple times by the time I see him. And now here is another person with another role asking details about a time in his life that he may not want to discuss for valid reasons. Sometimes, it is that people respond different. Sometimes people shut down and are not able to articulate what they told you in the office three months ago. I think they just shut down. Some of them sob and cry. It is difficult to relive some of these stories. Some of them present well. Some of them manage it better than others.

Linda emphasized the importance of storytelling in how youth "present" and "manage" their telling of their histories. Youth must be neither so emotional that it disrupts the history nor so detached that their trauma is no longer believable. Histories thus do not speak for themselves but are performances that Linda harnessed and directed.

Similarly, Julie explained that she was working on an asylum case for a girl whose family had been targeted by gangs. Julie had trouble working with the story because, in her words, "[The client] didn't seem to be afraid. I don't know if that is the defense mechanism. [. . .] I mean, I think she really has issues but it doesn't come across." Julie continued, explaining that she understood that trauma could manifest in different ways, but she felt unable to help in this case, as she did not have the skills of a social worker or psychologist that would assist in navigating those emotional issues. In the absence of visible fear, Julie struggled to show the veracity of the asylum claims.

Nancy expressed a similar dilemma, but she attempted to "solve" the problem of faulty presentation in explicit ways: "So they don't connect the abuse and the trauma to their coping skills now or the depression or anxiety now. . . . [Attorneys have to] help them attach it to the emotion. . . . I am almost trying to bring them to the point of crying and being emotionally tapped to that fear. It feels really awful and cruel, but I usually only do that when I have caseworkers nearby or they are about to go to therapy after." Nancy's explanation conjures images of a director attempting to produce realistic emotions in his or her actors. She was not particularly comfortable with her use of this strategy, but she felt that it was a necessary part of building a case.

The display of and expectations for emotional responses are experienced in intersectional ways. For young men, in particular, expectations regarding emotive responses to their histories may clash with their own identities and sense of self, especially since the process of migration can often be tied to masculine, adult identities.[21] Young men who have migrated alone—for whatever reason—may cling to a narrative of bravery as proof of their independence and success. So, when attorneys hope for these same young men to present histories of trauma with convincing emotional displays, they often come up short. Grace, an attorney, explained, "I think a lot about teenage boys who, in some ways, seem like they have to put forth a front or act. That can sometimes work against them in their case. You know, make it harder for the officer to want to approve their case." In this example, asylum officers and attorneys make the mistake of ignoring the social positions of young men who have migrated alone. Scholars have argued that masculinity itself is a performance and act, so when the court system requires a different presentation of self, it is failing to acknowledge the competing demands faced by these young men.[22]

This tension is further exacerbated when attorneys and other professionals place blame for the lack of performative emotions on racialized understandings of the young men. Rather than questioning the mechanisms that create a need for standard emotive displays, Nathan, an attorney, blamed the stereotypical culture of machismo for these young men's refusal to display emotions of fear and victimhood.

> There is a little more of the machismo culture that comes in. Acting tough, not wanting to be perceived as afraid to go back home or having been motivated out of fear as the reason why you don't want to go back home. That can sometimes be a challenge, so having to counsel those young boys to say, "Look. We are pursuing asylum. We are doing that only if you have a well-founded fear of future persecution. It does not mean that you are not manly. It doesn't mean you're not brave. It doesn't mean you're not courageous. . . ." We can't jeopardize our legal case here out of some silly macho man type of behavior.

This "silly macho man" behavior, according to Nathan, is a cultural barrier that young men need to address in order to effectively express their trauma. He delegitimizes the real pressures faced by young men who have grown up in violent communities, where displays of masculinity may be essential for survival.[23] Masculinity may, indeed, be the way the young men have learned to counter dominations and, by extension, may continue to provide an edge in the power-laden interactions with adult professionals in the United States.[24] Further, the use of machismo relies on tired stereotypes of Latino men that have largely been rejected by scholars of Latino masculinity.[25] So, while macho behavior is framed as a problem of individual young men expressing harmful cultural messages, a more productive understanding would explore the nuances of power in these men's lives.

* * *

When Cynthia sat down with me for her interview, it was clear that she knew how to tell her story. Although we had a personal relationship and had a conversational rapport at the beginning of the interview, when I asked her why she immigrated, I felt as if I had pressed a button and a narrative simply fell from her mouth. It was chronological, stiff, linear, and rehearsed. At one point, she yawned as she spoke about the trauma of crossing the border and the rapes she had witnessed, expressing through her body language a complete disengagement from the horrific story she was sharing. My stomach churned as I listened to the details, and yet she uttered them almost thoughtlessly. I returned multiple times to this yawn as I reread her transcript in the months that followed. Was this a coping mechanism to steel herself from unhealed trauma? Was this actually evidence that she had overcome this pain? Was this a memorized utterance that had been repeated to so many official people before me that she no longer engaged with the words that she was saying? Or, was the yawn simply indicative of the exhaustion she felt, coming off a long shift in health care with a two-year-old running about in the next room and a baby in her belly?

On the other hand, Nicolas, an eighteen-year-old from Ecuador, had arrived to the United States less than a year prior to our interview. His engagement with the court had been limited at the time we spoke, although a case for asylum was underway. In our conversation, he was fully present, painfully so, allowing me to bear witness to suffering that lingered from violence experienced both before and during his migration. Unlike with Cynthia's story, which, while detached, was easy to follow and progressed chronologically, I had to ask Nicolas follow-ups and write down dates in order to pull together his disparate commentary. Anthropologist Erica Caple James explains that authentic trauma narratives "have a pace of their own, are often non-linear, and are sometimes full of gaps and pauses," unlike stories that have been shaped by professionals, which have a "rational, linear, teleological format."[26] It was clear that Nicolas had yet to learn how to tell this story for its productive purpose.

Without fail, the attorneys that I interviewed were deeply committed to their work with unaccompanied youth. They were dedicated to helping youth stay in the United States, and they utilized all of the tools at their disposal to do so. However, the creation of the borderland legend relies on the decontextualization of youths' histories, the medicalization and Westernization of the stories that youth tell, and the standardization of emotional display, outside of the complexities of actual human emotion. This process effectively decenters youths' voices and works as much to maintain American hegemony as it does to protect youth.

3

Educating Immigrant Youth

Marco was sixteen when he decided to emigrate from Guatemala to the United States. Although he was in contact with his parents at that time, he explained that they had essentially abandoned him when he was younger, and he had grown up with his grandmother. Since his grandfather had passed away when Marco was four, Marco took responsibility to be the man of the house from an early age. By sixteen, he was working at an Internet café, and his high school graduation was on the horizon. He explained that the day of his graduation was not a day for celebration. Instead, he went immediately to the university exams, so he would not miss a beat in continuing to pursue his goals. His dream was to be a civil engineer, and enrolling in a university was the next step. Marco passed the exams, but he soon realized that although the university program itself was free, he simply could not afford the extra costs associated with enrollment and studying full-time. This was the reason he decided to immigrate to the United States. He planned to work for five years to earn enough savings to return to Guatemala and pursue his university dreams. "I wanted to keep moving forward and to have a different life," he told me.

Marco began to make arrangements for his migration north. Although his parents had not been a part of his life in any meaningful way, he reached out to them, and they stepped up to help him pay the coyotes. He left just a week before Christmas. The journey was difficult and frightening. He did not trust the other men he traveled with, so he was on constant alert. He explained that when the group arrived at the border, he was essentially left to himself and told to walk straight until someone picked him up. I asked what he felt during that long, lonely walk, and he explained, "What I had in mind were my dreams. That was my motivation. I'm going to get there. I'm going to be someone."

Marco's plan was to work for five years and return to Guatemala, but that plan was diverted once he was apprehended at the border and de-

tained with the Office of Refugee Resettlement. He was eventually released to a family friend, and he took very seriously the ORR mandate to
go to school—something that he had not planned to do but for which he
was grateful. However, when the family friend lost his job and housing,
Marco found himself in a precarious position. He seriously considered
dropping out of school so that he could work full-time; he did not want
to do this, but he did not see any other option. Fortunately, Marco connected with a member of his church, who agreed to provide him a cheap
place to live so Marco could focus on his education. His new plan was
to finish high school in the United States, where he had already joined
the Reserve Officer Training Corps and been accepted into a civil engi-
neering program. Once he graduated, he hoped to join the military and
continue towards his dream of becoming a civil engineer—although this
dream had been transferred to the United States.[1]

Marco was an impressive young man. When we met for his interview, he exuded exceptional confidence and self-assuredness, and he
was steadfast in his commitment to his goals. When Marco reflected
on his history, it was clear that the pursuit of education had been one of
the most important drivers in his life. Although he did not plan to continue education in the United States, his migration was spurred by these
dreams and, once he entered the school system in the United States, he
found that education gave him a solid support system to continue to
move toward his goals. He felt grateful for the opportunities afforded to
him in his high school, and he was convinced that this education would
get him one step closer to the life he envisioned.

Indeed, education in the United States is often painted as a pana-
cea to social inequality. It is well known that high school graduates can
expect to earn more than those who do not graduate and that salary
compensation increases with further education.[2] High school graduates can expect higher rates of full-time employment.[3] Plus, high school
students benefit from the social support, services, and mentoring available in many American schools.[4] For vulnerable student populations, a
strong educational community can act as an important safety net. For
example, sociologist Roberto G. Gonzales explored the experience of
the 1.5 generation of immigrants and found that for them, high school
acts as a site of entry into society and may temporarily suspend their
experiences of legal liminality.[5] That is, while enrolled, even undocu-

mented students have access to many of the opportunities afforded other American children.

In my research, some schools demonstrated an intentional and thoughtful commitment to all students, including undocumented, unaccompanied immigrant youth. When caring people existed in the schools, and when districts were open and welcoming to immigrant youth, schools could be the foundation for youths' access to a wide range of services. Youth and educators told me stories of a myriad of ways in which schools and teachers stepped up to help vulnerable youth. Attorneys frequently reported that they became connected to youth through teachers and the school system. Food pantries run by schools provided important resources for youth who could not make ends meet. Extra-curricular programs such as soccer leagues aimed at migrant students provided what one educator characterized as "cheap therapy." And, schools with strong wrap-around services could connect students immediately to everything from medical assistance to language buddies to trauma-informed therapy.

However, despite these benefits, the reality is that the impact of local schools varies tremendously throughout the country. At their worst, school systems participate in the marginalization of the poor and of communities of color. Theorist Garrett Albert Duncan calls this "education for subordination," in which marginalized students receive an education meant to further entrench their subordination in society.[6] Schools frequently inculcate students into racial, gendered, and class systems.[7] Education researchers have similarly pointed to the school-to-prison pipeline, where the confluence of zero-tolerance policies, police presence, and harsh disciplinary practices lead students out of school and into the criminal justice system.[8] Plus, some schools fail to respond to high rates of student drop-outs, related to students' undocumented status, financial difficulties, community contexts, or discriminatory profiling and punishment.[9]

Within this context, the experiences unaccompanied youth have with the education system can best be described as precarious hope. Stories such as Marco's demonstrate that this institution is as important as the state and the family in the well-being of many young people. Indeed, as unaccompanied youth navigated the legal system and settled into (or were left out of) families, supportive educational systems played an essential role in their success. On the other hand, some districts failed to live up to these promises by passively or actively blocking youths' access to education, and youth themselves were often forced to make difficult decisions between school and work. These issues were further exacerbated by youths' precariousness within their families, within the legal system, and within the framework of a normative life course. Accordingly, youths' experiences in school were always intimately connected to their experiences with labor, family, and the state.

School, Work, and Participation in Adolescence

Education is an essential socializing institution in society, teaching students about the values of the community in which they live.[10] One of the latent functions of education in the United States is its use as a marker of life course. High school students are viewed as distinct from adults, in part because the majority of their time is spent on school, rather than work.[11] For immigrant adolescents, high schools therefore work to socialize youth into American understandings of life stages. By attending schools, unaccompanied immigrant youth find themselves in the midst of "normal" American adolescence, where they are instructed to focus on finishing an education in order to receive the financial and social benefits that a high school degree holds. Simultaneously, they are asked to withdraw from the work world, or at least place more emphasis on education than on labor. When these migrant youth enroll in school systems and participate fully in this institution, they are both learning the American values attached to childhood and demonstrating their adherence to these values.

The importance of education in socializing unaccompanied youth into American adolescence is not just symbolic. Indeed, high school enrollment helps to make immigrant youth legible as minors in the court systems. A common pathway to legal relief for these youth is the Special Immigrant Juvenile Status. Several of the requirements of this status work to implicitly demonstrate a youth's position as a minor: there is an age limit, the young person must have a legal guardian, and the youth must not be married. Although school enrollment is not written explicitly into this law, attorneys stress that a judge will read school attendance favorably, and it also provides evidence that residing in the United States is in the best interests of the youth.[12] Dan, a midwestern attorney, explained that the ideal youth client should "acquire positive equities" such as "developing friendships and relationships with people who can be character references" and, notably, "doing well in school." School attendance proves that youth are focused more on the activities of children (preparing for work) than the activities of adults (working). While a legal guardian is a marker of a child's dependency on adults, schools mark youths' dependency on institutions. Judges read high school enrollment as proof that youth are enacting appropriate versions of childhood and thus can receive assistance that is designated only for children.

Schools are therefore exceptionally important in helping youth to assert themselves socially as minors and then access legal relief. However, their participation in schools is simultaneously mediated by their need to work. This is not so much the casual "pull" of the work world: for many, it is a matter of survival. Not working is not an option. For these students, it is important to find labor that complements, rather than competes with, their school schedule. However, as sociologist Ranita Ray explains in her study of working-class youth, when youth keep a foothold in both work and school, it is often their education that suffers.[13] This reality is further complicated by exploitative practices among American employers. Although the Fair Labor Standards Act prohibits long hours, employment during school times, and specific types of employment for minors, the young people I interviewed frequently reported countless violations of these laws.[14] In my interviews, young people worked in a wide range of settings, including restaurants, golf courses, and car washes, and many reported work in industries explicitly prohibited for minors, such as roofing and manufacturing. They worked all hours of the day in shifts that far exceeded the federal time limits. Their jobs were often dangerous and dirty and frequently lacked the safety protections required by law. Yet, youth did not complain to me about these exploitative conditions; they reflected that they had to work to pay rent, support their families, and comply with their financial responsibilities. Indeed, several young men with whom I spoke talked about the difficulty they had in finding employment when they first arrived, especially when they looked young. This intertwined exploitation and necessity presented an ethical dilemma for professionals working with youth. Professionals did not want to report exploitative jobs because they knew that youth needed these very jobs to survive.[15]

One issue that contributes to this reality is that youth who are undocumented are often unable to access jobs that coincide with child labor laws. Paul, an educator in a West Coast district, explained that youths' ability to access jobs that work with their school schedule is often dependent on their documentation status.

> [Attorneys] are often able to get help with a work permit as part of that legal service, which then, with a work permit, [unaccompanied immigrant youth] are more likely to be able to find an evening or night job. Without work authorization it seems like most of the opportunities are day laborers, you know, like landscaping, so they need to be out waiting for jobs that are available for work in the mornings. So, it is a real domino effect. If they get the attorney and the attorney helps them get the work permit and they can find an evening job working at a restaurant or something like that, then they can stay in school during the day.

This is a catch-22 for unaccompanied youth: in order to get documents, they must act like minors by attending school. In order to survive, they must work. In order to work and go to school, they must have documents. Unaccompanied minors must deftly hop between these competing realities of their status as immigrants and as minors.

This reality is not lost on youth, who are often fully aware of ways in which their life course has unfolded in opposition to the structures around them. This was evident in my interview with Jesus, a young man from Mexico who had arrived in the United States at age sixteen. I met with Jesus at the end of his school day, and we spoke in his English classroom in the little time he had between his last class and the beginning of his job. Jesus explained that he was living with his parents in Mexico when his brother, who had been working in a Chicago suburb, offered to help Jesus migrate. Jesus had recently gone through a heartbreak, when his girlfriend of several years had cheated on him, and so the prospect of leaving the country was especially enticing. When he arrived to the Midwest, he immediately started working and was entirely focused on paying rent and sending money to his siblings back home: "I am trying to do my best to give my siblings a future," he explained. However, after about a year, a friend at work mentioned to him that he was still young enough that he had the opportunity to enroll in the local high school. The friend helped Jesus navigate his enrollment, and Jesus was thrilled to have the opportunity to keep studying. Since Jesus had been enrolled in school up until the week of his migration, he found that it was relatively easy to return to the classroom. However, he found balancing work and school very difficult. Talking about himself and a friend who was also an unaccompanied minor, Jesus explained,

> Sometimes it is really difficult to work and study. Working is necessary for money to pay bills. And sometimes school is hard because we don't do the homework. There is no time. And we don't study much because we get home from work, and sometimes you want to sleep, to rest, and the next day is the same. Get up early and return to school. It is the daily routine that we have. Sometimes we want to find a better job but we can't because we don't have a social security card. That's the problem. . . . I'm trying to find a better job. I found one, but they asked for the social security card. So that complicates things, since I don't have it.

Jesus had tremendous support from his teachers, who worked with his schedule and did not penalize him when he was unable to complete his homework after the school day. However, Jesus realized that his situation was not sustainable. He hoped to make it to graduation, and although he wanted to attend college, he realized he would have to work for a few years to save money before that could happen.

Jesus was also keenly aware that the pull of the work world, his responsibility for himself and to his family, and the trajectory of his life separated him from the other students in his school. "I think like an adult already. Rather, I realized that when I was sixteen, I could no longer act like a child, knowing that I was old enough to know what I needed to do. Sometimes when I'm at school, I see how other people act. For example, my classmates, we are in class and they start to play and all that. . . . It's what I don't like about them. Or rather, I think more like an adult than a teenager." This remark reveals an interesting reality: while school enrollment may be interpreted by courts as evidence of a normative life course, it is often not experienced as such by many immigrant youth who must also work. Indeed, these youth understand that their lives straddle multiple competing realities. They must be both students and laborers, adults and children in order to survive and continue moving forward.

Precarious Households, Precarious Enrollment

The tension among labor, education, life course, and legal relief is further mediated by youths' precariousness in households and families. Put simply, when youth are unable to act as children within their family structures, they find it more difficult to enact childhood and adolescence for the education system. For some youth, the ability to enroll in school is dependent on being simultaneously enmeshed in a family structure. Although educational policies vary by state, many youth are reliant on legal guardians to enroll them in school. At the very minimum, a lack of a legal guardian creates multiple bureaucratic difficulties for school systems. Marta, a community social worker in the Southeast, explained her frustration with this issue when she described a father who had recently been reunited with his adolescent son after the son's detainment with the Office of Refugee Resettlement. The father was an undocumented field worker and could not take time off to register his son for school, as was stipulated in the young man's release requirements. Marta prodded the father for months, and finally threatened to take the son away if he did not comply. Finally, at the risk of losing his job, the father acquiesced, took time off work, and enrolled the son. For this family, school enrollment depended on a traditional relationship between parents and children, in which parents are both willing and, importantly, able to take charge of the child's business. However, for this father and son, the father's ability to act in this capacity was even further limited by his own undocumented status and precariousness as a laborer. Midwestern advocate Veronica expressed frustration with these types of policies: "When it is a young person, they are even more limited because if they wanted to do something on their own, they can't. They're dependent on the adults they live with."

When youth are in households that do not function like a traditional household, their initial contact with the education system can be stymied. Further, these youth might also find that their ability to participate in the education system after enrollment is further compromised. The obligation to work is particularly strong when a youth's position within the family is unstable. That is, education is a privilege for only those who can afford to live socially as minors. Karen, an advocate for special populations in her midwestern district, explained, "[If youth] were taken into a family that often times was already struggling in terms of housing and food and transportation, they are either told you need to work, or they feel like they are a burden, and they go to work." She further explained that some youth also have the pressure of sending remittances to their families in their home country. Implicitly, therefore, youths' access to education is also dependent on the opportunity they have to act as a minor within a family unit.

On the other hand, while traditional household structures support schooling, school systems also play an important role when families or households fall apart. As discussed in chapter 1, for many unaccompanied youth, homelessness is an ever-present threat. In some cases, youth are released to nonfamily sponsors who may be undocumented. Although these sponsors step forward to help youth get out of immigration detention, they may not feel safe once youth are in their households. Out of fear of the extra attention from courts, attorneys, and government workers, these sponsors may ask the youth in their care to leave. Similarly, financial situations may change a sponsor's willingness and ability to keep a young person in their home. Several youth told me that their original sponsors asked them to leave because of financial concerns. For example, Marco, whose story opened this chapter, had been released to live with a family friend in the Southeast, after months of failed attempts to find placement with relatives. He lived with this friend for only a short period, before he was asked to find a new home: "[My sponsor] was also an immigrant here, and he didn't have papers," Marco explained. "He had problems at work, and since here people work and the job gives them a place to live, that was a problem. So I had to find an alternative living arrangement because he couldn't keep me anymore." So, when the sponsor became homeless at the loss of his job, Marco, too, found himself without a place to live.

If youth are enrolled in school, teachers are often the first to witness this kind of housing instability, and so they are also the first to provide youth with safety nets. Lisa was an immigrant advocate for her school district, a midwestern suburb with a large immigrant population. She explained that she often went to her own social networks and church in order to help homeless immigrant youth. She successfully found both temporary and long-term homes for her students by posting on social media and asking church members for support. Even more surprisingly, some of Lisa's colleagues actually allowed students to stay with them. Lisa introduced me to the English teacher in one of the schools in which she worked, and as we walked into the classroom, we discovered that the teacher was in the middle of problem solving an unaccompanied student's recent homelessness. They motioned for us to come in, as they continued their conversation. "You can always stay with me," the teacher was suggesting to the student. "But I'm afraid it would be a really long drive for you to get to work." The student asked how far her home was, and the teacher explained that she was a half-hour drive from the school. The student agreed this might be too far, but in the end, they decided that he could stay there if no other place could take him. As it turned out, this particular student had just been kicked out of his sponsor's home—the same sponsor that the Office of Refugee Resettlement had placed him with—because the sponsor was afraid that the youth's presence was putting his own undocumented status on display.

Teachers were often the first line of defense when youth faced instability in their homes. However, some schools also institutionalized services to support youth in their families. Several districts across the country have recognized the trauma faced by youth who have been reunited with their families and have worked to provide a variety of interventions. There is a wide range of this kind of programming, from free parenting classes for immigrant families, which by extension serve reunified families, to programming specifically created for the reunified families. Amy, a specialist in a midwestern school district, worked in an after-school program that targeted transnational households. She saw multiple families that had recently been reunified with their children, and so she witnessed many of the tense relationships that existed in the previously separated families. Amy explained that her program would attempt to work with parents on interacting with their children and provide therapy for the family to work through the separation issues. This type of support was sanctioned by the school and was a way for the school to encourage safe and supportive home environments for its students, thus intervening before youth faced voluntary separation from their parents. Another program on the East Coast targeted reunified families specifically. In this model, the school district meets first with the parents in reunified families to try to help them understand the experiences, and often traumas, faced by their newly arrived children, often by encouraging parents to reflect on their own experiences in the first few years after arriving to the United States. At the end of the program, the whole family attends a session together, to discuss their experiences reuniting. Yasmin, who often moderated these sessions, explained that many families have found them to be uniquely valuable and have asked the district for expanded programming.

Individual teachers and institutionalized policies often provided important interventions when students' living situations fell through. However, even when administration or teachers themselves did not provide support for homeless youth, youth themselves found that the physical school building could operate as a safe space. Karen, the special populations consultant for a midwestern school district, explained that one of the unaccompanied students at her school became homeless in his first year and did not trust anyone to help. However, he used the school building when he had nowhere else to go. She explained,

> We had a kid who actually slept in his school for two months before anyone noticed. That clearly should never happen. Somebody should have noticed. But he was also really smart and really quiet and kind of just blended in. And he would sneak back into sporting events or after-school clubs that were going on and just kind of disappear. When they found him he was in the boiler room because that was the warmest spot in school at night. . . . He was a really resourceful kid. He didn't want to be put into a system. He was afraid of being locked away. He was afraid of being detained. He was afraid of being arrested.

In this situation, the young man held a deep distrust of the institutions around him, and Karen lamented the fact that the student felt he could not seek help. Yet, the school building played a critical role in the young man's survival, even if it did so unwittingly.

When Schools Are the Problem

School is clearly an important institution for youth. Despite the necessity of labor, youths' legal status, and youths' precarious household membership, schools can provide important support for unaccompanied, undocumented students. They allow youth to enact a version of adolescence that can be essential for youths' legal cases, and they provide important safety nets when family systems and households fall apart. However, throughout my interviews, youth and community members reported a wide range of difficulties with their school districts, from the unintentional deterrence of immigrant students to the targeted harassment of these youth.

Florencio was a prime example of the unintentional ways in which local districts fail to enroll unaccompanied students. Florencio had been living with his parents in Mexico and was attending school when he decided to migrate. He had been frustrated with his life, as he felt that the lack of resources in his family prevented him from reaching his full potential. He was also frustrated in his household, as he felt that his parents prevented him from doing the things he wanted to do. He was tired of being told what to do, and he was ready for a change. He wanted to set out on his own to see if his life could get better. His plan was to work for three years, make money, and then return to Mexico. His real dream, he explained to me, was to buy some musical instruments and begin a band. Florencio planned his migration over the course of several months, and during a break between school semesters, he finally left and headed north.

Florencio was very enthusiastic to start working when he first arrived to the United States. He had settled in a Chicago suburb, where there was a large immigrant population. At age fourteen, he had a difficult time finding a job at first because he was so young, but eventually a friend helped him start at a car wash. Soon after, he transitioned to a factory job, where he remained for several years. He loved the independence that came from having his own job and living on his own, but soon his life turned into a never-ending cycle of work and sleep. He was depressed that he was not seeing friends, and he began to regret that he had never finished school. He explained, "I wanted to return to school to keep studying. But I thought that schools wouldn't accept me because

I was past the age. Every school has its age limit. And that's why I never went. But I did want to keep studying." Florencio felt that his time had passed for any assistance. He did not know whom to talk to or where to go to find out if this was true or to explore his options. When I asked if he had ever tried to go to school, Florencio laughed and said that he had not. "I never found a job that would allow me the opportunity to go to school. Or, that I could both go to school and support myself. That was one problem. Also, when I got here, nobody told me: 'If you want to study, I'll give you a hand,' or something like that. I also didn't really want to study. I mean, I thought about things differently when I came here, but I think differently now, too. I guess I matured a little more." I spoke with Florencio when he was eighteen years old, and as the conversation turned to his education, he began to ask me as many questions as I was asking him. He wanted to know if there were programs that would still take him, if there was a school that could work with his schedule, and what other options he might have. In reality, Florencio lived in a school district that would have been able to provide tremendous support to him. There was a large Spanish-speaking population in his community, so his local school had resources to work with English-language learners, and although his district was not particularly wealthy, there were plenty of educators and staff who could have provided important assistance for him.

Yet, for Florencio, attending an American school felt out of the realm of possibility, even though at age fourteen when he migrated, he had been well within the age limits of traditional high schools. Florencio's inability to connect with a local school district was due to the mutual invisibility of the young person and the school. As a young person who had not been apprehended at the border, Florencio was not connected to the Office of Refugee Resettlement and therefore had no mandate to attend school. He was also not connected to institutions outside of the workforce that could have helped to guide him. His lack of resources and knowledge about his own rights meant that he did not have the information he needed to walk through a school door. He was unaware of how to approach schools and had no social or institutional support to do so. Schools were invisible to him.

Invisibility goes both ways, however. Just as school was invisible to Florencio, Florencio was invisible to the local school. Even when he was a young teenager, local school districts had never seen Florencio. Even if his school district had engaged in migrant outreach, they had failed to see him. Florencio is not unique in this respect, of course. School districts around the country often fail to see undocumented, unaccompanied students in their areas. Even schools with the most progressive policies around unaccompanied youth were aware that there were many young people in their communities who were falling through the cracks. Several school districts engaged in recruitment in migrant camps, but these policies were incomplete at best and still failed to reach youth who worked in other industries, such as food service or construction. Paul, an outreach specialist in a progressive West Coast school district, explained that his school did outreach in local migrant camps, but despite the best intentions of the school, they were not able to contact all of the unaccompanied youth in their community: "We're losing tons of students [due to a lack of explicit outreach]," he explained. "We have to do extra work. We [have started] regular outreach to day laborers and try to find students who are just, you know, going straight to work." Yet youth who are more dispersed throughout the community—working in car washes and factories, for example—often stay under the radar of even the most intentional schools.

However, not all schools are intentional about finding and helping unaccompanied students. In fact, some schools actively exclude youth from enrolling in their mainstream programs. In some cases, schools block youth on the basis of their legal status. Although schools are required to enroll undocumented students, there are frequently cases in which schools use loopholes to reject this statute.[16] Journalists across the country have documented cases in which schools refused to enroll students, and my participants from multiple different locations reported the same issue happening in their communities.[17]

This discrimination was sometimes covert, wrapped in the shroud of bureaucracy and based on loopholes, including age and English skills. Two community workers in a large, urban, southeastern district explained that they had contacted the Department of Justice to complain about their local district, because schools were refusing to register unaccompanied students or were rerouting the students to alternative programs where they would not receive the same education as in a traditional high school. Yesenia, one of these workers, explained,

When we were registering some of the kids, [the schools] were saying, "No, you're already old." Some were [only] sixteen, seventeen. [Schools were] telling them, "No, you should go to a night school. You belong in night school." Because probably of the English barrier, or because their levels were low compared to wherever they belonged. And then . . . the school counselors wanted them to sign up for a school called East Side, but then we discovered that East Side was a school for kids that come out of jail or were detained. Those are troubled kids. I don't think you would want to send a refugee kid to [those schools], because they are not coming from that side of the surge. They are fleeing violence.

The social workers were continually frustrated by the district and what they saw as the systematic and intentional rerouting of these immigrant students. Youth were marked as too old or too criminal, despite the realities of their ages and histories. In this way, the bureaucracy was weaponized as a tool for exclusion.

Beth, an education advocate in an urban East Coast region, saw a similar situation in her community. She complained that many of the unaccompanied immigrant students in her school district were funneled into an adult program. The explicit purpose of rerouting students in this district was to provide them with a more flexible learning environment to work with their work schedule. However, Beth felt as though this was a lose-lose situation, as the students did not receive the benefits of the traditional school, and the rules of the program were still not flexible enough to actually meet the needs of the students. For example, the school's policy was to automatically withdraw a young person after fifteen absences. Students could get some absences excused with a doctor's note, but since most students did not have health insurance or an understanding of the medical system, this was little help to the unaccompanied youth population. For youth who were balancing work and school, a limit of fifteen absences over the year was an onerous requirement. Beth expressed concern that the inflexibility of this rule systematically unenrolled unaccompanied students.

Bureaucratic requirements were not always intentionally set for exclusion. Lisa was a liaison in a well-off suburban school in the Midwest, and although her school had a stated commitment to helping migrant youth, she found that she was still often working against the bureaucracy. In one case, she was working with a young man who was eighteen already but wanted to finish high school in order to provide evidence for his legal case. However, he did not have paperwork to demonstrate his compliance with vaccine requirements, which meant that he might not be able to finish his education. Although the solution should have been easy—get the vaccines—Lisa explained that they were trapped by the bureaucracy at every turn:

> Based on the funding and everything else that I don't understand, the [local mobile clinic] isn't able to give him any more vaccines, because their vaccines are only for [minors]. Supposed to be just for students. The public health department doesn't have vaccines. The community clinic, they cannot provide vaccines to anybody who is eighteen and younger. So I said, okay, what do we do? He needs to get the vaccine to stay in school. He is going to be out of compliance with this health requirement if he doesn't do that. It took us almost a week calling every pharmacy in the city to see who had that vaccine.

Yet, even once Lisa was able to identify a place to fulfill this bureaucratic requirement, the price tag reached two hundred dollars, and the young man was not able to afford it. Again, he found himself in a bureaucratic cage; while the school had money to help students in need, it was not earmarked for vaccines. Finally, Lisa was able to petition the school administrators to foot the bill, just so the young man could stay enrolled in school. In this case, the young man's existence on the edge between adulthood and childhood barred him from accessing basic services needed to get him into the school system. It was the school itself that broke out of the bureaucratic requirements to help fund the young man's vaccines to keep him enrolled.

While bureaucracies could prevent a student's enrollment in both intentional and unintentional ways, some schools were even more overt in their exclusion of unaccompanied migrant students. I interviewed several professionals (educators and social workers) who worked with unaccompanied youth in the same region in the rural Midwest, and all of them explained that they faced explicit discrimination throughout the educational process. Allison was a foster care worker in the community, and she often helped her unaccompanied immigrant clients in the enrollment process. She explained that in one school, "The secretary would not even take the paperwork. Would not enroll the child. Told us that we are not taking thugs here, so you better turn around and leave."[18] Allison was constantly pushing back in these types of situations, but she feared that such blatant racism at the outset created impossible environments for the students. She explained that even after an attorney would fight to force a school to educate a student, the student would "get in the classroom and experience so much racism and discrimination" that the environment itself made it difficult for students to stay enrolled. Michelle, who was an educator in the same region, provided a vivid example of what this harassment looked like in her school:

> Our school didn't have a whole lot of respect for other cultures and languages. A lot of [teachers] would scan the hall and say: "Don't speak that language in here! We speak English!" A lot of that kind of thing. My community in particular has [migrant farm workers], so they're seen almost as if they are owned by the farmers' kids, and that has been said and portrayed many of times. [Migrants] live on [the farmers'] land: "You live on my land, in my little houses, you work for me, and my family is the reason you are here." That was said to them many times.

Research is clear that blatant discrimination can have devastating impacts on a person's mental health and their ability to integrate into an institution.[19] Students, in particular, are vulnerable to these messages, and unaccompanied youth in these environments quickly learn that they are not welcome.

The professionals I interviewed came from school districts across the country and from all types of communities—rich and poor, rural, suburban, and urban. Yet the stories they told about school exclusion were strikingly similar. Schools systematically weeded out unaccompanied, undocumented students through their bureaucratic requirements, the rerouting of students, and hostile environments. These actions stigmatize and criminalize immigrant students, and the balancing act between labor and education that so many unaccompanied youth face becomes almost impossible to maintain. Karen, an advocate in the Midwest, explained that youth often made cost-benefit analyses of their likelihood of finishing their education, when they simultaneously needed to make money to support themselves and sometimes their families. Karen noted, "[Youth] look at school and say: 'Am I likely to graduate or not? And if I'm not, or it doesn't look like I'm going to, then I can go to work right now and make that money and make a difference.'" Youths' ability to stay in school thus involves an analysis of the time spent and money lost on an education, and when school environments are implicitly biased at best and actively adversarial at worst, youth have even less incentive to finish their degree.

Mentorship and Resilience

Families, the state, and education are intimately woven together in youths' lives. These institutions are co-constituting in many ways, such that precarity in one leads to precarity in them all. However, the youth I interviewed were nothing if not resilient, and their resiliency was located outside of any of these institutions. As previous research has demonstrated, social networks among migrants are often essential in migrants' well-being.[20] In my research as well, youth found support through one another, stepping in when institutions failed and providing an array of help to each other.

In a very early stage in my research, I heard a rumor of a country club in a wealthy Chicago suburb where several unaccompanied minors worked and lived. I attempted to connect with these workers first by going through management, but I was quickly denied access. Instead, on the basis of a rumor about a dormitory where workers lived, I drove around the grounds until I located the building. I was able to intercept a man coming off his shift, and when I told him about my research, he helped me to connect with several unaccompanied minors who were employed by the country club. The first person I spoke with was a young man named Andres. Andres had migrated by himself from Mexico at age fourteen with the intention of supporting his younger siblings' education. He had entered into the country without being apprehended, and had virtually no connections to institutions within the United States. In the beginning he bounced around between living situations and jobs, living at times with an uncle and occasionally working in a factory, where he lived in a trailer with forty other men. Eventually, he reunited with a friend from home, who was only a few years older and who had also migrated alone as a minor. This friend, Isaiah, took Andres under his wing, helping him find the job at the country club, where the pay was better and where he could live in the dormitories—a step up from the tight quarters in the factory trailer. Then, Isaiah began to speak with Andres about the possibility of enrolling in the local high school. Andres explained the conversation they had:

> [Isaiah] asked me, "How many years have you been here?" I tell him I had been here for three years. "How much money do you have?" Well, I didn't really have any money. And he asks, "Do you know English?" I said I didn't. He says, "There are two options. The first is that you study so you can get a better job. One that pays better." That made me think. He says, "Because if not, you are always going to be like this, without money." So, that made me think. I said, right. . . . I told him, "If you help me, why not?"

From there, the two young men went to school, where Andres was told he needed to have a legal guardian to enroll him. Isaiah, who was in his early twenties at the time, agreed to take on this responsibility. He worked with Andres's parents, who were in Mexico, to get guardianship rights for Andres, and eventually Andres was able to start his education. When I interviewed him, at age eighteen, he was a junior and was still making progress towards graduation.

After speaking with Andres, I was thrilled to be able to connect to Isaiah as well. He was in his midtwenties when we met and had enrolled in a local community college. He had also come to the United States as an unaccompanied minor. Isaiah had long valued school, but he had been forced to drop out when he lived in Mexico due to financial strain. However, when he came to the United States as a teenager, he was eager to enroll again. He had moved in with an older brother upon arrival, but he soon found that work took up all of his time and was preventing him from enrolling in school. He ended up having a conversation with his older brother about his desire to enroll, and his brother agreed to help him matriculate and also to reduce rent costs so Isaiah could focus on his education. When Isaiah reflected on this, he was grateful for his brother's assistance, but still wished he had more moral support: "Finan-cially, my brother helped me. Financially, when I arrived here, he had an apartment, I could live with him, and he didn't charge me rent. So that was a big help. He brought me to school, he helped me take the first step. He brought me to school and registered me. But once I was in school, he never said: 'Oh, yes, you can do it! Keep studying!' . . . I understand him. He had to work. . . . So I was the one that encouraged myself: keep on going, keep on going, keep on going." Isaiah was proud of himself: he continued working and still graduated high school. In fact, he did so well that several teachers took him under their wing and raised money for him to attend the local community college, even though he was undocumented. Isaiah understood that many young people like himself did not see the point of an education, especially if their undocumented status would restrict their future job prospects. Isaiah vehemently disagreed: "My mentality is this: it is good to go to school, get your degree. No one can take away the education that you have. The English that you learned . . . who can take that away. Absolutely no one. People can take away your money, maybe you lose it all. But I believe, I have always thought that education is necessary to have a life." It was with this mindset that Isaiah felt strongly about bringing his peers along with him in his educational journey. He believed that success was a combination of financial assistance, moral support, and personal resiliency, and he was willing to bridge the gaps as much as he could among his friends.

Isaiah and Andres were not the only friends who pulled each other forward, particularly in their educational goals. Similarly, Mariana and Angelica leaned on each other for support, even when outside institutions failed them. From Honduras and El Salvador, respectively, the young women met each other while attending school in the Houston area. Unlike Isaiah and Andres, both Mariana and Angelica had gone through the Office of Refugee Resettlement after being apprehended at the border. Through the ORR they had been placed in families and had been encouraged to enroll in school. However, for both girls, the placements from the ORR failed. As discussed in chapter 1, Mariana was placed with a father who was eventually deported due to domestic violence, and Angelica was placed in an uncle's home, where she did not feel comfortable. The two girls bonded immediately when they met each other, especially due to their similar histories and shared precarity. They leaned on each other emotionally as they struggled with traumatic memories, homelessness, violence, and the more mundane difficulties of school. When Mariana received assistance from a local family, after losing her housing when her father was deported, she made sure that the family cared for Angelica as well. Their friendship sustained them, and to this day, they credit one another with their individual successes.

* * *

Education for unaccompanied youth functions in conjunction with numerous contradictory factors in these young people's lives. It is woven into youths' experience with adolescence in that it both proves one's status as a minor and also depends on youths' ability to enact that status. It is experienced in conflict with the necessity of labor. It depends on youths' involvement in families; but it can also mediate the fallout when students are separated from families. Finally, even social circles are important in youths' access to education. All of these variables are further dependent on local contexts, school flexibility, and racialized beliefs about immigrant youth. Because of this, for unaccompanied youth to access the benefits of an education, advocates must think broadly and comprehensively about making the education system a truly welcoming institution.

4

Institutionalizing Paradoxes

In the three years before I took office, more than 150,000 unaccompanied alien minors arrived at the border and were released all throughout our country into United States' communities—at a tremendous monetary cost to local taxpayers and also a great cost to life and safety.
—Former President Donald J. Trump, 2017

MS-13 is particularly violent. . . . These are animals.
—Former President Donald J. Trump, 2017

Why are we having all these people from shithole countries come here? . . . We should have more people from Norway.
—Former President Donald J. Trump, 2018

Former president Donald Trump is notorious for his off-the-cuff, tell-it-as-it-is rhetoric, and he saves a particular vehemence for his talk about immigrants. To listen to Trump tell it, migrant youth have taken American towns hostage. Gang members from MS-13 are "pouring into our country,"[1] and communities throughout the nation are "under siege."[2] He frequently and explicitly makes connections between migrant youth and gangs, often highlighting when arrested gang members are undocumented[3] and focusing on the brutality of MS-13 as a particular threat to American safety. In truth, immigrants are less likely to commit crimes than native-born individuals,[4] and although brutal, MS-13 as an international criminal organization is relatively powerless.[5] Nonetheless, the claim that unaccompanied youth are linked to dangerous gangs goes beyond Trump's unscripted rhetoric and into official government statements. A news release by the Department of Homeland Security in February 2018 made the explicit claim that the "influx of unaccompanied alien minors . . . creates recruiting opportunities for brutal gangs such as MS-13."[6] Notably, this memo relied on anecdotal evidence, admitting that there are "no official statistics on the number of UACs [unaccompanied alien children] involved with gangs."[7]

Violence is not Trump's only focus when it comes to immigrants. Trump is not anti-immigrant, he claims. He just wants the "right" immigrants. In January 2018, Trump made his now infamous remarks in which he referred to Haiti, El Salvador, and countries in Africa as "shithole" countries and lamented that the United States should have more migrants from countries such as Norway.[8] Commentators were quick to notice the racial and classed implications of this statement, which suggests that the right immigrants are wealthy, educated, and white. Policies implemented just a year later followed suit. These policies sought to expand the definition of "public charge" as a way to deter immigrants who could potentially request public benefits. In an August 2019 statement, USCIS acting director Ken Cuccinelli explained that this change was meant to encourage "self-reliance and self-sufficiency for those seeking to come to, or to stay in, the United States."[9]

Unfortunately, Trump's rhetoric is not isolated. Whether or not Donald Trump is in the White House, these sentiments and policies have long impacted the experience of migrants. Migrants in the United States walk a tightrope of expectations and contradictions, which permeate every aspect of life, including the humanitarian apparatuses that seek to provide assistance. Unaccompanied migrant youth, in particular, find that as they navigate the institutions of family, the state, and the education system, they encounter several paradoxes that govern their behavior. They are criminalized at the same time they are scrutinized for their ability to enact narrow versions of worth based on personal responsibility. They must demonstrate that they are dependent on adults and institutions in order to prove their status as minors, but they also must demonstrate agency and responsibility in taking care of themselves. Simultaneously, they must demonstrate steadfastness, mental fortitude, and focus—elements of personal stability—all while enduring the trauma that is necessary for access to legal relief.

Criminalizing and Decriminalizing Youth

They had me locked up for one day. They lock you up. I don't know, I had never been to jail, but maybe that was it. They lock you up with metal,

cold, with a stiff, ugly blanket. I cried, I yelled, I apologized: "Why did I come? Why? Why?" I kept throwing myself on the floor, getting up again, and crying.
—Cynthia, who migrated from Guatemala at age fourteen

For Cynthia, it was nothing less than shocking when, after a harrowing journey across Mexico, she was placed in jail. She describes being exhausted, shaking with cold and hunger, and feeling deeply ashamed. She was devastated by her incarceration, and her response was to apologize to the border agents, to beg for forgiveness for her apparent misdeeds. The message she received was loud and clear: she did not belong, and her desire to pursue a new life was criminal.

The criminalization of young migrants is pervasive. For some youth, particularly boys, the poor, and indigenous youth, this criminalization starts in their home country. It follows them throughout their journeys and into the United States, where the markers of criminalization are present through their apprehension, detainment, and release. It also spans temporally, in the sense that criminality exists in the past, in the present, and as a looming possibility in the future. However, youth must actively resist this label, even while it is nearly omnipresent in their lives. On a national level, public sympathy and political will is dependent on the perception of migrant youths' innocence. On a personal level, youth who carry criminal labels have a greater difficulty accessing legal relief and other resources. For example, school districts are more open to youth who have been victims than to youth marked as criminals. Even accessing foster families is easier for youth who are able to avoid the criminal label. This results in a particular paradox for the professionals who work with youth: they participate in structures that criminalize youth while also actively working to decriminalize the same youth.

Moments of Criminalization

The criminalization of migrant youth is pervasive before youth leave their homes and in the context of the circular flow of migration and deportation. Across Latin America, particularly in the neoliberal context, youth culture is often met with violent political repression, particularly for poor and indigenous youth.[10] *Mano dura* policies, translated literally as "firm hand" policies, are common throughout Latin America and follow the US model of strong penalties for minor offenses, the use of police force, and the reduction of legal rights. These policies have transnational implications. For example, anthropologist Elana Zilberg shows that the criminalization of young men in both the United States and El Salvador is linked. Violence and insecurity create migratory flows from El Salvador to the United States. However, when young Salvadoran men in the United States are criminalized, especially in the context of the War on Drugs, they are penalized for minor offenses and may ultimately face deportation back to El Salvador. Because El Salvador has adopted many of the same policies, these same young people face continued criminalization upon their return. Youth find that they are also criminalized as they make their way north. The United States has pressured Mexico to cut off the flow of migrants, which has led to the increased surveillance and arrests of Central Americans in the country.[11]

When youth arrive to the United States, they are not treated as children who have undergone a traumatic and often violent journey. Instead, they are immediately placed for up to seventy-two hours in a processing center that is known colloquially as "*La Hielera*," or the Ice Box. This is a physical description of a painfully cold, cement building where detainees are provided no warmth outside of crinkly foil blankets. Many migrants report being fed only frozen sandwiches and receiving persistent harassment from the guards.[12] *La Hielera* came up in most stories youth told me about their entry into the United States. For many, *La Hielera* was among the most painful experiences of their migration, due to the combination of the physical suffering in these buildings and also the emotional torment of this marker of criminalization. Nicolas, the young man from Ecuador, perceived immigration detention as a punishment. He explains that once he was apprehended by border enforcement, "they brought us to jail." I asked how he was treated and he explained, "Well, in the jail, it was really hard because we weren't used to that, and when I was in jail it was really. . . . They didn't have anything to sleep on, there was just like a cement bench that you could sit on, that was it. If you wanted to lie down, it was on the floor. That was really difficult. . . . You couldn't see if it was day or night, everything was closed up and they have the lights on day and night, as if it were always day." Whether or not this temporary detention center is supposed to be a jail, it is very clearly read by youth as such. Instead of arriving into the arms of a country that wants to provide humanitarian assistance to vulnerable lives, they arrive into a cold, terrifying cell where they experience tremendous fear, desperation, and physical discomfort.

This criminalization continues when youth are transferred to the long-term shelter facilities run by the ORR. Although shelters vary according to the size, the contractor, and the security level, many of the criminalization practices exist in nearly all facilities. Youth have limited movement within the building—some buildings are fully monitored by security cameras—and youth are not able to go outside alone. Youth must abide by various rules regarding their dress and behavior; often, their clothing is picked out for them, according to the particular shelter's standards (for example, sweatpants, t-shirts, and sandals). Some workers reported that youth in their facilities were specifically issued sandals that made it difficult to run. Youth and workers report that youths' activities are monitored closely; for example, any drawings or sketches that youth make must be checked for gang symbols. Their phone calls are often monitored, and they may not be allowed to keep personal belongings, such as pictures of their families, in their rooms. Relationships between girls and boys are strictly controlled, and youth are often forbidden from sharing contact information with one another for the future (although this is often a futile effort in the age of social media). In one case I encountered, a young man was written up after being caught masturbating alone in his room. As Salma, a family reunification worker commented,

> While I was working [in the government shelter], I hadn't noticed because I had never been in a prison before, but then when I did visit a prison, I was like, this is exactly . . . you're doing pretty much the same thing. And that was very disturbing to find out. It's in a way that's not necessarily . . . like the people that are doing it, like the staff on the floor don't acknowledge that necessarily and don't realize that what they're doing is cruel. Just like how the children would have to sleep with their doors open, and then [the staff] would come in in the night, do checks with flashlights to make sure they're in their bed and everything. And just like how they would have to be . . . file in line, they would get their room checked and turned over to make sure they don't have any weapons and stuff like that, which you know, they never really did. And just the way

they would be treated, wouldn't be able to go outside really, they were only able to go outside to this little backyard area that they had.

The Trump administration further tightened these practices by creating the Community Safety Initiative, in partnership with the Office of Refugee Resettlement. This initiative promised to keep gang-involved migrant youth out of local communities, and it did so by training shelter workers to identify these youth.[13] Most notably, these guidelines included explicit mention that youth in custody may reveal gang-related activity during their weekly counseling sessions. The guidelines request that the clinician thoroughly document the gang revelations and report to the Department of Homeland Security. The clinician therefore acts not as a mental health professional but rather as an arm of the security apparatus.

When border control agents and ORR professionals suspect youth of gang involvement or other criminal activities, they transfer youth to secure facilities or even to juvenile detention centers. Even youth who are transferred to shelters, instead of secure facilities, learn quickly that this placement is precarious. If they act out or reveal any connection to gangs, they can very quickly be downgraded from a homelike shelter to a youth detention center. Aurora, a child advocate on the East Coast, explained that her very first case as an advocate for unaccompanied youth was with a young man who was being held in a local juvenile detention center. However, the young man was very confused about why he was there. He had been apprehended at the border with drugs in his possession, but he insisted that he was a victim of a drug trafficking ring, and had been forced into this labor. Aurora also believed that he may have been sent to the facility due to a lack of beds in the ORR shelter network. He was angry and ashamed by this placement. Aurora explained, "He didn't understand why he was with other criminals. Like in a jail. But he had great behavior. People there had nothing but good things to say about him. . . . But definitely he felt that he shouldn't be there with all these other kids who committed crimes and horrible things, according to him." The young man clearly distinguished himself from the American youth around him, but he worried that others did not make this distinction. While the immigrant youth were supposed to be separated from the main population, they would sometimes mingle with others and would get in trouble along with everyone else. All activities were monitored and everything was scheduled. There was intense surveillance, and the young man complained about not receiving enough to eat and being constantly cold. Aurora went on to explain, "He was wondering why he was there. 'Why am I here? I didn't commit a crime.' And I always felt that it was such a punitive place to be in . . . for a victim of a crime. . . . I felt that it was such a contradiction, not only to place him there . . . [but also] to ask of them to be on their best behavior and to be all of these things. It was such a contradiction." Aurora's point about the contradictions of his detainment is apt. While the young man was a victim, he was perceived to be a criminal, he was placed with other youth labeled as criminals, and then he was expected to maintain a sense of self and behavior that demonstrated his innocence.

The reminders of criminality are also enforced through legal education. The Office of Refugee Resettlement provides a legal resources guide—a "Know Your Rights Handout"—to youth in their shelters.[14] It begins with the question "Why am I being detained?" The guide explains, "Many of you arrived at the United States border and entered without permission or without proper documents. Maybe some of you were already living in the United States without permission before being stopped by the police or immigration authorities. You may have even been arrested and detained and taken into custody by immigration authorities."[15] While the guide provides youth with information regarding their rights, it makes clear that youth have violated a law. In fact, in a misguided effort to make the form child-friendly, it features small clip art images, including a cartoonish police officer chasing a man and a set of handcuffs.

When youth are finally released from detention and establish lives in the United States, they enter into a world that continues to systematically criminalize them as youth, migrants, and people of color.[16] Further, they remain under government surveillance as they navigate their communities, social groups, and educational system. A report by the Immigrant Legal Resource Center demonstrates the wide range of ways in which immigrant youth are racially profiled and associated with gang membership.[17] For example, youths' social media posts may be analyzed, based on clothing in photos and the other people who appear with youth in pictures. These practices create a "school to deportation pipeline" wherein reports by school officials can be used as evidence for gang membership, even if the evidence is sparse.[18] This is particularly problematic in the context of racial profiling, both among school officials and among law enforcement officers. It also further ties the education system into the immigration system, so that even schools who hope to provide aid to immigrant youth must be wary of their collusion in the surveillance of these youth.

Criminalizing Youth to Get the Job Done

This context of criminalization increases feelings of hopelessness and contributes to chronic stress in young people's lives.[19] Within this context, professionals encounter a difficult paradox in their work with youth. They work within structures that criminalize youth, but they must also seek to remove these labels from youth. They must both criminalize and decriminalize youth at the same time. Attorneys, in particular, find that their job is to enforce the idea that youth have broken a law, even if their personal stance differs from this legal work. In fact, many of the attorneys in my research professed their own beliefs that youth had the right to seek asylum in the United States, and that they should be treated as humanitarian victims rather than as criminals. Yet, in order to help youth navigate the legal system, these same attorneys have to emphasize criminal actions to the youth. Susana explains how she communicates this to her young clients:

> I start off, you know, countries are like houses. You can't just come into a house, I mean, come into a stranger's house. You have to ask permission and get invited in. And that's how countries work. So I really just try to explain the whole process to them and educate them. And my personal stance is, I'm not here to judge anybody, so I hope that is what is coming across, too. I'm not here to judge you. I'm here to help you with any context that I might be able to help in this juncture in your life.

Susana's go-to metaphor positions youth as intruders into the American household and she grapples with presenting this metaphor while simultaneously taking a nonjudgmental stance towards youth. She recognizes that she must enforce the idea that youth have committed a criminal act while also making sure that they know that she personally does not judge them for these "criminal" actions.

Professionals must also actively guard against the possibility of youths' future criminal behavior. Attorneys, along with other professionals, indicated a preoccupation with any possibility that the youth in their care would commit illegal acts that could put their cases at risk. They often felt a need to remind youth constantly of their precarious legal position and the importance of remaining above the fray. Attorney Nathan explained, "I think as the kids get more advanced into the teen years, we do have to really be concerned about the company that they are keeping and the peer influence. . . . As kids get older, they are becoming their own people. There is a little rebellious streak that can sometimes occur, and we have to do our best to try to help them understand the consequences are going to be steep with them." Similarly, Nancy explains to her young clients,

> Until you become a US citizen, you are under the microscope of the government, so even after you get your green card, no drugs, you can't drink and drive, you can't get in a fight, you can't. Everything has to be above board. You have to be better than me. Because I was born here so I get to mess up left and right. . . . If you make similar mistakes, if they are very serious mistakes, they can put you in jail, take away your stuff, and then they can send you back. . . . Don't get yourself caught in these stupid situations that every kid in our country has a right to get caught in. . . . So everything you do, you have to be better than people who are born here.

Both Nathan and Nancy are often preoccupied with the possibility of their clients getting into trouble. Nathan sees this so-called rebellious streak as a normal, developmental stage, and in a sense, he expects youth to behave badly. He simply sees it as his job to control these impulses in his clients. Nancy, however, is more pained when she explains her worry to me. She does not relish having these conversations with youth, because she worries that her hypervigilance over her young clients will be read as suspicion by the youth. She is also concerned that her emphasis promotes stereotypes that all immigrant youth are at risk for criminal behavior.

Finally, while professionals help individual youth, they must often do so in a way that actively criminalizes another community. Indeed, one of the easiest ways to decriminalize one young person is to juxtapose them against a criminalized other. For example, in an attempt to explain why the youth with whom she worked should be not be sent to a "school for juvenile delinquents," a social worker explained, "Those are troubled kids. I don't think you would want to send a refugee kid to them, because they are not coming from that side of the surge. They are fleeing violence." Her language here is telling. "That side" suggests that there are two types of youth, and the youth in her care are the "good" ones. They are the refugee youth, fleeing violence, not the troubled kids, the youth perpetuating violence. While the intention behind these sentiments is always to help the individual, it does so by erasing the context of violence in youths' lives and delineating victims and villains. The risk here is that the individual child is saved at the expense of others who may come after.

Similarly, Marcy, a director of a shelter for unaccompanied youth, consistently emphasized to me the worth of the unaccompanied youth by comparing them to other American populations her nonprofit served.

> So the [American] kids are pretty angry a lot of times. And sometimes resentful. They come from a different background, and they come from—it is not their choice, how's that? Whereas the UAC [unaccompanied alien children] kids are looking at this placement as, everything is appreciated. Everything was welcomed. They took direction. They had no problems following rules, because they had a lot more to lose, one. And, two, it was their choice to make their journey to the United States, and they knew they would more than likely be caught and be placed in a facility like ours before they could finish their journey to their sponsors. But the kids' attitudes were completely different than a normal population. So, they were extremely appreciative, they wanted to go to school, they wanted to experience everything.

Marcy was effusive when talking about unaccompanied youth, and it was clear to me during the interview that she wanted to communicate in no uncertain terms that these immigrant youth deserved assistance. Throughout the interview, she repeated words like "appreciative," "refreshing," "heartwarming," and "grateful" to compare the differences between immigrant youth and other adolescent populations. However, the byproduct of such rhetoric is to exclude some populations from care and to enforce a very narrow set of behaviors as deserving.

Reading Crime and Innocence on the Body

Whether acting in a pro bono capacity or working for a legal aid center, every attorney I spoke with had limited time and resources to dedicate to unaccompanied youth and were therefore selective in who they were willing to represent. The same tension existed for social workers and educators, who often made personal decisions about whom to expend their time and energy on. In the context of criminalization, it was often more productive for these resources to be expended on innocent youth, rather than those perceived as criminal. Yet, with limited insight into youths' full history, professionals in the United States must use their own discretion in making these determinations and delineating the "criminals" from the victims. To do so, professionals find themselves reading youths' bodies as if they were canvases where past indiscretions were written. Just as refugees around the world have used the scars on their bodies to prove the veracity of traumatic histories, youths' bodies carry physical indicators that professionals can interpret as markers of either criminality or innocence.[20]

Attorneys have perhaps the highest stake in portraying their youth clients as innocent victims. Throughout our interviews, I would ask how these professionals would make determinations about the authenticity of youths' stories, and in particular, youths' claims to innocence. There were, of course, a wide array of tools that attorneys used in their authentication process, from gathering affidavits from individuals close to their clients to cross-checking youths' stories through news articles and weather reports. However, many attorneys also relied on "gut-checks," in which they used their intuition to make sense of youths' histories. After further probing, many attorneys revealed that intuition is often developed consciously or unconsciously through visible markers.

Jessica, an attorney, demonstrated her reliance on bodily markers as she reflected on my question of whether or not she trusts her young clients: "Most of the kids that I have run across came here because they were asked to be in gangs and they refused for a number of reasons . . . but I wonder sometimes if one or two of them are lying to me. But most of them are pretty young. None of them have tattoos. None of them seemed hardened, you know, like they've been in gangs or anything like that." Jessica makes these intuitive determinations regarding youth through physical indicators. "Pretty young," "no tattoos," and "seeming hardened" become the evidence that she uses to stake her own claim to trusting youths' stories of innocence. Even her suspicion that some youth might lie to her can be assuaged by bodily appearances of innocence. Similarly, Ashley, a social worker, emphasizes corporeal markers to argue the innocence of one of her youth clients. This particular young man had gotten into trouble in his school, acted violently against a teacher, and was sent to a juvenile detention center. But, when Ashley tells his story, she uses his stature to combat this evidence, explaining that although he was twelve, he "looked eight" and was a "really, really petite little guy": "He lost fifteen pounds, and he's a little itty bitty kid. He went from 80 pounds to like 65 pounds while he was in the juvenile detention center. Thought that he was going to be deported the whole time and he was petrified. . . . He is just this really, really sweet little kid but has had no guidance." For Ashley, his innocence, despite his actions, was an embodied and enacted quality. Whereas large, strong bodies are associated with masculinity and adulthood,[21] the "little guy" in her story could only be read as a child. Since he had not matured physically into a masculine, adult body, his stature and his weight gave him access to innocence in Ashley's assessment (although, notably, the young man was still deported in part due to his behavior).

These examples show how bodies can display innocence in the eyes of professionals. Yet, the reverse side of this coin is that bodies can also display criminality. Racial prejudices intersect with bodily markers such as size and physique to cue stereotypes of violence and aggression.[22] While none of the professionals I spoke with employed explicitly racialized language around their own beliefs, they frequently expressed concern that others in the immigration system would rely on racialized stereotypes in their work with immigrant youth. Ayana, an attorney, worried that stereotypes of dangerous Latino men would be activated by the ways in which young men were presented in court. She explained that with the increased use of the "rocket docket," which fast tracks the court procedures, youth would stand in front of a judge in groups based on similar histories and similar legal requests (such as extensions for their cases). Instead of working with one young person at a time, a judge would make blanket determinations for these groups. Ayana mourned that this practice of grouping young men erased the individuality of her clients and instead created momentary visuals of the rumored hordes of violent gangbangers.

There was one marker that was particularly salient as the embodiment of criminality: a tattoo. Tattoos were used specifically as evidence of gang affiliation, an affiliation that could obliterate the right of due process.[23] Because of this, the presence of a tattoo became a fixation for professionals working with youth. Aurora, the child advocate discussed previously who worked with the young man in the juvenile detention facility, tells one such story. She had been called to work on the case as the adolescent had expressed an explicit desire to return to his home country, and the social workers on his case felt that this was not in his best interests, especially due to his claims that he had been the victim of drug traffickers. Aurora's job was to learn more about his situation and work with him to learn about his best options. Aurora held the young man in high esteem: it was clear to her that he was a victim of circumstances and was highly vulnerable to violence and exploitation in his home community. She also explained that "he's witty, he's charming, he knows how to talk to people . . . he knows what people want to hear." However, her perception of him became complicated the moment she noticed a tattoo on his body.

> I saw a tattoo on his hands. . . . And I saw that tattoo, and I'm just, I'm like [deep sigh]. I knew something wasn't right. . . . I didn't ask him anything. I just took a good look and called a friend, a sheriff in a police department that does gang-related stuff. I drew it for him and sent it over, and he confirmed with me the gang affiliation. I'm like, oh man. I call the [social worker from his case] and am like, we have a problem. I don't know how serious this is, and I don't know if the detention facility has realized this yet, or if his attorney knows this, or how is this information at all going to, you know, not be so good for his case.

Aurora eventually decided to approach the young man directly about this tattoo. She strongly encouraged him to either remove or cover the marking. She was concerned both about how the tattoo would be perceived in court and by social workers and also about how the tattoo would complicate his relationship with other youth in the detention facility. The young man agreed that tattoo removal would be the best option, but he was transferred to another state before Aurora could do any follow-up with him.

In this story, the tattoo was an embodied marker that contradicted established beliefs of innocence. It was clear to Aurora that the body needed to be changed for both the safety and the success of this client. Many other attorneys reported similar experiences when they discovered a tattoo on a young person's body. Caroline told me about a new client whom she had recently started representing: "This particular young gentleman does have a tattoo. It is always good for me to research this. What were the circumstances for getting this tattoo? What does it mean? Make sure it's not gang affiliated. I still have some pending questions with him. I should just know all of the details and be clear and open because as you know, immigration is very serious about gang involvement. And I would like to have full disclosure and know exactly the circumstances of his tattoo." Linda describes a case that proved impossible to win, due in part to the tattoo: "One time I had a kid who had MS-13 literally tattooed on his forehead. You are probably not going to get an indiscretion. That kid was committed to the gang life. He just, it was the only place he could find family. He was here alone, had no support, that gang literally took him in. So when it was time to put in work for the gangs, he did it and he was very proud of it." Linda provides her own, nuanced analysis of her client's gang involvement. However, even though the young man was willing to explore tattoo removal, this was not sufficient for the judge, who issued him a deportation order.

Tattoos were not only purposefully revealed but also accidently discovered. Kathy told a story of a young man who had fled gang recruitment in his home country and had come to her for help on his case. As they worked together, he provided a strong testimony that he had not had any involvement in the gang and had actively avoided recruitment. To build the case, Kathy suggested that the client undergo a physical exam to provide corroborating evidence regarding violent acts against him. However, during this exam, the medical professional discovered a tattoo on his back, and this went into the medical report. While the young man maintained that this was not a gang-related tattoo, the judge remained focused on this embodied piece of evidence, asking what it meant and why he had gotten it. Kathy asks, "How do you prove the negative, that you were not involved in gangs, especially when you have a tattoo or appearance that looks otherwise?"

Similarly, Caroline told a story of an unaccompanied youth client who was living in the United States when he was assaulted by a gang with connections in his home country. He was taken to the hospital for treatment after the attack. An officer was present, and during his examination, multiple tattoos were revealed that had been otherwise hidden by his everyday clothing. These tattoos became part of the evidence linking the young man to gang involvement and thus permanently damaging his opportunity for relief in the United States. Both of these situations reveal the uncomfortable tension wherein hospitals who are supposed to heal or support evidence of trauma instead operate against the young people's cases.

These stories also expose the potency that tattoos have despite other evidence. A robust literature reveals a cultural preoccupation regarding the correlation between tattoos and other deviant behavior such as drug use, suicide, and criminal acts, including assault and homicide.[24] Doctors and other medical professionals often view tattoos as a symbol of gang involvement or as a clinical marker for high-risk behavior.[25] Criminologists John M. Hagedorn and Bradley A. MacLean show that jurors and judges frequently rely on their own folk knowledge of gang tattoos, often drawing incorrect conclusions that the existence of these tattoos represents a "deep commitment" to gang life, and by extension, a wide range of antisocial behavior. However, these researchers provide stirring evidence that tattoos—even with gang-related symbols—do not always provide a direct link to past deviance.[26] Further, these tattoos are often used as evidence without a simultaneous examination of the mechanisms that prompted the tattoo, such as the local community influence, a need for belonging, personal protection, or even self-expression. The tattoo itself cannot speak for violent acts, criminality, or immorality. Furthermore, people from a wide range of backgrounds use tattoos for a variety of reasons: to mark the passage of life milestones, to demonstrate commitment to a person or belief, to perform or eschew gender, to assert one's bodily autonomy, or to participate in a range of subcultures.[27] In fact, almost a third of Americans have at least one tattoo.[28] Yet, tattoos continue to serve as a false stand-in for deviance that is easily misinterpreted by stakeholders, specifically when the tattoo supports existing racial and ethnic stereotypes.

Tattoo removal is a viable option for some youth who have the resources and willingness to undergo this long, painful process. For some, tattoo removal is an empowering act, in which the individual can claim a new future against what they perceive as an oppressive past.[29] However, anthropologist Mauro Cerbino suggests that the criminalization of tattoos, along with the practice of removing tattoos in order to find belonging in society, represents a new institutional violence against poor young men from Central America.[30] Cerbino interviewed a young Honduran man who reported that getting a face tattoo was a positive experience in which he felt a sense of power and belonging. On the other hand, in discussing tattoo removal, Cerbino remarked of the man, "He only talks about the pain he experienced, the loneliness he has been through, the shame he felt, about his fall into a state of resignation."[31] Tattoos, Cerbino suggests, are a symbol of relative sovereignty over the body, while the removal of the tattoo "transforms a person into a passive or docile entity."[32] Similarly, unaccompanied youth in the United States find that their bodies are subject to scrutiny, and tattoos speak with particular force. While youth may choose to undergo tattoo removal for the sake of their case, this "choice" is simply an extension of state power and a reminder of their dependency on and their precariousness in the United States.

Proving Worth: Dependency, Responsibility, and Stability

At the same time youth deal with the persistent trauma of criminalization, they must also prove their worth by navigating a second paradox. On one hand, they are required to be childlike, dependent on various adult institutions and willing to give up aspects of adulthood and personal agency. But, they must also take responsibility for themselves. They must be able to demonstrate their stability and worth through specific versions of neoliberal personhood. Just as with criminalization, this paradox is present throughout the various institutions youth encounter and presents specific obstacles based on youths' multiple vulnerabilities.

Act like a Child: Institutionalized Dependency

The immigration shelters that detain youth shortly after apprehension are the first spaces in which dependency is required. As described in the previous section, the shelters are often highly regimented and many of the aspects that are used to secure the shelters also operate implicitly to infantilize the detained youth. Whether it is limiting movement, erasing choices, or controlling dress, shelters exert tremendous control over young people. Most rules are justified with the language of safety and best interest. Workers extol the virtues of schedules in providing trauma-informed care and helping youth adjust to the structured educational system in the United States. Practices such as monitoring phone usage, prohibiting pictures in the room, and forbidding youth from sharing contact information with one another are intended to combat the threat of human trafficking. Security cameras and limited movement are meant to keep youth safe from each other. But shelter workers often see youth struggling with these restrictions, and they observe that this is directly connected to youths' previous life experience. Rosa, a case manager in a midwestern shelter, expounds on the difficulties that many youth have when they first arrive to the shelter program.

> Sometimes they all go crazy because they are like, "I have never had structure in my life! I lived on the street! What the heck is this? Why are you telling me what to do? Fuck you!" . . . Teenagers who, some of them are working and have children or whatever (they certainly get to date) . . . really being like little adults working and providing maybe, and all of a sudden to be like, "Nope you can't get water from the water fountain until we say. . . . You can't leave your room right now."

Rosa notes that many of the youth have long surpassed many of the milestones associated with adulthood. By definition, they have undertaken an international journey without parents. They may have left the education system long before and have been working full-time. They may already be living without guardians and supporting themselves. They may already have developed intimate adult relationships of their own, sometimes being parents and partners. Many feel suddenly infantilized by an institution that will not allow them to get water without permission. This can be punitive, stifling, and humiliating for some young people.[33]

Once youth are released from detention facilities, they can continue to prove dependency through their relationships with legal guardians. As detailed in chapter 1, family reunification workers implicitly seek arrangements in which youth will enter into traditionally structured families. Workers attempt to ensure that the sponsor will take full responsibility for the youth. There is an expectation that within these families the youth will not work—or will work minimally—and that the adults in the household will provide youth with the basic necessities. This arrangement is further enforced when youth pursue legal relief, particularly if they want to pursue a Special Immigrant Juvenile Status. Like other immigration laws in history, SIJS implicitly requires that a youth not become a "public charge" by ensuring that there is someone who can account for that youth.[34] For youth without parents in the country, this requires that a sponsor take the legal steps necessary to become an official legal guardian.[35] As part of this procedure, attorneys have indicated that in order to arrange the necessary guardianship, they have had to pursue divorces for young people who have already married.

Connected to their relationship to legal guardians is the assumption that youth can and should be in school. As detailed in chapter 3, school attendance, although not required by law, presents favorably in front of a judge. It helps to establish character and dependence and works to show that staying in the United States is within the youths' best interest.[36] Sponsors must show that they understand their obligation to enroll youth into school, and when the government does a thirty-day check-up on families, school enrollment is one of the primary indicators that a placement has been successful. School attendance can be a complicated requirement. While a large portion of youth certainly saw the benefit of education, some youth need to work for their own survival. Some have already been employed for years and have families—parents, siblings, or even their own partners and children—to support. Karen, who worked with special populations in her school district, saw the tension in unaccompanied-youth students. She explains that while these youth were expected to behave like American, middle-class adolescents, they often had trouble doing so: "We see a lot of behavior issues. . . . That behavioral issue is often insubordination or what is viewed as disrespect of authority. I think a lot of that has to do with kids that have been acting as adults for a long time and then we try to get them to play school. And in a lot of schools, that is you know, sit down, be quiet, be in your seat. It isn't conducive to what they are already going through." Karen identifies the infantilization required by the institution as the problem, even noting the performative aspect of "playing school." She understands that this practice does not coincide with some young people's life courses or the reality of their needs.

Although some professionals, such as Rosa and Karen, identified the tension between infantilizing institutions and the realities of some youth, many others embraced the ideology of dependency. The rhetoric of these professionals highlighted their belief that the young people should act as dependents, but their reflections in this regard were highly gendered. In general, professionals discussed boys' dependency—or lack of it—as a frustrating obstacle to overcome, but one that was understandable. Many professionals were aware that young immigrant men are often pressured to support family members at home and may also deal with a self-concept that conflates this adult responsibility with their own masculinity.[37] However, some professionals framed boys' agency as an obstacle to overcome, rather than a reality to embrace. Nancy, an attorney, describes the difficulty of getting boys to comply with requirements of schooling, when their goal is often to work: "I have the hardest time with [teenage boys] because their impulse is to be: 'I want my work permit. I don't care what you do, just get my work permit.' I will say, 'Yes, I can get your work permit but it is here [motions far away] and we are still back here.'" For attorneys like Nancy, boys' agency is an annoyance, albeit an understandable one. Nancy and others feel that they must help to reign in boys' pull to adult activities in order to assist boys with their cases.

However, the rhetoric around girls' nonchildlike behavior took a different focus. Whereas boys' independent actions were understandable but bothersome, girls' independence was unbelievable and shameful. First, girls' existence as unaccompanied minors was often met with disbelief. For example, Kathy, an attorney, told a story about representing two sisters, both preteens, who had migrated to the United States in order to reunite with an older brother. The girls had initiated their own migration, but the judge could not wrap his head around this fact. Instead, the judge focused his questioning on the older brother, demanding to know how he could have let the girls migrate alone. Despite the girls' insistence that they had come of their own accord, the judge summarily dismissed their agency and continued to hold the older brother responsible.

Girls were also shamed when they acted in adult roles. Attorney Lavonne demonstrates this as she reflects on the girl clients she has encountered: "It is amazing to me how many girls come from Central America alone. And why they think they will be safe on that journey! Really, you didn't think that anybody would take advantage of you? You thought you could preserve your virginity on this trip? I don't know why you thought that. But that is a very hard subject to discuss with girls." Lavonne's comment is striking for several reasons. She ignores the structural realities that led to girls' migration, dismissing the possibility that girls often make informed decisions about the costs and benefits of crossing borders. She disregards the reality that sexual violence permeates girls' lives even before migration, and so avoiding migration does not necessarily mean avoiding this violence. Indeed, violence is often a thread that runs before, during, and after the migration of young people.[38] The particular vitriol she demonstrates here is in line with larger cultural patterns of blaming women for the violence they have experienced; she implies that girls can and should avoid the risks of assault and that it is their responsibility to protect themselves.[39] For Lavonne, girls who migrate are irresponsible, and their migratory agency is naïve and shameful.

Act like an Adult: Personal Responsibility

While institutions and ideologies demand dependency from youth, the paradox is that they also demand agency and responsibility. For children in general, the responsibility for success and failure is shared by both the child and the family.[40] However, when a young person has a precarious relationship to the family, that young person must often bear this responsibility alone. Reflecting on the experiences of children in foster care, social scientist Gerald Cradock argues that these particular young people are taught to enact personal responsibility since their claim to family life is tenuous.[41] Further, since their ability to exert control over their lives is limited, youth in foster care can "act out" in order to assert some agency over placements. However, Cradock explains that "such self-determination comes with a price. The freedom children purchase through acting out also brings responsibility for the self."[42] Similarly, I argue that unaccompanied youth operate within these same logics. The freedom they purchase through solitary migration (and the connected tenuousness in the family system) means that they are treated as neoliberal subjects who are required to exert personal responsibility as they simultaneously enact their dependency. This ideology of personal responsibility is often divorced from structural realities in youths' lives and fails to recognize the particular constraints that surround youths' decision making.

Unaccompanied youth face an array of structural barriers, many of which have been discussed throughout this book. From their responsibilities to their families to discrimination in their education to their legal liminality, youths' options are limited at every turn. Although professionals have a wide range of individual beliefs regarding the role of personal responsibility versus structure in youths' lives, they must operate in a way that privileges the role of personal responsibility. Throughout my interviews, professionals of all backgrounds discussed in detail the decision making of youth, emphasizing youths' personal responsibility and providing limited analyses of the structures constraining these decisions.

Attorney Julie, for example, explained to me her work with a young man who had lost his parents and had found support in a gang. She was working to get his green card, but she was worried about how the decisions he made would affect his case: "I told him very clearly you have got to change your ways, you have got to keep your nose clean. . . . You need to think like an adult here. You can't blame other people, you have got to take responsibility and realize what an opportunity you have. . . . I try to impress upon [youth]: it is hard, but you need to keep trying to talk to people and learn the language and not be afraid of saying the wrong things. That is how you learn. Go to school and study all those things." Julie emphasizes that the young man must act like an adult, not blame others, take responsibility, appreciate opportunities, and push forward. The language Julie uses here aligns with neoliberal personhood: the neoliberal subject embraces choice, self-regulates, and avoids vulnerability.[43] Unaccompanied youth must make no excuses for themselves. Julie articulated to me that she understood the limits in the young man's life, but in the eyes of the law, these did not matter. And in the end, she was not able to help the young man, who was eventually deported. As Gerald Cradock laments, "In neoliberal forces of governance, responsibility settles on the weak and unprotected."[44]

The emphasis on personal responsibility was rooted in a particularly strong belief in the American meritocracy. If youth behaved "badly" in their home country—perhaps participating in gang activity— professionals could create a story about structural influences on youth behavior. But if youth continued this type of behavior in the United States, this was no longer attributable to structure but to youths' personal flaws. Susana, an attorney, explained that she would lecture young people on the need to take responsibility for themselves once in the United States: "You're here, you have the opportunity to try to turn things around. If you behave in a way that you start associating with gangs over here, then it is like, okay, this is a pattern for you. But if we want to prove that you were just young or just did this out of need or coercion, it will look very good if right now you are just going to school, you stay out of trouble." Susana's uneven application of personal responsibility is telling. Whereas a story can be created in which youths' indiscretions in their home countries were structural, the same indiscretions in the United States are read as personal. This effectively erases the limitations and barriers that youth face in the United States and assumes that youth have entered a neutral environment where their histories and responsibilities vanish and barriers such as legality and discrimination disappear.

The tension between dependency on institutions and the requirement of personal responsibility plays out in a story told by Ricki, a social worker. Ricki compared the experiences of two boys ("Abel" and "Byron") from the same country, who both had family members in their home country whom they needed to support, and who initially lived in the same foster home for a period of time. The foster home was barely adequate, providing little more than food and shelter, and Abel was quickly transferred to a more supportive family. While in this new foster home, he completed high school, attended community college, and obtained a green card. Byron was not transferred to a new foster home.

He dropped out of school, left his foster family, and started working without a permit. There is an obvious structural difference in the boys' lives in the change of foster families, but when I asked Ricki directly why the two had differing outcomes, he suggested, "Their priority was different. Byron's priority was more: 'I want to do my own thing. I don't want to listen to anybody. I get in trouble, and every time I get in trouble I go back to [the social service agency] for help.' Abel saw the opportunity of really changing his life. And also the responsibility back home of helping the rest of his family. And so he made that decision of continuing education. . . . Abel was able to see the light at the end of the tunnel. Byron was short sighted." In this example, success has been boiled down to the decontextualized idea of "priorities," especially as those align with particular enactments of agency and dependency. Byron, the "less successful" youth, refused to perform his dependency on the foster family; as Ricky paraphrased him, "I want to do my own thing. I don't want to listen to anybody." Yet, when the young man needed help, he turned instead to the social service agency, which Ricki saw as an inability to take responsibility for himself. Abel, on the other hand, displayed appropriate dependency and life course decisions regarding his foster family and education. The language here emphasizes his choices ("saw an opportunity" and "made a decision") and his willingness to depend on institutions such as education. There is a lot left out of this analysis. The boys' only similarities are their countries of origin and their initial foster placement; beyond that, this narrative ignores the differing histories, contexts, and structures of the two boys. It focuses, instead, on the ability of the young men to enact dependency while taking responsibility for themselves.

Personal Stability in an Unstable World

I recently encountered a situation in which a thirteen-year-old girl detained at an immigration shelter had received a determination to be released to foster care. She was put on a "list," waiting for an opening, but her placement never happened. Within a few months, she was taken off the list. It seems that no one in the foster system wanted to take in a girl with her background, which included traumatic experiences of sexual violence; and, her erratic behavior while in the shelter further exacerbated her unattractiveness to potential foster families. An attorney working on the case said to me in frustration, "It's like they only want to take kids who don't have problems. But if they didn't have problems, they wouldn't be here!"

This story demonstrates a specific variation of the theme of personal responsibility, which is personal stability. However, unaccompanied youths' lives are inherently unstable and often marked by severe traumatic events. Geographers Kate Swanson and Rebecca Maria Torres show how violence for these youth is transnational, a thread that ties their experiences in their homes and during their journey north.[45] Violence in their home country may include family abuse and severe forms of political and community violence.[46] Rape, torture, gun fights, assault, and extortion are not uncommon in the most unstable communities.[47] If the young person has not been a personal victim of this violence, he or she almost surely knows someone who has. Structural violence also affects young people prior to migration. Youth I worked with could tell me exactly how chronic hunger feels in the stomach, and they could recall the humiliations of extreme poverty. They watched people around them die of diseases that could have been easily cured had there been appropriate medical intervention, and they too often had the scars to show when they themselves had not had access to the medical care they needed. Crossing international borders in clandestine ways means that young people have been exposed to further sexual violence, theft, loss of limb, drowning, starvation, assault by gangs and police who prey on migrants, and the extortion of human smugglers. They may know intimately the terror of a gun to one's head or the feeling of being alone, thirsty, and hungry in the middle of the desert. In the United States, they face border militarization, the indignities of criminalization, and human rights abuses in detention centers, including the denial of basic needs and violence at the hands of the guards. They are often still not safe in American communities. For example, one young man I interviewed from the Miami region told me about consistent and sometimes violent harassment by gang members in his neighborhood. In this context, it is hard to imagine a young person without psychological scars. Yet, youth must exhibit personal stability as a way to navigate the institutions around them.

The performance of personal stability helps to oil the machine of the immigration system, so that youth can be processed quickly and efficiently. For example, as discussed in chapter 1, case managers who work with youth detained in government shelters must evaluate parents and potential sponsors for youths' release. If a young person is perceived as "stable," the family background check can process quickly. However, these background checks become significantly more rigorous when youth show signs of emotional instability or behavioral difficulties. In these cases, potential sponsors must demonstrate that they can "handle" the behavior of the youth. However, the markers used to determine personal stability can be broad, and arbitrary, and are often decontextualized. Mercedes, a case manager in a government shelter, explained her process of determining a young person's emotional health:

> Many of the minors, when they arrive here, they are super sad, super alone, and they can have depression. And it's fine. And you ask them in the interview, "Have you ever had any mental health issue?" If they use the word "depression," that's an automatic home study.[48] When they say "depression," I'm like, I don't want to hear this! So I try to be like, "Well, were you diagnosed with depression, or it was just you being sad and adjusting to the new life?" "Oh no, I was just feeling depressed." Okay, feeling depressed is another thing. But if they say "depression," then: home study.

Mercedes does what she can to help youth present themselves in a way that shows that their negative emotions are temporary and not a part of their core self. The difference between "feeling depressed" and "depression" is not clinical here—Mercedes is not a psychologist or a therapist—but she knows that the ways in which youth use this language will have significant consequences for their stay and release from the shelter.

If a young person "has depression," their stay in the shelter will be extended as their sponsors prove that they can support the child's mental health needs. Paradoxically, research shows that migrants who face long periods of time in detention show increased depression and anxiety.[49] Several facility workers commented on the detrimental nature of these long-term detentions on youths' mental health—a vicious cycle in which instability prevented a quick release that in turn caused more instability and more issues for case managers to work through.

This catch-22 of stable instability occurred, too, while youth pursued their legal options. I met with Nancy, a passionate attorney in the

Midwest, who explained how emotional stability affected her work by telling me a story about Josefina, a young girl from Honduras with serious mental health concerns: "All the kids have anxiety, all the kids have depression issues, but Josefina has, um, attempted suicide so she was in residential treatment on and off for a year. It has been hard to work with her only because I can't really get to her half the time because she does not—they don't want her to talk about trauma." Nancy explained that Josefina was the ideal candidate for asylum based on her history of persecution. But, it was this very trauma that had caused Josefina's mental health crisis. She was unable to stay in school, demonstrate her positive personal characteristics, and participate in an asylum interview: "There is no way she can go to the interview, talk to an officer for three to four hours—that is how long these interviews take to rehash all of her trauma. In fact, her therapist at the time was like, 'You can't talk about her trauma, you can't even bring it up because we are just trying to keep her stable.' So we had to withdraw her asylum claim." After trying to work with Josefina and her therapist, Nancy realized that Josefina was simply unable to pursue this legal option. I asked Nancy, apologizing for the callousness of my question, if all of these problems of instability could actually be beneficial. Trauma is the basis for relief, so despite the difficulty of getting Josefina to court and enrolled in school and emotionally stable, could this not just be proof of relevant suffering?

> Yes definitely. I think so. I think that is partly why I wanted to try for asylum for her, because she is so damaged from her life. . . . She is so damaged from her life, and the abuse that she has suffered, and the fear that her mom is going to come back and take her away, and she has no coping skills whatsoever. That would so clearly come through in an asylum interview. And here at the local courts for the family court stuff for her, especially the juvenile status visa, that clearly came through and continues to come through every time she checks her. . . . She is eligible for her relief, and it's manifesting very clearly in her, unfortunately, but in a way, it is helpful to her case.

In the end, Nancy decided to pursue a different legal route for Josefina and was ultimately successful in getting the Special Immigrant Juvenile Status. While Josefina's instability prevented Nancy from obtaining her best option for immigration relief, and while it caused significant barriers in completing basic tasks for the court, Josefina's mental health was ultimately proof of sufficient hardship within the law.

Personal stability is viewed as a package of personal characteristics and behaviors. Dan, an attorney, explains: "Ideally, handling a case in the immigration court system, you would love to have a client who is very stable, who is doing everything he or she is supposed to do in terms of acquiring positive equities, doing well in school, developing friendships and relationships with people who can be kind of character references." Youth can thus show their stability by engaging in a variety of actions that help in "acquiring positive equities." This ideal youth client has overcome the chaos in his or her life through sheer force of will. In this sense, personal stability is not something that just happens to youth. It is not a state but an action that can demonstrate responsibility and neoliberal personhood.

Youth are also responsible for doing the psychological work to overcome past traumas. In doing so, they help to shift the culpability for that trauma away from historical and structural inequalities and onto individual behavior. This decontextualization enforces that trauma is the problem of the individual.[50] It also individualizes the onus for healing. Professionals often attributed the success or failure of youth—whether that meant finishing school, gaining legal relief, or establishing themselves in their families—to their personal effort to overcome their trauma. For example, Allison, a foster care social worker, offered up a comparison between twin girls who arrived together as unaccompanied youth: one ended up in prison for child abuse while the other went to community college. When reflecting on why the community college youth had been successful, Allison commented, "A big part of this is that she recognized her own junk, her own trauma, and was like, I want to work on it. And so she would go to therapy and would talk to me about her issues. And she would talk to me about what she wanted to do about it and where she wanted to go in life." Allison called the difference "resiliency," and she implicitly suggested that the failure of the second girl was not due to structural inequities or historical barriers but to her unwillingness to deal with trauma in an effective way, that is, bring her trauma to a licensed therapist and discuss it with adults.

The ability to "recognize one's junk" and effectively deal with a traumatic past was seen as a transformative process and was often embodied. Just as proof of suffering and trauma must be accounted for in body or in affect,[51] the healing process is also embodied. Clara, a therapist, discussed a young woman who had experienced sexual assault: "She was sixteen and in her journey she was raped by several guys in the process, the coyotes. She got pregnant from that. She felt guilt. We were able to [work through this trauma]. When you see her now, she does her hair and her nails. She is a different person." Bianca, Clara's coworker, agreed: "You can see [unaccompanied youth] change [after therapy], dress like kids, get their hair cut. They are able to be more present here once they work through the trauma." In these examples, trauma and healing are embodied and enacted traits. The evidence of healing and personal stability is in the presentation of self.

The embodiment of healing can also take on a particularly ethnocentric bent. As established in literature on humanitarian efforts, humanitarian narratives are frequently buttressed by orientalist stories that position the United States as the modern contrast to savage, backwards cultures.[52] Narratives of personal transformation often used this same logic. Rosa, a shelter worker, told a story about a young woman who also "transformed" her suffering into an embodied and enacted healthy present.

> [The young woman comes from] a very patriarchal society, and so she is like fifteen and was married off, like was going to be married to this much older man, without any say. And she ran away. And she somehow came here. . . . When she first got [to the shelter] she was just . . . so shy, painfully shy. Like it just hurt you how shy she was and scared. You could see that she was scared, and she was like this little, so timid, and couldn't make eye contact. . . . It wasn't just super fear based but just this shyness and having no voice, no voice at all. And she blossomed into our most— her smile! She was never not smiling, and I don't ever remember having her mouth closed! I just remember her big smile. . . . She had this amazing transformation. She learned so much English and she got so much confidence.

For Rosa, the young woman's smile, voice, and eye contact operated as markers of her transformation. In Rosa's telling, the young woman had gone from being a timid, shy girl from a patriarchal culture to being an outgoing and confident Western woman. This transformation, according to Rosa, was made possible through the shelter and, implicitly, her contact with American culture. Lost in this description is an acknowledgment that the young woman instigated her own migration— presumably, an act requiring that she already was independent, before her contact with the United States.

* * *

The expectations of unaccompanied immigrant youth are high. When young people enter into the United States, they find themselves on a tightrope of humanitarian assistance. Their ability to navigate American guardianship, citizenship, and education is based on their ability to balance several paradoxes. Youth must prove their innocence while being perceived as criminal. They must show that they are dependent upon adults and American institutions while also demonstrating that they are able to act as adults and take responsibility for themselves. Finally, while their past traumas are necessary for legal relief, they must also show that they can transform these traumas into personal stability. The professionals who work with youth find that they must enforce these paradoxes, as well. While some professionals remain oblivious to these strains, many others are aware of the competing demands that they make of youth.

5

Making the System Work

MARIBEL: I'm an immigrant myself. I actually was one of the Dreamers that arrived when I was really young. I overstayed my visa, and my mom overstayed her visa, and so immigration was always really a big part of my identity. . . . I saw [an opening for a] family reunification position. I read what the position entailed, and I was like, this is perfect. This is exactly what I'm looking for. I've done case management before, so this is what I have experience in, but I'm doing it with a population that I feel really passionate about. So, I applied to the interview and got in.

EMILY: What did you think of the job once you started?

MARIBEL: It was a little bit more toxic than I expected. It was toxic, period.

Throughout this book, I have explored the tensions, paradoxes, and dilemmas that exist in the institutions that work to help unaccompanied youth navigate life in the United States. When youth confront detainment in the shelter system, the bureaucracy of family reunification, the narrow scripts of the legal world, or the politically charged climate of education, youth are not alone. They are accompanied by professionals who inhabit positions in their respective institutions, who carry out activities as required by law, and who keep the bureaucracy moving forward. Professionals are not anonymous cogs in the wheels of their institutions. They are often passionate, caring, and empathetic. And, they are often deeply critical.[1] As the quote with Maribel suggests, the professionals I spoke with had a lot to say about the nature of their jobs and their attitudes about the help they were giving. Not all were quick to critique. A few felt that the system was working as it should, and others—I believe—did not trust me enough to give me critical insight. However, most of the people I spoke with harbored grave concerns about the overall structure of support for unaccompanied youth and their own participation in it. As I explore in this chapter, professionals faced daunting challenges in carrying out their jobs while maintaining a sense of competence and ethical principles.

When I first began conducting this research, I had no intention of spanning into all of the institutions that I have touched in this book. As I explore in detail in Appendix A, my original intent was to focus the lens on the detention facilities that shelter youth. Yet, I quickly learned that the barriers around these facilities would make it impossible to start that research. For the sake of moving the research forward, I started to interview professionals from a variety of occupations working with unaccompanied youth. What began as a haphazard attempt to maintain momentum turned into a revealing and systematic exploration into the ways in which youth might experience the United States. As I encountered these professionals, I quickly realized that unaccompanied immigrant youth who arrive into the United States traverse multiple spaces, institutions, and geographical regions. They encounter a dizzying number of people who want to help them, from social workers in the shelters to postrelease workers, counselors, attorneys, and community activists. Any given youth might travel a wide geographical distance when encountering all of these people. The young person might be apprehended and placed into the temporary holding facility on the US-Mexico border. They might then be transferred to a shelter on the other side of the country—in Chicago, for example—where they encounter counselors, social workers, family reunification workers, attorneys, and advocates. From there, they might be placed with a sponsor in yet another region of the country—say, Miami—where they may (or may not) be connected to new counselors, social workers, attorneys, and, now, educators. Even from there, many youth change households, jumping from their government placement to the home of their choosing, sometimes in the same town, sometimes across state lines again. In a sense, I encountered professionals much as youth might: I would talk with an attorney in a city who could then connect me to a teacher, social worker, and activist in the same area, leading me into a tight-knit group of professional support. On the other hand, I might also contact a teacher in a rural community who had no one else she knew to connect me to.

For young immigrants, the geographic space traveled and the enormous number of adults encountered is bewildering. For professionals, the lack of stability and consistency is frustrating and can create significant barriers in providing the type of care and service that they intend. No professionals will see a youth's progress from their first entry into the United States until their eventual and final settlement into their homes. This means that while they might work in separate fields, they are often interdependent. This system is interconnected in that everyone is dependent on the success of youth in other fields, and it is also insular in that the communication among professionals of different fields is limited. I argue that professionals and youth who navigate this system do so with a combination of flexibility, creativity, and resistance. Many professionals also grapple with difficult questions about their role in the systemic oppression of immigrant youth.

Flexibility: Responding to Role Strain

Individual professionals in each field often held defined roles that were supposed to be limited to their institution. For example, family reunification specialists work directly in the institution of the family; attorneys work directly with the institution of the state; educators work directly with the institution of education. Yet, the most common complaints I heard from nearly all professionals was that they felt either inadequate in fulfilling these roles or unable to complete their duties without stretching these roles. The problems faced by these professionals fall under what sociologist William Goode termed "role strain": "the felt difficulty in fulfilling role obligations."[2] Specifically, Goode expounded on the idea of role ambiguity, when there is a "lack of necessary information available to a given organizational position," and role conflict, when the "behaviors expected of an individual are inconsistent."[3] Such role strain often arose when individual professionals were trained for a specific position but discovered that their training and expectations did not match the needs of unaccompanied youth clients. Indeed, role strain is widely prevalent in work with unaccompanied youth because each field is dependent on other fields for the overall success of youth, and yet the connections among fields are precarious. Because of this, personal flexibility and boundary spanning are both ways for professionals to complete their jobs while still abiding by the rules of their organizations.

Attorneys, in particular, were the most vocal about this role strain, ambiguity, and conflict, especially regarding the necessity of providing emotional labor to youth.[4] It is notable that sixteen of the eighteen legal professionals I interviewed for this project were women, reflecting a gendered bias in helping work, even though the American Bar Association reports that women make up a little over a third of the legal profession.[5] Women are not just more likely to participate in jobs that require emotional labor; they also feel differently about those jobs.[6] The American Bar Association reported that women are slightly more likely than men to believe that their pro bono clients need their help and that they are extremely passionate about doing pro bono work. They are also more likely than men to report that they would take more pro bono cases if they could.[7] In addition, when women and men do the same job, women are often expected to attach emotional qualities to that job.[8] So, in order to understand the role strain that attorneys feel, it is necessary to understand the gendered experience of these attorneys.

The attorneys I spoke with discussed having the education to deal with legal aspects of migrant cases but having no knowledge or training in dealing with the emotional or physical needs of youth clients. Samantha explained,

> Often times we do a lot more than you typically do as a lawyer for a client. Because if I don't do it, this kid is not going to be successful, and there is no one else to do it. I am often the only English-speaking, professional person that this kid knows. . . . So I'll call the school, I'll work with the school social worker, I'll help them set up their cognitive evaluation, I'll help them get into therapy. I'll do all kinds of social work-y things. It is not that I—it is more that it is not a lawyer role. But if I don't do it, this client's case is going to lose. We cannot win without these things. And my job is to help this person succeed.

Providing a long list of extra tasks, Samantha emphasized that she was the only person who could assist her client and that the success of her actual job—to win the case—was dependent on all of these things happening. Julie discussed the same strain, noting the emotional labor that she felt inadequate in providing: "It takes time to build confidence and get that [migration] story to come out. It requires some services and therapy and stuff and I am not. . . . I am a caring person, I want to help people, but I don't have the skills that maybe a social worker or psychologist would have to deal with situations like that." Julie lamented that she did not have the skills that a psychologist or social worker has, but it is notable that she emphasized that she "is a caring person" and she "wants to help people" anyway. She made sure to separate her personal, feminine characteristics (caring and helpful) from her professional training as an attorney. Similarly, Jessica explained that she often felt that she had to step into a social work role. I asked her what that meant:

> It only happens because the clients think that that is my job. So they come to me for that job. So I just have to sort of do it because that is what they think I am sometimes. I guess it has just been difficult because I am not one [a social worker]. Mostly it has just been trying to find services for them. . . . Some work hours have gone to just trying to find somebody to help them. . . . Sometimes we've referred them out to private therapists, if the family is able to at least pay a little bit. I feel like I am not equipped to deal with their issues, other than their legal case. Sometimes that is a little frustrating. . . . I don't think I'm a very good social worker. I'm a failed one.

Jessica, Julie, and Samantha all expressed similar concerns. They felt competent in handling legal elements of cases but discovered that they could not be successful in these elements if they were not also fulfilling other needs of the clients. They often felt underprepared to take on the emotional labor of therapists and expressed frustration about taking extra time away from their legal work to fulfill the social-worker role of connecting youth to resources. Additionally, research has suggested that when women attorneys carry out their job, they do so in the same way their male counterparts do, using the same language and techniques. But, clients respond to them differently.[9] So, when these attorneys note that their clients have expectations about their emotional labor, they are experiencing this particular gender bias.

One particularly gendered element of the client-attorney interaction went beyond the therapist/social worker role: some felt that they were asked to bridge parenting gaps as well. This is, quite literally, the "mothering" that sociologist Arlie Hochschild suggests is often subtly attached to women's job descriptions.[10] Susana told a story about a family who had been reunited with a teenage daughter:

> It is crazy because the parents, I think sometimes they are trying to get us to raise the kids, to help with the discipline. They will call and are trying to threaten the kids: "Hey, I'm going to call your attorney because you need to do this, if not you're going to get deported or something." . . . I'm always thinking, I can't raise the kids for you. It is a huge drain on our resources, actually, dealing with all of this. Mom will call me and say, "She ran away, and I know she is with her friend." I'm like, first, let's make sure she's okay. I try to get in touch with the child, I try to bring the child in, I try to refer them to the social worker, and then the parent will come in, and this whole time I could have been working on your case, but now . . . I'm playing mediator or psychologist, instead of really, really working on your case.

The responsibility to help raise children felt inappropriate to Susana but, just as the other attorneys expressed, it also seemed essential for the success of the job. This reality demonstrates once again the interconnectedness yet insularity of the various institutions that unaccompanied youth deal with. Attorneys know that youth need to be successful in schools and family in order to win their cases, but they also do not always have the needed connections with these other institutions.

Many attorneys who worked independently with youth clients (often in a pro bono capacity) did not have organizational support to provide for the variety of youths' needs. They attempted to fit youth into the client mold that adults typically inhabited, in which attorneys could place the bulk of the responsibility on the shoulders of the adults. However, attorneys learned quickly that immigrant youth clients did not always have the structural support or knowledge to navigate life outside of the legal system, so attorneys often made a choice to step in and fill that gap. Other attorneys worked for new organizations that were still scrambling to find funding and did not yet have the capacity to hire the necessary support staff. This was the case for Susana, who was eventually able to convince her organization to hire an actual social worker, which alleviated, although it did not erase, some of this burden. And, still others found that there were not the appropriate resources available to them at all. For example, attorneys working with rural clients did not always have access to Spanish-speaking therapists, and thus found themselves taking on this role as a last resort.

Attorneys were not the only professionals to experience role strain. Interestingly, social workers found that they needed to work as attorneys, too. Marta, a community worker in the Southeast, talked about needing to help parents locate their children in detention centers. The parents often could not afford legal assistance, so they would come to Marta and her organization.

> It was a big challenge. But the biggest one was learning how to do the paperwork, faxing it to them, getting in contact with the caseworker or the officer, using the ICE locator. It is not easy because they are minors, and they wouldn't show up [in ICE's system] with information about what you are looking for. But, thank God, all of us women working together, finally we got everything under control! [Laughs] We are still getting cases, and now we know how to do stuff, like when they change the venues from one state to another, all of that stuff.

Marta and her colleagues did not feel adequately trained to provide the legal assistance that their youth clients needed. As a social worker, she felt competent to provide for the emotional and physical needs of the youth, but when she and her coworkers confronted legal challenges, they felt stymied. In her community, youth often struggled to connect with attorneys, because the amount of pro bono legal help available did not meet the needs of the community, and many of the youth clients could not afford private help.

Professionals who dealt with role strain were successful when they were willing to be flexible with their own roles. In the above scenarios, each of the professionals described discomfort with her role but also conceded to the unwritten demands of the job, expanding her role to include other commitments. Individuals often justified their expanded roles and the time they put into these as a requirement for getting the job done and fulfilling their personal obligations to the client. Often, they viewed their own role flexibility as proof of their care for and dedication to their youth clients.

Another strategy that professionals used to deal with role strain was to facilitate connections outside of their particular field, also known as boundary spanning.[11] For example, attorneys often needed youth to enroll in school in order to complete an application for legal relief. The attorneys might contact the schools themselves in order to start the enrollment process. Sometimes, they would have to threaten schools with legal action when schools refused enrollment. Similarly, attorneys would frequently partner with therapists who could provide the emotional labor that the attorneys felt inadequate to provide. Clara and Bianca worked as therapists in a trauma-centered program in the Southeast, and they often worked with attorneys who represented unaccompanied clients. Bianca explained that youth would be referred to her when they were resistant to opening up about traumatic events to an attorney: "[One youth client] was leaving the most traumatic thing that brought him here for the last. . . . The client wasn't opening up to the attorney at all. So I told [the client] that here we are person centered. We are going to do whatever you want to work on, but in order for that evaluation to hold something and be strong and for the judge to see why he can't send you back, you are going to have to open up and tell me what happened." In cases such as these, attorneys relied on therapists to coax out the appropriate legal stories for the case, using the particular skills that the therapist could offer. However, this type of boundary spanning does not always work, especially when the service, such as therapy, is actually meant to fulfill an entirely different purpose, which was to build a legal case. Bianca and Clara were both frank that sometimes when attorneys sent them clients in order to work through a traumatic event, the client might not be interested in therapy. Clara explained, "Even though the lawyer may stress about it, [the youth] don't want to [go to therapy]. We cannot force anything." So, while boundary spanning provided occasional help, it still did not always create the necessary bridges to fulfill all of the needs of youth clients.

I was not immune to role strain. Multiple times during my research with youth, I was also asked to step outside of my role as a researcher to help youth navigate their lives. After one interview, a young man asked me to connect him with the local school district, as he did not know whom else to ask. Another reached out to me when he was unable to contact an attorney whom he had worked with, as she had left the nonprofit that had connected them. In both of these cases, the young men came to me out of confusion about how the education and legal systems worked, and I believe that the fact that they saw me as a trusted adult points to how difficult it is to get unaccompanied youth truly connected to American institutions. One of the most difficult situations of role strain occurred when I received a panicked message in the middle of the night from a young man who had received several threatening texts extorting him for money. The police had not helped him, as they believed the texts were fraudulent. The young man was not convinced, however, and reached out to me to ask what to do. Where I was able to help the other youth, drawing on my professional background in case management, I was truly at a loss as to how to help in this situation. I got a taste of how many professionals might feel, when asked to help in an area in which they had no training. I felt a deep sense of failure for my inability to provide the young man comfort or resources for dealing with these threats, legitimate or not.

Creativity: Disrupting Legitimate Practices

When professionals faced role strain, they were often able to work within legitimate institutional practices in order to respond to this strain. However, professionals often faced ethical dilemmas as well, which pitted their organizational roles against their moral obligations to help youth.

Anne-Claire Pache and Felipe Santos describe these dilemmas as competing institutional logics, where the need to maintain organizational standards conflicts with individual beliefs and identity.[12] For many professionals I interviewed, their identity and self-concept were often defined through service to youth, and this sometimes forced professionals to compartmentalize their requirements as professionals and their ethical obligations as individuals. This was particularly true when they dealt with youth facing difficult situations, such as homelessness or deportation.

Educators were the professionals who most frequently revealed issues with competing demands between their professional obligations and personal beliefs. Researchers have noted that teachers are expected to carry out the emotional labor of caring and connectedness with their students, but that this labor must have boundaries and be confined to the teaching role.[13] However, teachers often have a front-row view to the most severe problems that youth might face outside of the school building, including homelessness, domestic violence, or deportation. Being witness to these events prompted several educators to work outside of their institutionalized roles as school employees.

Michelle, an ESL teacher in a midwestern school district, provided one of the most compelling instances of how these dilemmas play out. She felt like the sole advocate for immigrant students in a district that she described as "not super respectful of other cultures." Her community was conservative, predominantly white, and middle-class; however, there was a small but growing population of immigrant students, and unaccompanied youth in particular, due to the area's agricultural economy. She explained that the few immigrant students who enrolled in her district were often treated with disrespect, including being scolded for speaking Spanish and being mocked about the status of immigrants in their community. Her school culture did not provide resources to support immigrant students, and Michelle was further confined by legal and professional obligations around her status as a teacher. Amidst the pressures of her local context and professional boundaries, Michelle had strong feelings about her personal, spiritual mission to her immigrant students. She explained, "There's white privilege, and I try to use it. I think there are way too many marginalized, and there are way too many of us who have the ability [to help]. It infuriates me when I see people who have the ability to step up and they don't. And it costs me nothing. It really doesn't. . . . If we don't use the privileges that we have to help someone else, I think it is wrong." Michelle was very emotional when she described her personal mission to help immigrant students. Her own husband was an immigrant, and so she felt intimately connected to the vulnerabilities of this population.

Michelle frequently confronted situations in which her professional boundaries and school culture—and sometimes even her legal obligations—went against her own personal moral compass. Michelle told numerous stories in which she went above and beyond her role as a teacher, often stepping outside of what are generally accepted professional boundaries for educators. She described working directly with youths' attorneys, taking youth to drug counseling, and becoming involved with youths' families. She even revealed that she had made the decision to ignore her duty to report child abuse, because she knew that the family was undocumented and that reporting this abuse could lead to the deportation of some of the family members. Instead, she took matters into her own hands, confronting the abuser and helping the young person locate safer housing. Michelle also frequently brought youth to her home to work odd jobs when they needed money. Sometimes these youth would end up living with her and her husband for months on end, when they found themselves with no other safe options.

I was curious about how the administration at her school responded to Michelle's unorthodox relationship with her unaccompanied migrant students. She explained that she "got away" with breaking institutional norms and rules because "there was an unspoken rule. I was the translator so it was like, you scratch my back, I'll scratch yours. My principal was very aware of what was going on. My assistant principal—'If you make my life easier, I'll make your life easier.'" So, while her institution did not explicitly support Michelle's decisions to maintain very personal relationships with unaccompanied migrant students, they were willing to look the other way because her skills were essential in her school district.

While Michelle's stories explored the gray areas of boundaries between teachers and students, there were also other types of professionals who had to work outside of their professional roles. These professionals would disrupt the very practices that were seen as legitimate in their jobs.[14] Ashley, who provided postrelease services to unaccompanied youth, described a case in which a sixteen-year-old was released to live with his father. The father and son had no relationship prior to this reunification, so Ashley was sent to support the family and to ensure the young man's safety. During her first visit, everything seemed to be proceeding as planned: the young man was enrolled in school and the family appeared to be getting along. However, when Ashley went to visit the family the second time, they were no longer residing in their apartment. She tracked down the father and discovered that he was no longer living with his son and, according to the father, the son had not left information regarding where he could be contacted. Through some creative detective work, Ashley discovered that the young man was residing in a different state with his eighteen-year-old brother. When she caught up to the brothers, they reported that they had left the house due to abuse and neglect. Although the brothers were safe living together and were making enough money to support themselves, they indicated that they wished to be enrolled in school, which they were unable to do while providing for themselves. Ashley began looking for legal placement options, but she discovered that Child Protective Services wanted them to go back with the father. Plus, due to their interstate move, neither state felt that it had jurisdiction to enforce the case. Ashley found herself in a position in which the institutionally legitimate options were not appropriate, and she was forced to be creative. Eventually, Ashley found a community organization that identified a family that agreed to take in both of the brothers. She described this as an "under-the-table foster placement." By looking outside of the institutionally approved means of finding home care, Ashley essentially "disrupted" the legitimate practices in her field. She did so because her commitment to the safety and success of her client overshadowed her commitment to maintaining the legitimate practices of her organization.

Attorneys told similar stories of disrupting legitimate practices, when they found themselves needing to work on the edges of the legal system. Jessica, an attorney, explained how she and her colleagues would work around a particular judge who was, in her view, anti-immigrant. For attorneys to proceed with the option of the Special Immigrant Juvenile Status for youth clients, the youth first needed to have their guardianship with a sponsor approved in family court. However, this particular judge refused to issue guardianship orders to unaccompanied youth. Jessica explained, "That has been difficult, trying to navigate around that guy. And the few, the three or four kids who live in [the county], he absolutely won't issue them. That has been a hurdle. We were able to get around it by finding a guardian in a different county and applying in that county." In this case, Jessica worked to find her client a new family system altogether in order to circumvent the antagonistic judge. This was not an easy task, of course, and it required Jessica to take on a variety of new responsibilities. However, she was able to work with a new organization that had been founded recently to help with the influx of unaccompanied youth in her community. The organization was composed of local residents, predominantly native-born citizens, who wanted to be involved in immigrant youths' lives. Together, Jessica and the organization arranged coguardianship situations between counties and conducted background checks for the new families. The organization was essential for Jessica: "It is hard with so many cases to be a case manager for each one of them, so sometimes the organization does the case management stuff for me, because I don't have a paralegal, so I do all of my own work. . . . I get overwhelmed." Jessica's willingness to expand her own role, partner with local organizations, and disrupt the status quo in her field ultimately led to successful cases for several youth clients.

Resistance: Changing the Goal

Professionals who wish to help youth can do so within their institutions through expanding their roles or disrupting legitimate practices, as described in the previous sections. However, there were also a handful of individuals who felt that the best way to assist unaccompanied immigrant youth was to resist American institutions altogether.

In chapter 1, I argued that family and sponsor placement is not always adequate for the needs and histories of unaccompanied youth. I came across at least one alternative model that presented another option for youths' release that did not depend on the family institution. Joel was a community activist in Arizona who had been working in various capacities with unaccompanied youth since 2013. He had a brief stint as a case manager in one of the country's largest shelters for immigrant children, a job that he took "undercover" in order to better understand the system. At the time when I met him, he was involved with an activist method that he called "radical hospitality," which he described as being based both on his Quaker faith and on the Sanctuary Movement.[15] Joel worked with a network of individuals and families who sponsor youth to help them get out of shelters, particularly those who are turning eighteen and will be soon transferred to an adult facility. The goal was to get youth out of government shelters, provide youth an alternative to family placement, when family placement is not feasible, and help youth integrate into their community. Joel also emphasized that this intervention is necessary, as ORR does not provide the needed support for youth, once they are released: "I think the most important thing for people to understand is the extent to which youth are abandoned after they get reunified or are aged out. Abandoned at least by the system. I think that is not understood, even by people who are working in the system their whole lives. They imagine there to be these mythical resources out there. [. . .] But they are not out there." Joel has personally housed multiple youth, with

four young people in his house at any given time. He saw these placement options as significantly preferable to adult detention when youth
age out of government shelters or homelessness if youth cannot remain
in their original placements. Further, Joel observed that many youth do
not fare well in community organizations: "They would get kicked out
of the program. All of the stuff you would expect from a young person
who hasn't had a lot of positive mentorship and doesn't know how this
country works and didn't have any kind of family or social support here."
Joel and his activist colleagues experimented with different interventions, trying to determine what was the best approach to helping the
most vulnerable youth: "There's often the instinct to make things into
formal organizations, but I think an informal network is sometimes the
most effective. So what we have now is a network of people who just host
these kids and try to help them." Because of this, the network of individuals remained largely uninstitutionalized, although they had formalized one aspect of the movement, in that they began buying apartments
and then leasing these apartments to youth. Joel explained that youth
often have a difficult time renting when they have no credit history. This
program now has three apartments with four to five youth in each.

Joel was very careful not to project his own desires onto youth, specifically around their involvement in American institutions. He emphasized that the youth themselves have formed a mentorship network so
that they can support one another without government intervention,
especially as their involvement in American institutions is often precarious. I asked, for example, if the youth he has worked with have attended high school. He responded, "Some of them have. I haven't seen
great outcomes for that. But some of them have. I always hope that they
will, but I try not to let myself project my own cultural values on them.
So they know that high school is available to them and free and a good
idea in my opinion, but if they are like, honestly I just want to find a job
and work, then I try to respect that." For Joel, youth know what is best
for themselves, and it is his responsibility to provide the structures and
resources to help youth with whatever path they choose to take.

However, Joel did not sugarcoat the difficulties of this activist movement. It is difficult to find households willing to take in youth, especially
if there is no exit strategy. Households often prefer to take in girls, although most of the cases they work with are boys. Some of the most

generous activists do not live in communities that are appropriate for integrating these youth. And, youth bring in a wide range of needs based on cultural backgrounds and traumatic histories that many homes are not always adequately prepared for. Joel himself faced his own dilemmas, especially as he grappled with how trauma histories turned into present-day behaviors that he found deplorable. He explained that he had become the legal guardian for one young man, in order to help him pursue legal relief. However, the young man had an abusive relationship with his girlfriend. As Joel described him, "He is violent. He is controlling. He is in one of the sick patriarchal controlling abusive relationships. [. . .] He is also a kid who has seen a lot of violence and who is traumatized himself. How do I reconcile those truths without making excuses for abuse?" Joel still grappled with how to respond to such cases. He did not want to criminalize young people. He also did not want to implicitly support this ongoing violence. Joel worked with several other community members, had frequent meetings with the young man, worked separately with his girlfriend, and tried to intervene in a multitude of ways. However, in the end he cut off ties: "I don't think any of us have a sense of clarity in terms of exactly where the ethical lines were."

Disappearing as Resistance

Joel's networks provide an alternate option for youth to migrate to the United States and find success without needing to integrate themselves into the institutions that the immigration system depends on. Fundamentally, he viewed the traditional family and the performance of childhood as options only for a select group of youth. Plus, he saw the legal system and the education system as institutions that are, at best, not welcoming to immigrant youth and, at worst, adversarial. Joel and his colleagues were not alone in their assessment. Young people, too, often held a deep mistrust of the protection American institutions offered. For these young people, an alternative option was to disappear.

Disappearance was a common occurrence that professionals in my research discussed with some frequency. Youth who "disappeared" were youth who dropped out of institutions or lost contact with professionals, despite frequent attempts by professionals to reach out. Professionals had a wide range of hypotheses about these disappearances. Some who discussed disappearances believed these to be a result of a conscious choice on the part of youth, albeit a choice with which many professionals strongly disagreed. Others blamed disappearance on the deep mistrust that youth harbored towards American institutions.

Karen, an educator, saw unaccompanied migrant students disappear from her school regularly. Living in a rural midwestern district, she believed that the kids "end up disappearing to Chicago," but she did not have a satisfying understanding of why this happens: "Some of them will hear bad news from home and go back. . . . Some of them leave because they're trying to get siblings up, and so they'll go back to try and help the siblings make the journey up. Others, though, just disappear and we don't know what happened. Sometimes we find out much, much later that they were detained and they're in deportation proceedings. But other just completely go off the grid. Where do they go?"

Attorney Jessica told the story of a disappearance that she believed to be intentional. The young man was applying for SIJS. He had turned eighteen, which made getting a guardianship order difficult, although not impossible. She had told the young man that he needed to be in school for the judge to "buy our arguments." She explained,

> This young man just, unfortunately, didn't see how beneficial it would be to have legal permanent residency. In other ways, he had a really good SIJS case. His father was alcoholic and abusive, so it was a good abuse SIJS case. He just, he didn't want it. . . . We couldn't, no matter how much we tried, get him to see the value in becoming a legal permanent resident here. How lucky he was to have an opportunity to do that, since so many people here have zero path to citizenship or to legal permanent residency. And he dropped out of school, decided he just wanted to work, he didn't want to pursue it anymore. That was kind of devastating that we had tried for a little while to convince him. Someday I think he'll regret that decision.

In Jessica's telling of this story, she centered the youth's decision, emphasizing that he will regret his choice later. She made mention of his desire to work, but did not consider other constraints that might have influenced his decision. Nancy provided a similar scenario of a young man who refused to engage further in his case because he preferred to work:

That was devastating because you put a lot of work into his asylum and his special juvenile visa, and he had a great case. But he couldn't . . . I think he couldn't handle, number one, not working. . . . Especially the boys, you know, they are working since age eight or something. . . . If you go to the US, you better send money home. You need to pay for the coyotes. Sometimes [coyotes] are causing trouble back at home looking for the money. The amount of pressure I think that he felt, I'm guessing it came from the need to get out and work and do his own thing.

Unlike Jessica, Nancy provided a more nuanced understanding of the pressure that this client faced. She knew that his desire to work stemmed from his need to send money home or pay for a coyote who might be making threats. His disappearance could be better understood as a result of limited options and his belief that American institutions were only distracting him from his most pressing needs.

Another common hypothesis was that disappearances were the result of fear and distrust. Ashley, a postrelease service provider, described these disappearances as youth "going into hiding" because they do not trust the legal system. Ayana, an attorney in the Midwest, explained that disappearances for her frequently occurred when her first claim for that client had been denied. After having divulged so much information to the court and committed so much time and energy, the first denial was extremely disheartening for her clients. While Ayana would still see a path forward, she found that clients would often disappear after this, unwilling to spend more time trying to fight their case. They lost trust in the court system and found it easier to try to remain in the shadows. Similarly, Nancy told a story about another young man for whom she had pursued a green card. However, as he was waiting for his green card, he disappeared. He called Nancy several months later, a bit mysteriously, and asked that the green card be mailed to a different location. Nancy explained, "You could just see that these kids have so much anxiety, and they are so afraid. They do not even know what getting a green card means, even though we have been over it and over it and over it. It is still scary to them. It is still the immigration process that has so much mystery. They can't handle it, so they just run away. It is how they got away from the bad stuff that happened in their home country." In this case, Nancy saw disappearance as a fearful response that had served youth well in their past. Other professionals called this "survival mode," explaining that youth who grew up in unstable environments often do not trust adults or institutions in the United States, either. However, this idea unfairly suggests that youth *can* trust the legal system to protect them. Indeed, disappearance is perhaps an entirely rational response when youth are faced with a state body that has taught them to believe that they are criminals and do not belong.

I, too, had several experiences with these disappearances. I was excited when I got a phone call from a young man whose attorney had referred him to me for an interview. He was eager to meet with me and tell his story, and he spoke highly of his attorney, who he said had "put up with him" even though he disappeared on her for months. I hoped to be able to ask him more about his self-described disappearance to help shed more light on the reasons youth decide to circumvent—if only temporarily—American institutions. However, I had overbooked myself to meet him, and I messaged him several days prior to reschedule. He responded that he was confused, and then he disappeared. He did not return future phone calls or private messages via social media, which he had started using to communicate with me regularly. If it was not for his active social media presence, I would have been concerned that something had happened to him. To this day, I have not heard from him, and I cannot help but think that he had actively disappeared from me as well.

Around the same time as this disappearance, I was advocating for a young man being detained in a midwestern shelter. I had promised to assist him upon his release, to help him enroll in school and seek legal relief. He was to be released to his mother, who seemed to comply willingly with all of the requests and demands made by the Office of Refugee Resettlement. The young man had a clear path to legal relief due to the very visible scarring on his body as a result of persecution in his home country. The attorneys and social workers I spoke to about his case felt optimistic that he would continue to abide by the processes and procedures that would allow him to assimilate into what is regarded as normative American adolescence.

He was released to his mother, and I was given the responsibility to follow up with him. I was able to reach him by phone after he was released from the shelter, and he also attended his first court date. Everyone remained optimistic about his legal case. However, within three weeks, I tried to reach out again, and his phone numbers had been disconnected. I called regularly for several weeks to no avail. Eventually, I reached his mother, who very quickly hung up the phone, saying that she did not know where he was. It was clear that she was no longer interested in speaking with me. I was never able to reach the family again, and the young man failed to turn up to court in the following months. I do not know what happened to him, and his disappearance left me unsettled. He had clear pathways for all of the typical goals for unaccompanied youth: he had legal options, he had a family system, and he was enrolled in school. And yet, with this disappearance, he effectively exited all of these institutions.

Like other professionals, I can only provide conjecture regarding the reasons for these disappearances. My feeling, in the case of the potential interview participant, was that I had broken his trust by canceling our initial meeting. However, I am at a loss regarding what happened with the young man I volunteered with. I hope that his disappearance was a decision to live his life on his own terms. However, I am fearful that this decision was prompted, instead, by his deep mistrust of the people around him. I am also concerned for his safety. I hope that his mother was lying when she said that she did not know where he was—a lie that would clearly arise out of her own mistrust of the system. I am frustrated at the outcome, disappointed in my own inability to establish trust with the family, and deeply worried for his well-being and future.

The Right Side of History?

I think people, Latinos especially, originally sign up because they want to help, but then they're actually just being maneuvered by the system to do these things to other Latinos.
—Salma, family reunification worker

This is how you get a group of good people that are in a position to try and do good, and slowly pivot them to do bad.
—Doug Stephens, former asylum officer who resigned in protest of the Trump administrations attack on asylum[16]

Nearly every professional I interviewed believed that the system of immigration is broken. Nearly every professional I interviewed wanted to help.

Yet helping youth to navigate a broken system creates an array of dilemmas. Some of these are small: the stresses of trying to do good work with limited time and resources. Some are much more significant: making ethically fraught choices about breaking professional obligations to provide care or engaging in civil disobedience to provide alternative options for youth. Yet, there is a much larger question that surrounds this work. If you help people to navigate a broken system, are you complicit in that system? How close can you stand to it before you become a part of it?

Does the presence of case managers and therapists in the shelters implicitly condone the detention of children, when their intent is to provide a safe space? The nonprofits that run these shelters would argue that they are providing a public good.[17] But Rosa, a shelter worker, explained that the situation is more complex on the ground: "We are a nonprofit, or whatever, but really, this is ORR we are representing. Everything we do is regulated and funded so we're technically, kind of representing the federal government and their immigration system. That is weird because it is like, the kids are held by ICE initially and then they come to us. It is like, oh, now you are here, and this is different. But we are not different. We are all part of the same system, and that part is weird in an existential way." Should family reunification workers be held responsible for prolonging the separation of families, when they are just carrying out convoluted government policies to the best of their abilities, with as much compassion, insight, and efficiency as they can? "Is this a good thing?" Mercedes, in family reunification, asked me. "Sometimes I just want to open the door and say 'Run, run, run . . .' But I can't. I've never done it."

What about those who work outside of child detention? Are their hands clean? If your job as an attorney is to mine for the correct trauma, can you sit comfortably with your own conscience? "It feels really awful and cruel," Nancy said of her process of building the legal case around youths' greatest suffering. What if your choice for the individual is the right thing to do, but in making that choice you criminalize other youth? As a child advocate, I have asked myself these same questions. I do not work as an employee of a shelter that detains children, but I enter those facilities in order to do my job in determining the best interests of the young person. I meet with youth on a weekly basis until they are released. I mine trauma in my own way, to use it to recommend the best interests of the child. I am supposed to provide an outsider's lens into the facility—a type of accountability. On one hand, this volunteer work is a badge of honor, something that others often view as a good, noble deed. I am helping immigrant children, am I not? But, I think about this role often and ask the same questions of myself. *Is this a good thing?* Or, am I standing too close to a system I abhor?

I have felt most useful when I can stand next to a young person as they present themselves before a judge, filling as much of the courtroom with my presence as I can, so they know they are not alone. One young man with whom I worked while he was detained told me he appreciated talking with me every week. He felt as though he could *desahogarse*— unburden himself—with me. Another called me long after her release, just to talk. She was deeply hurt that no one from the Office of Refugee Resettlement had reached out to her. In these moments, I feel that I am doing right by the young person. I am a caring adult who has reached them in moments and places that are so often unreachable. But—a child should not have to stand before a judge alone in the first place. The young man should not be detained so long that his anger and anxiety about his life fester and burn. The young woman should not have been spit out by an institution that did not care for her long-term needs. Most often, I have felt useless. I have been just another person asking for a story and pushing elements of the bureaucracy forward—or, just asking other people to push bureaucracies forward. At worst, I have felt complicit. I have used a young woman's story of sexual violence as a tool, in order to assist in her release, and I have sat on my hands and watched as the detainment of young people stretched for months and months.

In mid-2018, I was waiting for a child whom I had been advocating for, sitting in the kitchen of a very small shelter for tender-aged children. At the table, with a plate of food in front of him, was a young boy, maybe six years old. He would not look up from his plate, but he also would not eat. He was motionless, almost unblinking, and the heaviness that sat in the air around him was impenetrable. His trauma seeped from him, from his skin, from his eyes. A worker sat down next to him, occasionally trying to puncture the air around him with a smile or a wink or a gentle plea for him to eat. He would not look at her. When she caught me staring at them, she mouthed to me that he was one of the separated children. He had been forcibly removed from the arms of his parents just hours before.

This was not the child whom they were supposed to work with, but here we were, an inadvertent arm of the state that had forced families apart in the most inhumane way imaginable. The Trump administration policies had broken any moral ground that one could stand on while working in this system, because one could no longer contend that the shelter was the safest place for the child when that child had been ripped from the hands of a loving parent. Yet, does it matter that his separation was at the hands of the border enforcement under one of the most anti-immigrant administrations in our history? Every child who is detained in government shelter has been separated from their parents at some point, recently or long ago: international borders, legality, poverty, violence, deportation. Separations of immigrant youth from their families are so commonplace that we forget they happened at all. We have learned to decontextualize the child from his or her family. The child I was there to meet had been separated, too, but not because of the Trump administration's policy. He was with an uncle who had no papers to declare legal guardianship, and so despite the fact that the young man was blind and had received a diagnosis on the autism spectrum, he had been taken away from the family member he traveled with. It happened during Trump, but it could have happened during Obama or, now, Biden.

There was another separated child at that same shelter. He did not like to sleep alone, so he often napped on a mat at the feet of one of the shelter employees, as she typed case notes into her computer. I would enter the building through her office, and she would motion me to be quiet as I came through, her fingers clicking away on the keyboard and the young boy softly snoring under her desk. She asked me to help move him at one point; she needed to work in a different part of the building, so we each took a side of the mat and hoisted him through the house. I can still feel the weight of his body on that mat. My hands tingle thinking about the cruelty that put him there.

Professionals working with unaccompanied youth wanted to do good. Nearly everyone I spoke with entered their work with the explicit commitment to help immigrant youth. Yet work with unaccompanied youth—particularly when it is institutionalized—is at its core fraught. It always has been. Now it is worse. Perhaps one of the greatest challenges for professionals is grappling with where to find the moral ground when their greatest desire is to help youth in the midst of an oppressive world.

Conclusion

In late 2018, I attended a meeting of activists in a predominately Latinx neighborhood on the south side of Chicago. We met at a community center that was nondescript on the outside—just a house among rows and rows of houses—but was buzzing with life on the inside. The hosts had made a vegan meal for the audience, and the rooms were packed with dozens of activists, lounging on the floor, squished into sofas, and huddled in groups in every corner of the building. These audience members were mostly white and young, although some individuals of color and older activists were part of the group as well. Among the items on the agenda, the meeting was convened to teach the audience about the inhumane treatment of unaccompanied migrant youth in Chicago. The audience expressed their fury at the current system of immigration, and they had created targeted campaigns against nonprofits in the area that held contracts for shelters that detained migrant children. The activists used language such as "baby jails," "child jailing," and the "lucrative child-captivity business"—and all for good reason. This was in the midst of Trump's family-separation policy, and the moral foundation of care and protection that the system had once claimed—albeit precariously— had crumbled entirely.

Yet, I left the meeting feeling apprehensive. I agreed with their assessment, but I also knew that the people who worked in this system— especially those working in these shelters or the attorneys who helped youth navigate immigration law—had more nuanced analyses. This system of humanitarian intervention for unaccompanied youth is complex, and nonprofits, individual workers, and volunteers make complicated decisions about their participation, often wrestling with the line between care and complicity. The foundations of crimmigration, racialized child welfare, and neoliberal humanitarianism have made it very difficult to institutionalize aid for immigrant youth.

In this sense, it is easy to criticize the aid apparatus. I have done so throughout this entire book. It is much more difficult to find solutions, and ones that both address the root causes of the issue and also ease the suffering in the present moment. The reality is that in this present moment, youth arrive at the United States border by themselves, as they have always done. The root of the problem, which goes beyond the scope of this book, is a world system that controls human movement through the use of borders and the destabilization of countries of the Global South through unfettered capitalism, global warming, and political interventions, resulting in insupportable poverty and violence.[1] Perhaps we must dismantle this entire system.

However, for the foreseeable future, borders remain, violence goes on, poverty endures, and youth will continue to arrive alone at the borders of the United States. The question for practitioners is how to operate in this current world while minimizing the suffering that is written into this system. That is, what progress can be made within the current structure, until more revolutionary change can occur? In my imagination, I picture a response that looks very different. In this imaginary world, there are no border agents, only social workers and therapists, who encounter youth at the edge of the country or, even better, at a consulate in their home country, prior to the youth making any international journey at all. Youth would be treated with care and respect from the moment of the first encounter, and efforts would be made for immediate reunification with family members in the United States. If young people are truly alone and they must stay at a facility for any length of time, these would only be homes, run by social workers, with full transparency and freedom of movement, or foster families. There would be no more converted Walmarts warehousing thousands of youth, or secretive locations, or monitored behaviors. Through trauma-informed practices and immediate triage with youth and family members they identify, a plan would be created and implemented within days to get youth to the homes where they wish to reside. Monitoring for victims of trafficking would remain at the forefront but would not be used as a guise to maintain the separation of families. Additionally, families would have no reason to fear coming forward as their children's safety would not be connected to their legal status. Those youth who do not have family members in the country would have the option to connect with networks of homes, which would be run by culturally sensitive, trauma-informed practitioners, who would allow youth to work, go to school, or engage in any combination of the two that makes the most sense for the young person's life. There would be no need to perform versions of adolescence or adulthood to appease institutions; lives would be lived in ways that support the needs of the individual alone. Families would receive wrap-around services, where they would have assistance in repairing the wounds of transnational lives, and these services would have no bearing on or connection to legality and the surveillance of immigrants. There would be no such thing as deportation proceedings or adversarial court procedures. Rather, youth would work with a team of social workers, attorneys, and therapists—at no cost to their families—to determine the best long-term options for their futures. Trauma would be approached therapeutically, rather than productively. Gang affiliation and criminal background would not be used as weapons in court. They would be addressed through providing structural supports that allow for new options and different choices. Rural communities would be able to plug into resources outside of their area, where best practices from more experienced locales would be freely exchanged and applied.

To move us closer to these possibilities, several practical interventions are available that can reduce harm in the moment. Using these interventions, we can work within the current system and chip away slowly at the suffering that is written into the structure. However, these are not revolutionary changes. Because of this, professionals whose desire it is to help must still grapple with their complicity in the oppression of immigrant youth. I do not believe there is a way around this in any form of the current system. Yet, we cannot be paralyzed by this reality. We must match and challenge our complicity through our mindful engagement, transparent personal practice, sustained critique, and the constant, tireless push for broader reform.

First, with the Trump administration in the rear-view mirror, there is a lot of work to be done to simply return the system to what it was prior to the barrage of explicitly anti-immigrant assaults. The list of damages is long, and it includes the inhumane family-separation policy, attacks on the *Flores* settlement and asylum law, the Migrant Protection Protocol, known widely as the "Remain in Mexico" policy, and Title 42 Expulsions, which returned children and families to their home country with no due process under the guise of public health during the coronavirus pandemic.[2] Some of the most egregious results of these policies included the emergence of migrant camps at the US-Mexico border, where asylum seekers faced ongoing threats of violence, extortion, kidnapping, and grave health concerns.[3] The danger of this situation has forced many migrants to make difficult decisions about returning to their home countries or staying in a perilous limbo. Some families have chosen to send their children across the border alone, rather than continue to live with them in the dangerous and unsanitary camps, effectively creating a new population of unaccompanied youth.[4] Fortunately, backlash to these policies has been swift, and activists have continually pushed against these changes, often winning legal battles in the larger war. In the beginning days and months of the Biden administration, I expect to see more of these policies overturned.

Beyond reversing the human rights abuses carried out by the Trump administration, there is work to be done within the system that has existed for years prior to Trump. If we are to reduce harm within the current system of child detention, one of the first issues is to increase the transparency and accountability of these facilities, including opening the facilities to research. Further, in accordance with the spirit of the *Flores* settlement, the government should not contract with programs that participate in the warehousing of youth but rather create small, homelike environments. Shelters must also sever ties with DHS. Historically, the Office of Refugee Resettlement's custody of migrant youth was meant to resolve the tension that existed when the INS had the responsibility to both protect and prosecute unaccompanied youth. However, DHS intervenes in the ORR in ways that harm children and disrupt the pretense that the ORR is in place to protect children. Disclosures to shelter therapists and behaviors during detention should not be used in court. Finally, there is a strict age-out policy for youth in shelters and for access to certain types of legal relief. These age-out policies do not acknowledge the nonlinear nature of youths' lives and respond punitively to youth on their eighteenth birthday. Shelter workers with whom I spoke discussed the terrible experiences of youth being removed in handcuffs from shelters on their eighteenth birthday and placed in adult detention facilities, where they no longer had access to the resources and support in youth shelters.

In the legal realm, there are several movements I would like to high-light, led by organizations including the American Civil Liberties Union, the National Immigrant Justice Center, Kids in Need of Defense, and the Young Center for Immigrant Children's Rights. First, I join immigrant advocates in calling for expanded asylum opportunities based on gang persecution and domestic violence. The Trump administration attempted to limit these options, but even prior to these attacks, gang-based violence was a difficult asylum claim, although not impossible.[5] Related, there are already numerous calls for youth to have expanded access to attorneys, including the proposition that youth should have the right to an attorney. The Funding Attorneys for Indigent Removal Proceedings Act, for example, would guarantee right to counsel for children and other vulnerable migrants, including those with disabilities, at the expense of the government.[6] In addition, the Young Center for Immigrant Children's Rights has proposed a "Best Interest Visa" that would expand legal relief options for children who do not have SIJS or asylum claims. This visa aligns with the United Nation's Convention on the Right of the Child in providing a legal option to remain in the United States, when that is in the best interest of the child.[7] This also helps to limit practices of mining for "appropriate" trauma.

In the field of family reunification, change needs to begin at the border. It should go without saying that children should never be separated from their parents, as was practiced by the Trump administration, and parents should not have to make a decision between family detention or separation. These heinous policies, meant as deterrents, violated the basic human rights of migrants, and the trauma for the families involved will be long term.[8] Beyond this practice, there needs to be further nuance in the way family is defined. Even prior to the Trump administration, youth were routinely separated from family members who did not have legal guardianship, including aunts, uncles, and siblings. I have personally worked with a child with significant disabilities who was separated from an uncle at the border as the uncle was not his legal guardian; similarly, my research participants have told equivalent stories, including the separation of deaf children who speak no formal sign language and can communicate only with the family they traveled with. This is an issue that intersects migration and disability, in particular, but the continuation of separations puts the rights of all children and families at risk. We must create more nuanced processing procedures with expanded definitions of family, in order to actually reduce the number of unaccompanied youth in the system in the first place.[9]

When children are truly unaccompanied and must be reunified with family members, one of the most significant barriers to a quick release is the current criminalization of immigrant parents. Under the Trump administration, parents who had paid for human smugglers for their children could be prosecuted and deported.[10] Further, DHS and ORR have entered into an agreement in which they share information about parents who are to be reunified with their children. We must end this sharing practice.[11] First, it impedes trust and breeds fear in immigrant communities. Second, the argument that these policies are meant to protect children is called into question, when deportation will do even further damage to children and families. Further, this policy is based on numerous faulty assumptions that I have challenged in this work. It assumes that parents made the decision to bring their children to the United States, ignoring the fact that youth themselves often make these decisions. Finally, these policies assume that being smuggled into the United States is more dangerous for youth than staying in their home communities. For youth fleeing gang violence, smuggling may very well be the safest option for their lives.

When youth begin their lives in their local communities, they would benefit from increased support. In current practice, the ORR conducts just one follow-up for youth and provides postrelease services for only the most vulnerable. However, my research suggests that these policies do little to care for the long-term needs of immigrant youth in their new homes. Further, many families and young people are wary of these supports, as they have legitimate concerns about being on the radar of the US government. Once again, it is essential that help to youth is in no way connected to their family's legal status. Further, networks among immigrants, particularly among young people themselves, are a great source of strength. I do not recommend institutionalizing these networks, because this would risk the cooptation of organic support. Rather, I encourage the ORR and community organizations to understand the potential of young people and support what already exists. This would diverge from current ORR policy, which prohibits young people from sharing contact information and remaining in touch with one another upon release from facilities (a rule that is unenforceable in the era of social media).

My research shows that schools can act as tremendous safety nets for youth. However, districts often need further training on how to connect with and support young immigrants in their areas. Rural schools, in particular, could be more effective at identifying the unaccompanied young immigrants in their communities. This effort includes addressing misinformation about immigrant youth in the schools, and misinformation about education among immigrant youth. Additionally, as I have explored in chapter 3, the type of schooling that a young person needs is truly dependent on the individual's situation. On one hand, some young people want a traditional classroom where they can focus only on their education. On the other hand, other youth faced frustration when dealing with a full-time school day and the need to work simultaneously. These youth would have benefited from alternative school models, where they could still pursue the education that they wanted but are also not discouraged from working to support themselves and their families. I do not mean to suggest that I think youth *should* work. Rather, in our current reality, some youth *must* work, so until the foundations of poverty are addressed on a global scale, education systems must be willing to respond to these tensions. In any case, youth need school districts to work with them to find the most suitable arrangement.

Around the country, an array of programs has sprouted to help unaccompanied immigrant youth. Many existing programs provide just one service to youth: for example, a legal aid organization only provides legal assistance. And yet, attorneys have stated that they cannot be successful if the youth is not also being served by a therapist, a social worker, a stable household, and a supportive school system, ideally all culturally sensitive and in the same language as the young person's. The most successful programs are those that are able to connect family, the legal system, education, and, sometimes, the work world. Increased funding to add a wide range of job titles to these organizations would provide youth with the holistic assistance that they need. There are, of course, a handful of programs that currently exist that provide grouped services. For example, community organizations may have attorneys, therapists, and social workers in the same building. These organizations could be even more effective if they could also reach into the local school district. Of course, there are many organizations that do not have the means of adding multiple staff. In this case, programs may consider creating close connections with other services. An educator could forge a connection between the school, a local attorney, and a therapist to create a team of services for youth. In rural communities, these connections can be made virtually, so teams still exist, even when there is little support on the ground. Finally, Spanish-speaking professionals are essential in these fields. However, with increasing numbers of indigenous youth arriving to the United States, programs need to consider linguistic diversity as well by tapping into the local ethnic communities.

A final insight that was echoed by professionals in every institution was the need for trauma-informed training for all professionals who interact with unaccompanied youth. As the current relief system for youth is based on their ability to communicate their history of suffering in a productive manner, nearly all professionals must currently engage in multiple conversations with youth about their traumatic experiences. Yet, very few of these professionals have undergone any, much less extensive, trauma training. Professionals report feeling vastly underprepared in working on sensitive issues with youth. Those professionals who do have training in trauma-based counseling report being dismayed by their fellow professionals' misunderstanding of trauma. Government-funded organizations, such as shelters, should be required to implement training in trauma that is extensive and ongoing. Nongovernment organizations should include the same programs and provide the resources for volunteers, such as pro bono attorneys, to undergo similar education.

* * *

Several of the young people I interviewed for this book have remained in touch with me and given me updates on their lives.[12] Happily, many of them are doing well today. Collectively, there have been graduations, marriages, and children. Some of them have had recent successes with their immigration cases. Cynthia, the young woman from Guatemala who escaped an abusive home, recently received her citizenship. She is working as a certified nursing assistant, and she and her husband recently took their young family to Disneyland. Nicolas, the young

Ecuadorian man who explained that his life was a series of traumas, has received asylum. He is currently waiting on his green card, so he can begin to work legally in order to support his new wife and their two young girls. Mariana, who escaped violence in Honduras, is a nursing student at her local college. She also received a green card and continues to receive support from a family in her local community.

Not all of the stories have had these positive outcomes. Angelica, the young woman from El Salvador, has married the boyfriend that she moved in with after several failed family placements, and he continues to be an important source of emotional and financial support. However, she has not been able to adjust her immigration status. In late 2019, she told me that she had a date for her final asylum hearing. She did not have an attorney and would be facing the judge alone, but she was feeling optimistic about the outcome. I did not feel as hopeful. I immediately looked up asylum denial rates in Houston, where she was residing. They ranged from 87.8 percent to 100 percent.[13] I asked if she had connected with nonprofits in the area, to see if she could get a pro bono attorney; she could not afford to pay for an attorney herself. I even sent her a list of nonprofits to connect with and tapped into a few of my networks. However, she had already met with attorneys in these nonprofits, and as her case was not particularly strong, no one would use their limited resources to help her. In the end, she faced the judge alone. Her asylum request was denied.

* * *

I completed the final touches to this book on January 20, 2021, the day of President Joe Biden's inauguration. I am riding the wave of hope that comes along with the change of administration. As President Biden signs a flurry of executive actions, repealing some of the Trump admin-istration's policies around immigration, I anticipate that we are in a moment that is ripe for tremendous change. For Angelica's sake, and for the thousands of other young people like her, I have big hopes for new policies, pathways to citizenship, and support for struggling commu-nities. However, to truly support immigrants, we must actively disrupt the foundations of border securitization, racialized child welfare, and neoliberal humanitarianism that have guided work with unaccompa-nied youth thus far.

ACKNOWLEDGMENTS

It takes a village to write a book. It also takes a village to raise a child. And, to do both during a global pandemic and ongoing political unrest takes a pretty special one.

First, I would like to acknowledge the institutional support I received. Thank you to all of the following sources for financial assistance in this project: the 2010 and 2011 Chicago Area Studies, funded by the National Science Foundation (SES 0921414), the Russell Sage Foundation, and several units at the University of Illinois at Chicago (Institute for Policy and Community Engagement, Institute for Research on Race and Public Policy, Great Cities Institute, and Office of Social Science Research); the Chancellor's Graduate Research Award, the Provost Award for Graduate Research, and the Dean's Scholar Fellowship through the University of Illinois at Chicago; the Rue Bucher Memorial Award for Qualitative Studies; and finally, the Faculty Summer Research Grant through Elmhurst University. I am also immensely grateful to the team at New York University Press, along with the anonymous reviewers, whose support, ideas, and insight were essential in this project.

There are so many people who participated in this project that I cannot name, but I am deeply grateful for the young people who shared their stories with me and all of the professionals who took time out of their days to give me their perspectives. It is a true privilege to know you and to provide witness to your lives and your work. I am also grateful to the staff at Bethany Christian Services, the Young Center for Immigrant Children's Rights, the Humanitarian Respite Center, and the Dilley Pro Bono Project. These organizations did not participate in my research, but I was able to spend time volunteering for each, and these experiences have been truly transformative in how I think about the world.

I would like to thank many individuals at the University of Illinois at Chicago who have provided immense support to me. Andy Clarno, Claire Decoteau, Patrisia Macías-Rojas, Nadine Naber, and Laurie

Schaffner all provided invaluable feedback and support. Thank you also to Nilda Flores-González, who always made me feel that I had something to offer. I cannot overstate the importance of her encouragement in getting me through my own imposter syndrome. And, a huge thank you to Lorena Garcia, who has the rare ability to provide critical feedback that builds, rather than tears down. At Elmhurst University I am grateful for the supportive community, and in particular, I am grateful to Andrea Krieg, Carrie Coward-Bucher, Teri Walker, Connie Mixon, Bhoomi Thakore, Catherine Gaze, and Chris Travis for providing me professional guidance, and Michelle Reidy and Karen Musser for their support. Michelle did so much leg work in helping collect data on education, and I am particularly grateful for her proactiveness and innovation! Also, thank you to the student researchers who have assisted in this project over the years: Eliza Choi from UIC and Jailene Ascencio, Elizabeth Melvin, and Lillian Solis from Elmhurst University. I am so proud of their work and contributions. Outside of my immediate university communities, I have found a research kindred spirit in Lina Caswell-Muñoz, and I am so thankful to her for the countless hours—mostly on Zoom—that we have spent discussing these issues. I must also thank Dennis Kass, who acted as a research participant advocate, and Lauren Heidbrink, who agreed to act as a mentor in the early stages of this research. Lauren's own work on migrant youth is exceptional, and it continues to inspire me.

I would also like to thank a whole host of friends who have bolstered me in a myriad of ways. Thank you to Rachel Lovis, Jes Cook-Qurayshi, Laura Landers, Carolina Calvillo, Melissa Govea-Von Velasco, Tim Adkins, Rupal Satra, David Springer, Billy Mzenga, Herrica Telus, and Lu Rollins, who listened when I needed a sounding board, acted as both friends and colleagues, and were always up for a writing date. Related, thank you to the staff of Brew Brew, who provided a hot drink and a warm atmosphere that never failed to put me in the writing zone. I missed you terribly during 2020, but I hope to write at your tables again soon. Thank you to Tiffany Adkins, who allowed me to use long runs with her to troubleshoot issues in my research. Thank you to Amanda Chapman for being the best travel buddy, when research took me across the country. And thank you to Angelina Scianna, Ashley Bovin, and Holly Boot for cheering me on during our semiannual breakfasts. Thank you to Becky Karnes, who has been an important cheerleader throughout my life. Finally, thank you to the Acamamas 2019 group; your collective love and support have been vital in my attempts to navigate motherhood and research. There are also other friends who were essential in some of the practical elements of this project. Veronica Fonseca gave me support in translation, and Sara Rose Vruggink was a wonderful editor to work with, when I found myself in a last-minute scramble to format my project. Finally, thank you to Catalina Arias Maldonado, whose help with my family was the most important thing that kept me writing through a global pandemic. I don't think we would have made it without you.

I am truly blessed to have a family supporting me in everything I do. Thank you to my parents, Elwin Ruehs and Mary Magee-Ruehs, for believing in me. Thank you to my brother, Christopher Ruehs, who, along with my mom, spent hours over the 2016 holidays helping me with this project. Thank you to my husband, Jaime Navarro, whose own story and worldview have deeply affected my understanding of this world. Thank you to my sisters-in-law, Mela Navarro and Heydy Gonzales, who cared for my new baby in order to let me finish this manuscript. Finally, thank you to my beloved Sofia. If I am honest, you were not actually that helpful in writing this book. Between the morning sickness and the exhaustion, and now the sleep deprivation and your adorable but constant bids for attention, you slowed me down a bit. But, your miraculous presence has transformed me, and more than ever, you inspire me to seek sweetness in this world, to be ever more earnest in my compassion, and to be unwavering in making this world a better place for you to exist in.

APPENDIX A

The Borders of Knowledge

This project was shaped in significant ways by the level of access I had to participants. I quickly learned that borders are built not just around the limits of a country but also around knowledge. Throughout my research, I found myself stymied by gatekeepers of information about unaccompanied youth migrants. In this appendix, I explore the barriers I faced from government agencies and reflect on the purpose of these barriers.

When I set out to begin this research, my first proposed site was at a government shelter run by an organization in which I had formerly been employed. I had worked as a case manager in its refugee resettlement division and had occasionally conducted trainings and activities with unaccompanied youth in its youth program. In addition, I had volunteered as a mentor in the unaccompanied-youth program for several years. I had left the organization in 2010 on good terms, maintaining connections with many employees. In my exit interview, I was encouraged to "come back any time" to conduct research.

I was more than happy to take up that offer and planned to work directly with this organization's unaccompanied-youth program. I contacted them as I planned out my research, and although there were new employees by this time, my resume and enthusiasm got me back in the door for a meeting with a supervisor and several staff members. They were thrilled about the prospect of research when I proposed a partnership and an ethnographic study of their shelter program. I was warned that I would have to seek approval from several overseeing bodies, but this was little deterrent for me, and we promised to be in contact once I finished my research plan.

Several months after this initial meeting, I decided to move forward with gaining approval to access the site. The director of the program explained that I would need to have board approval from its governing organization as well as approval from the Office of Refugee Resettlement (ORR). I began immediately, optimistically, composing a letter to the ORR, inquiring into the process of requesting approval for research.

Within days, I received a response, stating simply, "ORR policy does not permit access to the children for purposes of research or media inquiry. This applies to children in shelter care as well as those in foster care, to ensure their privacy and protection while they remain in federal custody. Even with IRB [Institutional Review Board] clearance, I'm afraid we cannot grant access to the children in our care."[1] After wrestling with vacillating feelings of panic and frustration, I composed another email to ORR, asking to speak with someone about the blanket research ban, emphasizing the importance of research in creating better systems and institutions for the youth. The immediate follow-up email explained that "the policy is designed to protect the privacy and security of the children while they await further immigration proceedings, for as long as they are in federal custody."[2] I was then invited to submit an official proposal although I was advised that "access has not been granted in the past, and we do not anticipate it being granted in the near future, for the reasons specified previously."

Only a day later, I receive another email, this time from my former employer: "ORR contacted us today and reminded us of this policy and also indicated that children who are in both federal and state jurisdiction cannot give consent for a project like this. Of course any adult is able to make the independent choice to be interviewed by you, but we were advised to not participate (i.e. provide contact information on previous clients) as it would appear that both [the organization] and ORR participated in the research, which is not allowed under policy."[3]

I was dumbstruck by these emails. I had anticipated a long approval process with numerous hoops, but I had not anticipated being completely blocked at the outset. I was also astonished at the thoroughness of ORR, to reach out to the organization to remind them of their obligations of confidentiality.

I created and sent out a proposal and did not hear anything for several weeks. Three weeks later, I emailed again, inquiring whether my proposal had been received. Two days after that, I received a one-sentence response: "After careful re-consideration of your proposal, we are unfortunately still unable to grant permission for this study to be conducted with children in ORR's temporary care."[4] With this exchange, my relationship with both ORR and my former employer effectively closed.

Returning to the drawing board, I decided that if I could not observe or interview youth under federal custody, I would focus my efforts instead on the people whom the youth encounter in the United States. Yet, this too was fraught with difficulty. After I received an email from the ORR, the gates were effectively closed with my former employer. Yet, I hoped that other organizations would be less wary of my requests to talk with employees.

The ORR's official policy on researchers at the time was stated on their website in two sentences and pertained particularly to researchers requesting to visit ORR facilities: "Interested parties, including advocacy groups, faith-based organizations, researchers, government officials, and other relevant stakeholders who wish to visit a care provider facility must request a visit through ORR. ORR considers various factors when responding to these requests as described in 5.2.1 with the best interests of the child of paramount importance."[5] The ORR more thoroughly documents media inquiries. This written policy suggests that grantees may use discretion when responding to these requests:

> *ORR requires that grantees make a case-by-case evaluation of each media inquiry in a timely manner,* while recognizing the overarching mission of providing for the physical and mental well-being of unaccompanied children in our care.
>
> ORR funded care providers may be approached by members of the media for background information, requests for interviews with staff and unaccompanied children, and requests for tours of the facility. *ORR grantees can respond to any and all media inquiries about their organization and any of the organization's activities* as described in 5.1.1. ORR works with the ACF Office of Public Affairs (OPA) to address media requests that are outside the scope for care providers as described in 5.1.2.[6]

Sections 5.1.1 and 5.1.2 allow grantees to discuss their own organization but suggest that grantees should refrain from providing information on specific cases or the addresses of facility locations. Further, section 3.1.3 suggests that the media may interview children in exceptional circumstances, and it outlines questions that should be addressed when grantees consider these interviews.

Within these guidelines, it is clear that although researchers may not tour facilities without ORR approval, grantees are, indeed, able to provide information about their organizations and even provide occasional interviews with youth in exceptional circumstances. Yet, in practice, many organizations did not feel comfortable speaking with me. Some simply failed to respond to my email requests, and others rejected my requests altogether. Despite the written policy, there remained a culture of caution towards researchers. I believe this to be primarily due to how the official policy was communicated by the ORR to the grantees: my impression was that despite the relative openness of the written policies, organizations felt that the subtext was that they should not communicate information to the media or researchers. Of course, it would be an exaggeration to say that all government-funded agencies felt hesitant to talk. Indeed, several were very open to researchers, sharing in great detail their day-to-day operations and stories of their successes and failures.

Through my personal networks across the country and through social media, I was also able to contact workers within organizations that had declined to participate in the research. I would approach these individuals to ask for interviews not as employees of the organizations but as individuals with experience in this line of work. This was the most successful way for me to gain access to professionals—as individuals instead of members of institutions. In several communities, I was able to break into a network of these individuals, each passing my name on to the next in a clandestine manner. These workers approached interviews with trepidation, expressing strong concerns about confidentiality but feeling that the risk they took in the interview was a moral protest again the ORR's ban on research. The irony of the situation was not lost on me: to create knowledge on the borderlands, I was using covert means to circumvent the walls that were built by borderland institutions. Knowledge production paralleled the lived experience of migrants in the borderlands.

Workers in non-government-funded organizations were far easier to access: counselors, attorneys, and workers in community centers gladly provided their insight into unaccompanied youths' experiences. Once I broke into these networks through persistent emails and phone calls, I rode a wave of accessible interview participants for several months. Accessing educators who worked with unaccompanied youth proved much harder. I had developed a list of districts that were known to have high rates of unaccompanied youth, and in the beginning, I attempted to simply contact individuals in charge of the districts. I discovered very early on that when I contacted a school or district, asking to speak with a teacher or counselor who worked with unaccompanied youth in their school, I was immediately directed to the Institutional Review Board (IRB) at their school—a process that would take months and was simply not a reasonable use of my time, considering that I was looking for just one or two interviews in each district. In these cases, I would attempt to explain that I was not interested in researching their schools; I only wanted the opinion on a much larger issue from one specific employee. This argument never proved fruitful. So, once again, I would circumvent the system, no longer emailing general school addresses but instead searching for specific educators within school systems who might be willing to speak with me—as individuals and not representatives of their districts. In one case, I had emailed both a school principal and a teacher. They both responded in the same day, the principal directing me to seek IRB approval and the teacher immediately responding that she could speak with me. I was open with the teacher at that point, explaining that the principal had directed me to receive IRB approval first, something that I could not do given the time constraints of my research. In her response, the teacher dismissed the rule in principle, applying my own argument that she could speak with me as an individual.

One of my last scheduled interviews was with a postrelease specialist for a large government-funded agency. I had gotten into contact with the worker out of sheer chance—she was a friend of a friend. She invited me to come to her office building to speak with her. As I sat across from her in her cramped office and passed her a consent document, there was a sharp knock on her door. Someone asked to speak with her quickly, and only a few minutes after she exited the office, she returned with an apologetic look. I found myself in the director's office soon after, feeling a bit like a child who had been called to speak with the principal. I explained to the director, one last time, the purpose of my research. With a smile that was hard to interpret, the director explained that the postrelease specialist would get back to me once they ran my research request past a "higher up." I left the building, knowing I would never hear from them again.

ON BEING IN AND OUT: AUTOETHNOGRAPHY IN SECRET SPACES

The second location for my proposed ethnographic observation was the Young Center for Immigrant Children's Rights.[7] It is the only organization of its kind in the United States, training volunteer child advocates and pairing them with unaccompanied youth in shelters to provide youth with an advocate as they stay in the shelters, navigate the courts, and are released to sponsors. I was excited about this hands-on experience, hoping to be able to pair volunteer work with ethnographic observations of shelter facilities in the Chicago area. I immediately applied for a position, and after a several-month waiting period, a two-day training, and multiple background checks, I joined their team of advocates.

However, by the time I was trained through the Young Center, I had received the emails from ORR declining my research request. Although I had been forthcoming with the Young Center that I was also a researcher, I had been waiting for ORR approval before approaching the Young Center regarding conducting official research through my work with the center. At this point, I found myself in a delicate situation. I was effectively "in," entering buildings that were blinded on maps, accessing courtrooms that were closed to the public, speaking with the youth who were hidden from the media. And yet, I was still officially "out," unable to conduct any formal observations of the spaces and stories I encountered, as all of these spaces resided firmly and entirely under the auspices of the ORR. Furthermore, I had signed multiple waivers with the Young Center, promising confidentiality and promising to decline media inquiries into my work. Of course, maintaining youths' confidentiality was never a conflict: as a researcher, I, too, have the obligation to maintain complete confidentiality and privacy of my participants. However, what happens when you are the "media" that you are supposed to decline?

Being in and out encouraged some ethnographic flexibility; while I had no official permission to observe the spaces I encountered, I could observe myself in these very spaces, mindful of my own movements, aware of every interaction I had with youth. I could deconstruct my thought process, as I navigated the fog of truth and memory, as my heart opened and closed upon witnessing these truth-telling moments. I could witness my own grappling, as I navigated the hidden bureaucracies of unaccompanied minors programs. Although autoethnography is often marginalized as a social scientific method, self-reflection has been used successfully to unveil wide-ranging lived experiences, including experiences of gender, disability, and mental illness.[8] These projects, and others like them, provide evidence that deep insight can be revealed when the self is the subject of analysis. In my work, I argue that I can more fully understand how humanitarian logics are created and employed when I am one of those very creators. While it may not be feasible to base this project solely on autoethnography, I believe that I can provide more nuanced insight as I analyze myself as a professional.

WHY IS THERE A RESEARCH BAN?

The question that these experiences leave us with is, of course, why the ORR is so adamantly opposed to research. Indeed, it was not long before I discovered that the denial of my research request was not personal but systemic. Informal conversations with other researchers as well as recorded conversations with interview participants suggested that the research ban was far-reaching. For example, anthropologist Lauren Heidbrink, who published her book on the unaccompanied-youth detention system, details the great lengths she went through in securing approval to conduct research on the ORR.[9] She explains that her research was conducted in a political moment in which public outcry regarding the lack of ORR transparency was at an all-time high: "My request for access to the detention facilities directly benefited from the timing of these reports and public calls for transparency and supervision. Since then, the window has closed and several researchers have been denied access."[10] In my personal communications with her, she explained that she did not know anyone who had gotten permission to conduct research in recent years. Similarly, anthropologist Susan Terrio reports that she faced significant barriers in accessing specific areas of the ORR system, with her requests to interview federal field specialists and the directors of ORR being ignored or denied.[11]

Similarly, one of my participants who conducts psychological evaluations on children in ORR custody complained that this lack of research impeded her ability to accurately perform her duties:

> I am very research oriented. . . . So I have tried repeatedly to make [my work] into a clinical research project allowing me to use that archival data [that I've already collected]. . . . I am a psychologist and it is horrifying to me that I am giving questionnaires that have never been normed. . . . So I am comparing unaccompanied immigrant minors to norms based on kids from Cincinnati or something like that. It is absurd. And [my request for research] has just been repeatedly shut down by ORR. And I totally understand that they have concerns about the kids and they don't really get what it is that research is trying to do, and I think that they are trying to err on the side of safety, but that really blocks the science. We can't move forward as a community of providers if we can't use any of this data.

She explained the absurdity of her particular situation, as a person who already interviewed children and wanted to use deidentified data to create better tools for her work: "I was continuously routed to public relations people who were like: 'We are sorry but we need to decline your interest in interviewing the kids.' I was like, I don't want to interview the kids for the 7 o'clock news. I already interviewed the kids." Her frustration in my interview with her was palpable, as another individual who is already in the system and knows that research is imperative for the better functioning of the programs the government provides.

While there is no official research ban, the ORR explains that its hesitancy to participate in research is for the protection of the young people in their care. With ORR's emphasis on safety, perhaps one cannot be too critical of the tension that the ORR faces. There are, indeed, exceptional needs for privacy in situations with migrant youth, who are in high-risk situations for human trafficking and exploitation and who have become objects of ridicule by anti-immigrant activists who have staged protests outside of facilities. Numerous interviews that I conducted with professionals detailed the great lengths they went through to protect a child from returning to traffickers and described how youth have faced anti-immigrant protesters when the location of the facility was revealed in the media. The safety of children should be of the utmost importance to researchers and government agencies alike.

And yet, this very idea that youth safety is the priority begs the question, Who is the keeper of safety? Historical precedent suggests that the US government has had little accountability in this regard. Human rights reports have long been critical of the US response to unaccompanied children and immigration detention, even after a 1997 settlement, *Flores v. Reno*, required the Immigration and Naturalization Service (INS) to make significant changes in its treatment of children.[12] In 2003, custody of unaccompanied youth was transferred from INS to ORR, and while conditions for youth seemed to improve under the new oversight, there were still questions about how the ORR policy integrated standards implemented by the *Flores* settlement and the use of former INS facilities.[13] Other reports explore the problems with the immigration system, specifically the lack of representation for the children, and the significant issues arising in the current repatriation of unaccompanied children without a clear policy.[14] In addition to this history, there are inherent tensions in a system built to both care for and prosecute children, raising constant dilemmas for practitioners.[15] Finally, over the last several years, the Trump administration has participated in a wide range of practices, such as family separation, that have received international criticism for their treatment of children.

Given a history of questionable treatment and the tensions that are inherent in this work, it is my view that accountability *is* child safety; these are not competing or opposing interests at all but rather interests that go hand in hand. Anthropologist Didier Fassin suggests that "criticism becomes critical" when one is analyzing "a social world that presents itself as imbued with a sort of moral supremacy—a world, therefore, that claims it needs not to submit to any external oversight."[16] Thus, I join the leagues of frustrated researchers in imploring ORR to reopen access to its shelters for researchers to help maintain the accountability of a system that claims to have children's best interests at heart.

APPENDIX B

Demographic Details of Professional Participants

TABLE B.1. Interviews with Professionals

Pseud-onym	Job Title	Region	Interview Year
Attorneys/Legal Field			
Caroline	Attorney in Immigrant Legal Aid Nonprofit	Midwest	2015
Nancy	Attorney in Religious Immigrant Legal Aid Nonprofit	Midwest	2015
Lavonne	Pro Bono Attorney, working in private practice	Midwest	2015
Jennifer	Attorney in Religious Immigrant Legal Aid Nonprofit	Midwest	2015
Dan	Director of Immigrant Legal Clinic	Midwest	2016
Jacqueline	Attorney for Human Rights Legal Aid Nonprofit	Northwest	2016
Nathan	Attorney in Religious Immigrant Legal Aid Nonprofit	Midwest	2016
Grace	Attorney in Religious Immigrant Legal Aid Nonprofit	Midwest	2016
Ayana	Attorney with Child Justice Clinic	Midwest	2016
Samantha	Attorney in Immigrant Legal Aid Nonprofit	Midwest	2016
Jessica	Attorney in Immigrant Legal Aid Nonprofit	Midwest	2016
Julie	Pro Bono Attorney in Corporate Immigration Office	Southwest	2016
Linda	Pro Bono Manager in Corporate Law Firm	East Coast	2016
Victoria	Pro Bono Coordinator for Immigrant Legal Aid Nonprofit	Southwest	2016
Kathy	Pro Bono Attorney from Corporate Law Firm	East Coast	2016
Heather	Attorney in Religious Immigrant Legal Aid Nonprofit	Midwest	2016
Susana	Attorney with Immigrant Community Organization	East Coast	2016
Vanessa	Paralegal with Immigrant Legal Aid Nonprofit	Midwest	2019
Family Reunification/Services			
Ashley	Postrelease Case Manager; Home Study Case Manager	East Coast	2016
Mercedes	Family Reunification Case Manager	Midwest	2016
Stephanie	Foster Care Case Manager	Midwest	2016
Ricky	Foster Care Case Manager	Midwest	2016
Nicki	Family Reunification Case Manager; Home Study Case Manager	Midwest	2016
Brenda	Family Reunification Case Manager; Postrelease Case Manager	Southeast	2016
Lindsey	Family Reunification Case Manager	Midwest	2016
Taylor	Postrelease Case Manager	Southwest	2016
Lourdes	Family Reunification Case Manager	Midwest	2019
Maribel	Family Reunification Case Manager	Midwest	2019
Jane	Postrelease Case Manager; Home Study Case Manager	Midwest	2019

TABLE B.1. (cont.)

Claire	Family Reunification Case Manager; Home Study Case Manager; Community Advocacy	East Coast	2019
Lillian	Home Study Case Manager; Postrelease Case Manager	Southeast	2019
Salma	Family Reunification Case Manager	Midwest	2019
Other Workers in ORR-Contracted Organizations			
Riley	Shelter English as a Second Language Teacher	Midwest	2016
Rosa	Shelter Case Manager	Midwest	2016
Marcy	Shelter Manager	East Coast	2016
Allison	Mentor Volunteer Coordinator	Midwest	2016
Andrea	Freelance Psychological Evaluator, contracted by various shelters	Southwest	2016
Celeste	Shelter Clinician and Care Worker	West Coast	2019
Educators			
Janet	School Counselor	Midwest	2011
Don	School Counselor	Midwest	2011
Brad	Principal	Midwest	2011
Stephanie	School Counselor	Midwest	2011
Valerie	School Counselor	Midwest	2011
Lisa	District Latino Advocate	Midwest	2016
Tiffany	English as a Second Language Teacher	Midwest	2016
Karen	District Special Populations Advocate	Midwest	2016
Michelle	English as a Second Language Teacher	Midwest	2016
Layla	District Unaccompanied Youth Advocate	West Coast	2016
Luisa	Immigrant Student Registration and Services	Southeast	2016
Paul	Program Director for Outreach to Immigrant Students	West Coast	2019
Efrain	School District Unaccompanied Youth Specialist	West Coast	2019
Beth	School Social Worker	East Coast	2019
Itzel	School District Unaccompanied Youth Specialist	West Coast	2019
Amanda	Outreach for Immigrant Students	West Coast	2019
Yasmin	Reunified Family Support Specialist	East Coast	2019
Social Service Providers, Nongovernment Contractors, Community Activists			
Veronica	Advocate, Paralegal in Immigration Law Firm	Midwest	2015
Mario	Consulate Worker	Midwest	2016
Luis	Consulate Worker	Midwest	2016
Yesenia	Case Manager with Immigrant Outreach Program	Southeast	2016
Marta	Case Manager with Immigrant Outreach Program	Southeast	2016
Clara	Counselor with Trauma-Informed Therapy Center	Southeast	2016
Amy	After-School Program Worker	Midwest	2016
Bianca	Counselor with Trauma-Informed Therapy Center	Southeast	2016
Joel	Community Activist, Health Advocate, Radical Hospitality	Southwest	2016
Emmanuel	Counselor with Latino Outreach Program	Midwest	2016
Kendra	Community Activist	Midwest	2016
Aurora	Advocate	East Coast	2016

APPENDIX C

Demographic Details of Youth Participants

TABLE C.1. Youth Participants

Pseudonym	Age at Arrival	Country of Origin	Office of Refugee Resettlement (ORR) Placement Details, while minor
Interviewed in 2015–2016			
Cynthia	14	Guatemala	Placed with foster family (Midwest)
Javier	15	Guatemala	Placed with parents; moved in with uncle (Southeast)
Marco	16	Guatemala	Placed with cousin; moved in with church member (Southeast)
Mariana	16	Honduras	Placed with father; moved in with community members (Southwest)
Nestor	17	Honduras	Aged out; no placement (Southwest)
Nicolas	17	Ecuador	Placed with father (Midwest)
Interviewed in 2011			
Andres	14	Mexico	No contact with ORR (Midwest)
Carlos	15	Mexico	No contact with ORR (Midwest)
Edwin	13	Honduras	Placed with family friend; moved to father and then independent living (Midwest)
Florencio	14	Mexico	No contact with ORR (Midwest)
Isaiah	14	Mexico	No contact with ORR (Midwest)
Jesus	16	Mexico	No contact with ORR (Midwest)
Nacho	17	Mexico	No contact with ORR (Midwest)
Salvador	17	Mexico	No contact with ORR (Midwest)
Angelica	16	El Salvador	Placed with uncle; moved in with boyfriend (Southwest)

NOTES

INTRODUCTION
1 United States Customs and Border Protection, 2020.
2 United Nations World Food Programme, 2017.
3 World Bank, 2021.
4 United Nations High Commissioner of Refugees, 2015, 6.
5 According to a UN report, between 2000 and 2010, lethal violence increased by 12 percent in Latin America—the only region in the world in which lethal violence increased in this time period (United Nations Development Programme, 2013). Human rights groups criticize the Latin American governments for being unwilling or unable to protect their citizens. Yet, the history of US intervention in the region has had a devastating impact on the stability of these governments. In El Salvador, US political intervention and influential zero-tolerance policies have created international gangs and supplied weapons for violent political forces (Zilberg, 2007). In Honduras, the United States helped to militarize the country, inadvertently creating death squads that ruled with impunity (Kruckewitt, 2005). Similarly, in Guatemala, the United States played an important role in the overthrow of the government, an ongoing civil war, and the arming of the country (Jonas, 1991). With economic and security interests in mind, the United States has supplied technology and military training to Mexico (Norget, 2005). Neoliberal policies and trade agreements such as NAFTA have undermined the Mexican corn economy, as Mexican farmers could not compete with subsidized American farmers, ultimately destabilizing that economy and resulting in increased migration flows (Babb, 2004; Bank Muñoz, 2008; Gonzalez, 2011). And, the strengthening and militarization of the US-Mexico border has done little to decrease the undocumented population in the United States, but it has created greater dependence on networks of human smugglers (Guerette and Clarke, 2005; Payan, 2006; Angelucci, 2012). Some scholars argue that reliance on these networks ultimately strengthens other criminal syndicates (Laufer, 2004; Slack and Whiteford, 2011). Thus, an analysis of the push factors for Latin American youth migration is not complete without acknowledgment of the important role the United States has played in the region.
6 United Nations High Commissioner of Refugees, 2015, 8.
7 Nazario, 2006; Cammisa, 2009.
8 For a complete analysis of the types of smugglers that are available, see Spener, 2004.

9 United Nations High Commissioner of Refugees, 2015.

10 For a further analysis of the ways in which these youth create community and support networks, see Canizales, 2014 and 2015.

11 Gonzalez-Barrera et al., 2014; Isacson et al., 2014.

12 Gonzalez-Barrera et al., 2014.

13 This right was challenged by the Trump administration, particularly through a Title 42 order, which returned unaccompanied youth to their home countries, ostensibly for public health safety during the COVID-19 pandemic. This practice was overturned by a judge in late 2020, with the help of a global coalition of rights-based organizations.

14 Throughout the book, I use the term "shelter" to describe the system run by the Office of Refugee Resettlement. Because the ORR uses this term, I have chosen to maintain this language for the sake of consistency and to distinguish between the ORR system and the detention facilities run by CBP and ICE. Furthermore, "shelter" acknowledges the explicit purpose of care that these centers purport to provide. However, "shelter" alone fails to recognize the forced detainment of young migrants. "Shelter" falsely implies that youth are free to come and go and receive assistance on their own terms. In this sense, the term "detention" more adequately addresses the nature of detainment. Because of this, throughout the book I modify the word "shelter" with the term "detain" (as in, "youth are detained in the shelter"). The conscious coupling of the two words is meant to draw attention to this contradiction.

15 United States Department of Health and Human Services, 2016.

16 See Heidbrink, 2014, and Terrio, 2015, for extensive analysis of these facilities.

17 United States Department of Health and Human Services, 2017.

18 United States Department of Health and Human Services, 2017.

19 United States Department of Health and Human Services, 2016.

20 As I will argue in chapter 3, I am suspicious of this data as it does not coincide with my data or personal experience. My suspicion is that a thirty- to thirty-seven-day follow-up does not allow enough time for problems to arise and is thus not truly a good indicator of placement success.

21 Faries, 2010.

22 See Caswell, 2016, for an analysis of the ways that these mentoring programs work.

23 Taxin, 2016.

24 This administration has waged a full attack on universal rights to seek asylum, which, in turn, has a chilling effect on youth migrants. In June 2018, then attorney general Jeff Sessions attempted to crack down on so-called private violence as a means to asylum. In particular, he claimed that domestic violence and gang-related violence could no longer be considered viable categories for asylum claims (Office of the Attorney General, 2018). For unaccompanied youth, many of whom find a pathway to relief because of their history of gang persecution, this policy would have been devastating. Fortunately, advocacy groups across the country,

such as the American Civil Liberties Union, waged a successful suit against the administration over this policy. However, other attacks on asylum have been more successful. The Migrant Protection Protocol effectively eliminated due process for migrants by creating new barriers to migrants who wish to obtain legal counsel and closing courts to the public (Human Rights Watch, 2019b). While unaccompanied youth are one of the few categories of migrants that are not forced to remain in Mexico by this policy, it nonetheless creates a chilling effect for all migrants. Indeed, the government hailed this program as a success in that it has "effectively reduced the incentive for aliens to assert claims for relief or protection . . . as a means to enter the United States" (Department of Homeland Security, 2019b, 6). Indeed, in its initial nine months, the policy decreased the number of Central American families at the border by 80 percent (Department of Homeland Security, 2019b). More recently, the government implemented yet another policy that required asylum seekers to pursue asylum in the first country they enter after fleeing their home country and denies asylum seekers who have not pursued asylum in a third country (Department of Homeland Security, 2019a). The Trump administration has worked on deals with Guatemala (Trotta, 2019), Honduras (Miroff, 2019), and El Salvador (Kanno-Youngs and Malkin, 2019), forcing these countries to accept asylum seekers en route to the United States.

25 Frydman et al., 2014. While attacks on SIJS have received less press than the attacks on asylum, the Trump administration has also worked to chip away at this pathway to relief. One of the largest changes to this policy was to limit the age of prospective claimants. Where the law originally allowed for youth up to age twenty-one to pursue SIJS, the Trump administration moved the age limit to eighteen (Robbins, 2018). In addition, the Trump administration attempted to "crack down" on the "abuse" of this program. Since the beginning of the administration, the number of approvals decreased and the number of denials increased. (See Still and Rosenberg, 2019, for a visual on the changes in approval/denial rates for SIJS.)

26 Yee and Semple, 2017.

27 Chen and Gill, 2015; Frydman et al., 2014.

28 Nevins, 2000; Glenn, 2002; Gonzalez, 2011; Andreas, 2009; Barry et al., 1994; Massey et al., 1987; Balderrama and Rodriguez, 1995.

29 Andreas, 2009.

30 Massey et al., 2002, 2.

31 Massey et al., 2002.

32 Public Law 104–208, 1996.

33 Ackelson, 2005, 183.

34 Rana, 2011.

35 Correa, 2013.

36 Mason, 2013.

37 Barry, 2011.

38 Secure Fence Act of 2006.

39 Mason, 2013.
40 Office of the Governor Rick Perry, 2005.
41 Office of the Governor Rick Perry, 2006.
42 Menjívar et al., 2018.
43 Macias-Rojas, 2016.
44 Golash-Boza and Hondagneu-Sotelo, 2013.
45 Trump, Pence, 2016.
46 Exec. Order No. 13768.
47 Department of Homeland Security, 2017, 2019c.
48 Kelly, 2017.
49 Ong, 1995; Rose and Novas, 2005; Kraut, 1994.
50 Chavez, 2008; Gee, 2003; Peña, 2005.
51 Noah, 2012; Ngai, 2004; Chavez, 2008.
52 Ackleson, 2005.
53 Chavez, 2008.
54 Rosas, 2012.
55 Anzaldúa and Anzaldúa Trust, 2015.
56 Malkki, 2010.
57 Davis, 1999.
58 Zelizer, 1994.
59 Myers, 2008.
60 Hogan and Siu, 1988. McGowan, 2010, also shows that Black children today are less likely to be adopted than White children.
61 Platt, 2009.
62 Holt, 1992.
63 Gordon, 2001.
64 Adams, 1995; Colmant et al., 2004.
65 Torres, 2004.
66 Joyce, 2013.
67 Graff, 2008.
68 Kim, 2009, 856.
69 Byrne and Miller, 2012.
70 Loyd and Mountz, 2018.
71 Chan and Obser, 2015.
72 *Flores v. Reno*, 1993.
73 Byrne and Miller, 2012.
74 Somers, 2010.
75 White House, 2019b.
76 Barnett and Weiss, 2008, 11.
77 Redfield and Bornstein, 2010.
78 Harvey, 2005.
79 Steger and Roy, 2010, 37.
80 Braedley and Luxton, 2014, 10.

81 Thomas, 2014.

82 Silva, 2016; Doty and Wheatley, 2013.

83 Stewart, 2018.

84 Tyler et al., 2014, 14.

85 Longazel and Fleury-Steiner, 2013.

86 Calhoun, 2008, 94–95.

87 Ticktin, 2010.

88 Hernández, 2015.

89 Fassin and Rechtman, 2009.

90 Cantú et al., 2005.

91 Mohanty, 2003, 31.

92 Malkki, 2010, 60.

93 Malkki, 2010, 60.

94 Fassin, 2012, 180.

95 Taft, 2020.

96 Cook, 2011; Androff and Tavasolli, 2012.

97 Phillips, 2019.

98 Weizman, 2011; Khalili, 2013; Bonds, 2013; Williams, 2016.

99 Dunn, 1996, 29.

100 United States Customs and Border Protection, 2012.

101 Spener, 2004.

102 Williams, 2015.

103 Aries, 1962.

104 Lancey, 2008.

105 See Heger Boyle et al., 2007, for a full analysis of international treaties on childhood.

106 Martinez, 2009; Orellana, 2009.

107 Fulgini and Hardway, 2004; Perreira et al., 2007; Gonzales, 2011; Gonzales and Chavez, 2012.

108 For over a century, a wide range of feminist thinkers have conceptualized the ways in which oppression intersects. Activist Claudia Jones referred to the "triple oppression" of poor Black women, and activist Boyce Davis called this "super-exploitation" (McDuffie, 2011) During the second wave of feminism, the Combahee River Collective produced a statement in which they looked at their own positionality as Black women, some queer, and their relationship to three separate movements—the civil rights movement, the feminist movement, and lesbian separatism—showing ultimately that they must not just fight one or two separate oppressions but rather "address a whole range of oppression" (Combahee River Collective 1981, 214). Their different social locations were in no way separate and could not be viewed as such. Chicana author Gloria Anzaldúa refers to the "doubly threatened" undocumented woman, pointing to both sexual violence experienced as a woman and the simultaneous experience of a refugee, venturing into the unknown. "This is her home," Anzaldúa writes, "this thin edge of barbwire"

(Anzaldua, 1999, 35). Law scholar Kimberlé Crenshaw called this phenomenon "intersectionality" and used it to understand how different locations structure one another (Crenshaw, 1991). The idea of "intersections" conjures the image of a street in which different positions in society converge to create a unique experience of oppression or privilege (Collins, 2000).

109 Uehling, 2008.

110 Heidbrink, 2020.

111 Portes and Rivas, 2011.

112 Much of this work was led by sociologist Pierette Hondagneu-Sotelo. See, for example, Hondagneu-Sotelo, 1994, 2003; and Hondagneu-Sotelo and Avila, 1997.

113 Tamar Diana Wilson, 2014; Schmidt and Buechler, 2017.

114 Hondagneu-Sotelo, 1994.

115 Chavez, 2008; Foster, 2017.

116 Soto, 2018.

117 De Keijzer and Rodríguez, 2003; Huacuz and Barragán Solís, 2008; Hernández Hernández, 2012; Lozano Verduzco et al., 2012; Ruehs, 2016.

118 Hamilton and Bylander, 2016.

119 Rumbaut, 2004.

120 Malkki, 2010, 63–64.

121 Brindis et al., 1995; Waters, 1999.

122 Heidbrink, 2017, 37.

123 Hondagneu-Sotelo and Avila, 1997; Suarez-Orozco et al., 2002; Abrego, 2009, 2014; Dreby, 2010; Suárez-Orozco, Bang, et al., 2010; Dreby and Stutz, 2012; Baldassar and Merla, 2014.

124 Wessler, 2011; Enchautegui and Menjívar, 2015.

125 Levitt, 2001; Dreby, 2007.

126 Suarez-Orozco et al., 2002; Suárez-Orozco, Bang, et al., 2010.

127 Gingling and Poggio, 2012.

128 Salazar Parreñas, 2005.

129 Menjivar, 2000.

130 Hondagneu Sotelo and Avila, 1997; Dreby, 2009.

131 Dreby, 2009.

132 Dreby, 2007.

133 Baldassar and Merla, 2014.

134 Abrego, 2014; see also Carling et al., 2012; Dreby, 2015.

135 Taft, 2010.

136 For example, Oliva (2010) writes about immigrant youths' participation in immigration protests. Others have explored youths' active construction of their subjectivities. Bejarano (2007) examines how Chicano and Mexican youth negotiate borderland identities; Flores-Gonzalez (2010) explores how second-generation immigrants actively work to establish identities as immigrants and citizens; and Garcia (2012) explores second-generation Latina girls as they navigate sexual identities and experiences, not as a youth-in-crisis narrative but as a practice of

agency amidst structural limitations. Rosas (2012) approaches marginalized youth living at the US-Mexico border by understanding the ways in which they negotiate the structural forces of the borderlands.

137 Lofland et al., 2006.

138 There are, of course, limitations to such a broad net of data collection. I acknowledge that geography is important in understanding how both humanitarian and securitization techniques operate, and my research data cannot explore site-specific manifestations of these ideologies. I cannot speak to the nuances of place and the particular politics of a community. Further, I am not able to follow the details of a particular person's experience without the specifics of the environment around him or her. Future research would benefit from focusing on a specific location to explore how an individual community within a set location responds to unaccompanied youth.

139 I detail the difficulty of accessing youth participants in Ruehs, 2018.

140 Latina Feminist Group, 2001.

141 Chu and DePrince, 2013, 73.

142 American Psychological Association, 2019; Aubrey and Dahl, 2006; Chu and DePrince, 2013; Chu et al., 2008; Hemming, 2007; Kaminer and Eagle, 2010; Morse et al., 2008; Noroña and Safyer, 2018; Osofsky and Groves, 2018; Schäfer, 2012.

143 Kaminer and Eagle, 2010.

144 American Psychological Association, 2019.

145 Noroña and Safyer, 2018.

146 Aubrey and Dahl, 2006.

147 Hart, 1997; Osofsky and Groves, 2018.

148 Morse et al., 2008.

149 For a thorough description and analysis of advocates' work, see Caswell, 2016.

150 Chang, 2007, 209.

CHAPTER 1. LEAVING AND FINDING HOME

1 Booth et al., 2018.

2 Zilberg, 2007.

3 Booth et al., 2018.

4 Spener, 2004.

5 Wise and Breña, 2006; Babb, 2004; Bank Muñoz, 2008; Gonzalez, 2011; Aguila et al., 2012.

6 De Keijzer and Rodríguez, 2003; Huacuz Elias and Barragán Solís, 2008; Hernández Hernández, 2012; Lozano Verduzco et al., 2012; Ruehs, 2016.

7 Overseas Security Advisory Council, 2018.

8 Booth et al., 2018.

9 United Nations Educational, Scientific, and Cultural Organization, 2013–2014.

10 One situation in which youth are separated from their parents was not reflected in my data, which was collected mostly prior to the Trump administration. The Trump administration implemented the Migrant Protection Protocol, known

widely as the "Remain in Mexico" policy, wherein asylum seekers are no longer permitted to wait for their day in court in the United States. Instead, they are forced to wait in Mexico in dangerous border towns, where violence, extortion, and kidnapping of vulnerable migrants is commonplace (see, for example, Glass, 2019, and Rose and Smitherman, 2019). The danger of this situation forces many migrants to make difficult decisions about returning to their home countries or staying in a perilous limbo. For some families, one option is to separate their family in order to send their children to safety. In several reports, journalists have found that parents make the decision to send their children across the border alone, rather than face the danger of the camps (see, for example, Hennessy-Fiske, 2019).

11 McMillion, 2015; Linton et al., 2017.
12 United States Department of Justice, 2018.
13 For a thorough analysis of these tensions, see Heidbrink, 2017.
14 Reid, 2012.
15 Kelly, 2017.
16 United States Department of Health and Human Services, 2016.
17 Dreby, 2007, 2009, 2010, 2015; Abrego, 2014; Soto, 2018.
18 See Garcia (2012) for a fascinating exploration of the way Latina girls navigate sexual agency and safety, even amidst a host of gender and racial stereotypes.
19 In her book on poor youth of color, sociologist Ranita Ray eschews the at-risk ideologies that surround the romantic relationships of young people. She takes a more nuanced approach, arguing that "enacting romance under constrains of poverty and risk narratives meant that while romantic and sexual relationships generated resources, connections, support, and transcendental emotions of romantic love for the youth, relationships were often hard to sustain and efforts to nourish the ideal relationship often jeopardized the youth's pathways to social mobility" (Ray, 2018, 76).
20 Lam et al., 2011.
21 Fresnoza-Flot, 2015.
22 See the work by Menjívar and Abrego for a detailed explanation of legal violence (Menjívar and Abrego, 2012) and, in particular, how legal violence shapes the experience of immigrant Latina mothers (Abrego and Menjívar, 2011).

CHAPTER 2. LEGENDS FOR THE STATE
1 TRAC Immigration, 2014.
2 Collins, 2000; Senehi, 2002; Polletta, 2006; Swerts, 2015.
3 Bonilla-Silva, 2010, 75.
4 Hunt, 1997; Nguyen, 2010.
5 James, 2010b.
6 Fassin, 2012.
7 Gonzales, 2016, 27.
8 Nguyen, 2010; James, 2010a; Ticktin, 2011.

9 The work of Lynn Stephen provides an important look into the gendered structural violences faced by indigenous girls and women in Guatemala. See for example Stephen, 2018.

10 Carlson and Gallagher, 2015; Benner and Dickerson, 2018.

11 Buffalo Center for Social Research, n.d.

12 Collins, 2017.

13 Kruckewitt, 2005; Norget, 2005; Zilberg, 2007.

14 Lindo et al., 2013.

15 Diallo et al., 2013.

16 Basu and Tzannatos, 2003.

17 Clark, 2011; Ruppel-Schlichting et al., 2013; Vásquez and Bohara, 2010.

18 Ong, 1995, 1247.

19 Ong, 1995, 1244.

20 Ong, 1995, 1244.

21 De Keijzer and Rodríguez, 2003; Huacuz Elias and Barragán Solís, 2008; Hernández Hernández, 2012; Lozano Verduzco et al., 2012; Ruehs, 2016.

22 Connell and Messerschmidt, 2005; Schrock and Schwalbe, 2009.

23 Goffman, 2014; Rios, 2011.

24 Gutmann, 2007, 17.

25 Gutmann, 2007; Mirandé, 1979; Coltrane et al., 2004.

26 James, 2010b, 110.

CHAPTER 3. EDUCATING IMMIGRANT YOUTH

1 The military has been lauded as a pathway out of poverty for poor youth and young people of color, and as Marco's story suggests, unaccompanied immigrant youth are seduced by this promise as well. However, a critical perspective on military recruitment suggests that the recruitment of young people in schools is exploitative, predatory, and results in poor health outcomes for students who face structural limitations that prevent other pathways for prosperous futures (Hagopian and Barker, 2011; Scanlan, 2014). Further, Smith (2006) suggests that the military operates as a pillar of white supremacy in which some people of color can lift themselves out of poverty at the expense of their participation in global white supremacy.

2 United States Bureau of Labor Statistics, 2017.

3 United States Department of Education, 2018.

4 Suárez-Orozco, Onaga, and de Lardemelle, 2010.

5 Gonzales, 2016.

6 Duncan, 2000.

7 Martin, 1998; Bettie, 2003; Morris, 2005; Garcia, 2009.

8 Feld, 2017.

9 Solórzano et al., 2005; Gonzales, 2010; Castillo, 2014.

10 Parsons, 1959; Halstead and Taylor, 1996.

11 However, literature suggests that this clear-cut distinction is available only for a small, privileged groups of students. Students from poor and working-class

families often blur the boundaries between education and work. See, for example, Johnson et al., 2007, and Ray, 2018.

12 Kids in Need of Defense, 2015.

13 Ray, 2018.

14 United States Department of Labor, n.d.

15 Journalists with ProPublica have compiled detailed evidence about the issues surrounding undocumented and unaccompanied youth labor (Sanchez, 2020).

16 According to *Plyler v. Doe*, 1982.

17 See, for example, Burke, 2016, and other news articles about this topic.

18 This rhetoric is particularly notable given the political climate created by the Trump administration. While the narrative of immigrant threat is not new, Trump had a clear impact on how communities around the country perceived immigrant youth, and he often linked immigrants to gang violence and MS-13, in particular (Trump 2017, 2019a, 2019b). As a result, in a 2018 HuffPost/YouGov poll, 85 percent of Trump voters felt that MS-13 was a very serious or somewhat serious national threat, and over half of Trump voters felt that MS-13 was a threat to them or their families ("Huffpost," 2018).

19 Araújo Dawson and Panchanadeswaran, 2010; Liu et al., 2014; Sutter and Perrin, 2016.

20 Gomberg-Muñoz, 2011; Ramirez, 2011; Canizales, 2015.

CHAPTER 4. INSTITUTIONALIZING PARADOXES

1 White House, 2018.

2 Trump, 2017.

3 Trump, 2019b.

4 Landgrave and Nowrasteh, 2017; Light and Miller, 2017; Gunadi, 2019.

5 Dreier, 2018.

6 Department of Homeland Security, 2018.

7 The release cites a 2017 ORR report, in which the Department of Health and Human Services responds to a series of questions regarding gang membership among youth in custody. In this letter, acting assistant for legislation Barbara Pisaro Clark explains that in one count conducted in June of 2017, 35 out of 138 youth in medium- or high-security shelters were "voluntarily involved with gangs" (Pisaro Clark, 2017). Notably, this unofficial number only includes youth who were sent to secure facilities due to ORR's belief that they might pose a threat. It is not representative of all youth in ORR custody.

8 Dawsey, 2018.

9 White House, 2019a.

10 Coe and Vandegrift, 2015.

11 Pérez, 2019.

12 Details such as the cold temperatures, frozen sandwiches, and harassment have been reported by multiple outlets and are also corroborated by my own research. See, for example, reporting in the *Guardian* by Gumbel (2018).

13 United States Department of Health and Human Services, 2018.
14 United States Department of Health and Human Services, 2014.
15 United States Department of Health and Human Services, 2014.
16 See, for example, National Immigrant Justice Center, 2020a. Boyd and Clampet-Lundquist (2019) discuss the criminalization of youth of color specifically. Galli (2018) discusses the criminalization of unaccompanied immigrant youth in the Trump era.
17 Hlass and Prandini, 2018.
18 In addition to the report by Hlass and Prandini (2018), see Verma et al., 2017.
19 Boyd and Clampet-Lundquist, 2019.
20 Petryna, 2002; Ticktin, 2011; Ong, 1995.
21 Swain, 2003; Mora, 2012.
22 Wilson et al., 2017.
23 See Immigrant Legal Resource Center et al., 2019, for more information about how a gang label strips youth of due process.
24 Dukes, 2016; Liao and Chang, 2014; Carroll et al., 2002.
25 Roberts and Ryan, 2002, 1061.
26 Hagedorn and MacLean, 2012.
27 Kang and Jones, 2007.
28 Jackson, 2019.
29 Bazan et al., 2002; Phillips, 2011.
30 Cerbino, 2011.
31 "*Sólo habla del dolor que ha probado, de la soledad en la que estuvo, de la vergüenza que sintió y de la caída de un estado de resignación.*" Cerbino, 2011, 31. Translation is my own.
32 "*Intenta transformar a la persona en un ente pasivo o dócil*" Cerbino, 2011, 32. Translation is my own.
33 Notably, not all youth experience this structure in the same way, of course. In Cynthia's story in the previous chapter, this infantilization was a welcome reprieve from what she viewed as a stolen childhood, but for other youth, the structure is an assault on their self-concept and life experiences.
34 Gee, 2003.
35 United States Citizenship and Immigration Services, 2011.
36 Kids in Need of Defense, 2015.
37 Abrego, 2009; Ruehs, 2016.
38 Swanson and Torres, 2016.
39 Calhoun et al., 1976; Anderson, 1999; Davies et al., 2011.
40 Rose, 1990.
41 Cradock, 2007.
42 Cradock, 2007, 168.
43 Rose, 1990; Baker, 2010.
44 Cradock, 2007, 168.
45 Swanson and Torres, 2016.

46 See, for example, Bourgois, 2001, for an analysis of the normalization of brutality in El Salvador.

47 As an example of this violence, Ricky, a social worker, told me a story of a young man he worked with who had been deported back to his home country. Within three months, his body was found on a street corner. Ricky explained,

> They threw him in a corner with burns. Tennis shoes and clothes that he had the moment he was taken were not the same as the one that he had at the moment [he was found dead]. More raggedy. . . . So they throw him in a corner and put a sign with a . . . *narcocorrido* [narrative ballad, often dealing with the drug trade]. I don't know. I never found out what it was, what it said. But that is how they found him. Burned. Mostly his face is burned, chest, and he is tortured . . . and they throw him right in front of the corner with houses and all that. You can see the pictures [in the news]. That was the end of it.

48 A home study is a process that places further scrutiny on potential sponsors by requiring more evidence of safety and, often, in-person visits to the sponsor's home.

49 Keller et al., 2003.

50 Waldram, 2014.

51 Petryna, 2002; Ticktin, 2011; Ong, 1995.

52 Cantú et al., 2005.

CHAPTER 5. MAKING THE SYSTEM WORK

1 The professionals I interviewed were, across the board, passionate about the jobs they held. They had all started their work as individuals motivated to serve the needs of immigrant youth. However, these represent only a portion of the workers in the field, particularly those hired in the shelters that detain youth. With the influx of immigrant youth, contractors have bypassed safety procedures, and this haphazard hiring has resulted in multiple incidences of employee abuse of children (Moore, 2019).

2 Goode, 1960, 483.

3 Rizzo et al., 1970, 151.

4 Hochschild, 1983.

5 American Bar Association, 2019.

6 Guy and Newman, 2004.

7 American Bar Association, 2013.

8 Pierce, 1995.

9 Bogoch, 1997.

10 Hochschild, 1983.

11 Tushman, 1977.

12 Pache and Santos, 2013, drawing on the work of DiMaggio and Powell, 1983.

13 O'Conner, 2006; Aultman et al., 2009.

14 Zietsma and Lawrence, 2010.

15 See Daniels (2010) and Wilson (2014) for an exploration of radical hospitality in the Quaker faith. See Wiltfang and McAdam (1991) for an analysis of the Sanctuary Movement.

16 Stephens, 2019.

17 Nonprofits that run these shelters (in addition to the ORR) have been forced to publicly respond to such criticism, particularly with the increased critiques brought on by the Trump administration's policies. For example, the president of Heartland Alliance in the Chicago region issued a statement saying that they are distinct from Border Patrol detention centers and fully condemn the criminalization of immigrant children (Diaz, 2019). Similarly, criticism against Southwest Keys, the largest shelter system detaining unaccompanied youth, ultimately brought down the CEO, Juan Sanchez, who received significant financial benefits through this work (Barker et al., 2018; Raff, 2019).

CONCLUSION

1 In her TEDx Talk, "Imagining a World without Borders" (Anderson, 2011), sociologist Bridget Anderson invites the audience to "suspend your disbelief" and "imagine a world without borders." Imagination and creativity are essential in considering what could be and envisioning the possibilities outside of the finite systems we have thus far created.

2 United States Customs and Border Protection, 2021.

3 Glass, 2019.

4 Hennessy-Fiske, 2019.

5 An advisory by the National Immigrant Justice Center explains that "despite difficult case law and a challenging adjudicatory system," these cases "remain winnable with proper case preparation and adept lawyering" (National Immigrant Justice Center, 2020b).

6 FAIR Proceedings Act, 2019.

7 Young Center for Immigrant Children's Rights, 2011.

8 Pesonen and Räikkönen, 2012; Miranda and Rupinder, 2019.

9 Peña, 2019.

10 Kelly, 2017.

11 Office of Refugee Resettlement, 2018.

12 Due to the ethical constraints of my research, I did not remain in touch with young people unless they initiated further contact after our interview. Several of these young people have connected with me through social media and have been forthcoming about the changes in their lives. Others did not contact me after the interview.

13 TRAC Immigration, 2020.

APPENDIX A: THE BORDERS OF KNOWLEDGE

1 Office of Refugee Resettlement, email message to author, March 19, 2015.

2 Office of Refugee Resettlement, email message to author, March 19, 2015.

3 Email message to author, March 20, 2015.
4 Office of Refugee Resettlement, email message to author, May 11, 2015.
5 United States Department of Health and Human Services, 2015.
6 United States Department of Health and Human Services, 2015, italics my own.
7 The Young Center did not participate in or endorse this research.
8 Lucal, 1999; Polczyk, 2012; Orr, 2006.
9 Heidbrink, 2014.
10 Heidbrink, 2014, 13.
11 Terrio, 2015.
12 Ehrenreich, 1997; Amnesty International USA, 2003; Barraza, 2005.
13 Byrne, 2008; Nugent, 2006.
14 Frydman et al., 2014; Thompson, 2008.
15 Byrne, 2008; Heidbrink, 2014.
16 Fassin, 2010.

REFERENCES

Abrego, Leisy J. 2009. "Economic Well-Being in Salvadoran Transnational Families: How Gender Affects Remittance Practices." *Journal of Marriage and Family* 71: 1070–85.

———. 2014. *Sacrificing Families: Navigating Laws, Labor, and Love across Borders.* Stanford, CA: Stanford University Press.

Abrego, Leisy J., and Cecilia Menjívar. 2011. "Immigrant Latina Mothers as Targets of Legal Violence." *International Journal of Sociology of the Family* 37 (1): 9–26.

Ackelson, Jason. 2005. "Constructing Security on the US-Mexico Border." *Political Geography* 24: 165–84.

Adams, David Wallace. 1995. *Education for Extinction: American Indians and the Boarding School Experience, 1875–1928.* Lawrence: University Press of Kansas.

Aguila, Emma, Alisher R. Akhmedjonov, Ricardo Basurto-Davila, Krishna B. Kumar, Sarah Kups, and Howard J. Shatz. 2012. *United States and Mexico: Ties That Bind, Issues That Divide.* Santa Monica, CA: RAND Corporation.

American Bar Association. 2013. *Supporting Justice III: A Report on the Pro Bono Work of America's Lawyers.* Standing Committee on Pro Bono and Public Service. March. www.americanbar.org.

———. 2019. *A Current Glance at Women in the Law.* Commission on Women in the Profession. April. www.americanbar.org.

American Civil Liberties Union. 2012. "American Civil Liberties Union (ACLU) Statement on: Human Rights Violations on the US-Mexico Border." Submitted to Office of the United Nations High Commissioner for Human Rights Side Event on "Human Rights at International Borders," 67th Session of the United Nations General Assembly. October 25. www.aclu.org.

American Psychological Association. 2019. "Identifying Signs of Stress in Your Children and Teens." American Psychological Association. Accessed January 26, 2021. www.apa.org.

Amnesty International USA. 2003. *Why Am I Here? Unaccompanied Children in Immigration Detention.* New York: Amnesty International USA.

———. 2012. *In Hostile Terrain: Human Rights Violations in Immigration Enforcement in the US Southwest.* New York: Amnesty International USA.

Amuedo-Dorantes, Catalina, and Thitima Puttitanun. 2016. "DACA and the Surge in Unaccompanied Minors at the US-Mexico Border." *International Migration* 54 (4): 102–17.

Anderson, Bridget. 2011. "Imagining a World without Borders." TEDx Talks. September 22. YouTube video, 10:47. www.youtube.com.

Anderson, Irina. 1999. "Characterological and Behavioral Blame in Conversations about Female and Male Rape." *Journal of Language and Social Psychology* 18, no. 4 (December): 377–94.

Andreas, Peter. 2009. *Border Games: Policing the US-Mexico Divide.* Ithaca, NY: Cornell University Press.

Androff, David K., and Kyoko Y. Tavasolli. 2012. "Deaths in the Desert: The Human Rights Crisis on the US-Mexico Border." *Social Work* 57, no. 2 (April): 165–73.

Angelucci, Manuela. 2012. "US Border Enforcement and the Net Flow of Mexican Illegal Migration." *Economic Development and Cultural Change* 60, no. 2 (January): 311–57.

Anzaldúa, Gloria. 1999. *Borderlands/La Frontera.* 2nd ed. San Francisco: Aunt Lute Books.

Anzaldúa, Gloria, and the Gloria E. Anzaldúa Literary Trust. 2015. "Acts of Healing." In *This Bridge Called My Back, Fourth Edition: Writings by Radical Women of Color,* edited by C. Moraga and G. Anzaldúa, xxvi–xxviii. Albany: State University of New York Press.

Araújo Dawson, Beverly, and Subadra Panchanadeswaran. 2010. "Discrimination and Acculturative Stress among First-Generation Dominicans." *Hispanic Journal of Behavioral Sciences* 32 (2): 216–31.

Aries, Philippe. 1962. *Centuries of Childhood: A Social History of Family Life.* Translated by Robert Baldick. New York: Random House.

Aubrey, Carol, and Sarah Dahl. 2006. "Children's Voices: The Views of Vulnerable Children on Their Service Providers and the Relevance of the Services They Receive." *British Journal of Social Work* 36, no. 1 (January): 21–39.

Aultman, Lori Price, Meca R. Williams-Johnson, and Paul A. Schutz. 2009. "Boundary Dilemmas in Teacher-Student Relationships: Struggling with 'the Line.'" *Teaching and Teacher Education* 25, no. 5 (July): 636–46.

Babb, Sarah. 2004. *Managing Mexico: Economists from Nationalism to Neoliberalism.* Princeton, NJ: Princeton University Press.

Baker, Joanne. 2010. "Claiming Volition and Evading Victimhood: Post-Feminist Obligations for Young Women." *Feminism & Psychology* 20, no. 2 (May): 186–204.

Baldassar, Loretta, and Laura Merla, eds. 2014. *Transnational Families, Migration, and the Circulation of Care: Understanding Mobility and Absence in Family Life.* New York: Routledge.

Balderrama, Francisco E., and Raymond Rodríguez. 1995. *Decade of Betrayal: Mexican Repatriation in the 1930s.* Albuquerque: University of New Mexico Press.

Bank Muñoz, Carolina. 2008. *Transnational Tortillas: Race, Gender, and Shop-Floor Politics in Mexico and the United States.* Ithaca, NY: Cornell University Press.

Barker, Kim, Nicholas Kulish, and Rebecca R. Ruiz. 2018. "He Built an Empire, with Detained Migrant Children as the Bricks." *New York Times,* December 2. www.nytimes.com.

Barnett, Michael. 2008. "Humanitarianism as a Scholarly Vocation." In *Humanitarianism in Question: Politics, Power, Ethics,* edited by M. Barnett and T. G. Weiss, 235–63. Ithaca, NY: Cornell University Press.

———. 2011. *Empire of Humanity: A History of Humanitarianism*. Ithaca, NY: Cornell University Press.

Barnett, Michael, and Thomas G. Weiss. 2008. "Humanitarianism: A Brief History of the Present." In *Humanitarianism in Question: Politics, Power, Ethics*, edited by M. Barnett and T. G. Weiss, 1–48. Ithaca, NY: Cornell University Press.

Barraza, Javier. 2005. "Violation of the Rights of Unaccompanied Immigrant Children in the United States and the Need for Appointed Counsel." *Children's Legal Rights Journal* 25: 24–44.

Barry, Tom. 2011. *Border Wars*. Cambridge, MA: MIT Press.

Barry, Tom, Harry Browne, and Beth Sims. 1994. *Crossing the Line: Immigrants, Economic Integration, and Drug Enforcement on the US-Mexico Border*. Vol. 3 of the *US-Mexico Series*. Albuquerque, NM: Resource Center Press.

Basu, Kaushik, and Zafiris Tzannatos. 2003. "The Global Child Labor Problem: What Do We Know and What Can We Do?" *World Bank Economic Review* 17 (2): 147–73.

Battilana, Julie. 2006. "Agency and Institutions: The Enabling Role of Individuals' Social Position." *Organization* 13 (5): 653–76.

Bazan, Luis Enrique, Liliana Harris, and Lois Ann Lorentzen. 2002. "Migrant Gangs, Religion, and Tattoo Removal." *Peace Review* 14 (4): 379–83.

Bejarano, Cynthia L. 2007. *Qué Onda? Urban Youth Culture and Border Identity*. Tucson: University of Arizona Press.

Benner, Katie, and Caitlin Dickerson. 2018. "Sessions Says Domestic and Gang Violence Are Not Grounds for Asylum." *New York Times*, June 11. www.nytimes.com.

Berger, Lawrence M., Marla McDaniel, and Christina Paxson. 2005. "Assessing Parenting Behaviors across Racial Groups: Implications for the Child Welfare System." *Social Service Review* 79 (4): 653–88.

Bettie, Julie. 2003. "How Working-Class Chicas Get Working-Class Lives." In *Women without Class: Girls, Race, and Identity*. Los Angeles: University of California Press.

———. 2014. *Women without Class: Girls, Race, and Identity*. Los Angeles: University of California Press.

Binder, Amy. 2007. "For Love and Money: Organizations' Creative Responses to Multiple Environmental Logics." *Theory and Society* 36 (6): 547–71.

Blommaert, Jan. 2001. "Investigating Narrative Inequality: African Asylum Seekers' Stories in Belgium." *Discourse & Society* 12 (4): 413–49.

Boehm, Deborah A. 2012. *Intimate Migrations: Gender, Family, and Illegality among Transnational Mexicans*. New York: NYU Press.

Bogoch, Bryna. 1997. "Gendered Lawyering: Difference and Dominance in Lawyer-Client Interaction." *Law & Society Review* 31 (4): 677–712.

Bonds, Eric. 2013. "Hegemony and Humanitarian Norms: The US Legitimation of Toxic Violence." *Journal of World-Systems Research* 19 (1): 82–107.

Bonilla-Silva, Eduardo. 2010. *Racism without Racists: Color-Blind Racism and Racial Inequality in Contemporary America*. 3rd ed. Lanham, MD: Rowman & Littlefield.

Booth, John A., Christine J. Wade, and Thomas W. Walker. 2018. *Understanding Central America: Global Forces, Rebellion, and Change*. 6th ed. New York: Routledge.

Bourgois, Philippe. 2001. "The Power of Violence in War and Peace: Post–Cold War Lessons from El Salvador." *Ethnography* 2 (1): 5–34.

Boyd, Melody L., and Susan Clampet-Lundquist. 2019. "'It's Hard to Be around Here': Criminalization of Daily Routines of Youth in Baltimore." *Socius: Sociological Research for a Dynamic World* 5: 1–10.

Bracero History Archive. 2014. "Introduction and Background Information for Teachers." Accessed January 26, 2021. http://braceroarchive.org.

Braedley, Susan, and Meg Luxton. 2014. "Competing Philosophies: Neoliberalism and the Challenges of Everyday Life." In *Neoliberalism and Everyday Life*, edited by Susan Braedley and Meg Luxton, 3–22. Montreal: McGill-Queen's University Press.

Brindis, Claire, Amy L. Wolfe, Virginia McCarter, Shelly Ball, and Susan Starbuck-Morales. 1995. "The Associations between Immigrant Status and Risk-Behavior Patterns in Latino Adolescents." *Journal of Adolescent Health* 17 (2): 99–105.

Buffalo Center for Social Research. N.d. "What Is Trauma-Informed Care?" Institute on Trauma and Trauma-Informed Care. Accessed December 31, 2019. http://social-work.buffalo.edu.

Burke, Garance. 2016. "Report: Immigrant Students Blocked from Enrolling in School." Associated Press. April 11. https://apnews.com.

Burke, Garance, and Adrian Sainz. 2016. "Migrant Children Kept from Enrolling in School." Associated Press. May 2. https://apnews.com.

Burnett, John. 2017. "ICE Has Arrested More Than 400 in Operation Targeting Parents Who Pay Smugglers." *All Things Considered*. National Public Radio. August 18. www.npr.org.

Butler, Judith. 1990. *Gender Trouble: Feminism and the Subversion of Identity*. New York: Routledge.

Byrne, Bridget. 2006. "In Search of a 'Good Mix': 'Race,' Class, Gender, and Practices of Mothering." *Sociology* 4 (6): 1001–17.

Byrne, Olga. 2008. *Unaccompanied Children in the United States: A Literature Review*. New York: Vera Institute for Justice. www.vera.org.

Byrne, Olga, and Elise Miller. 2012. *The Flow of Unaccompanied Children through the Immigration System: A Resource for Practitioners, Policy Makers, and Researchers*. New York: Vera Center on Immigration and Justice. http://archive.vera.org.

Calhoun, Craig. 2008. "The Imperative to Reduce Suffering: Charity, Progress, and Emergencies in the Field of Humanitarian Action." In *Humanitarianism in Question: Politics, Power, Ethics*, edited by M. Barnett and T. G. Weiss, 73–97. Ithaca, NY: Cornell University Press.

Calhoun, Lawrence G., James W. Shelby, and Louise J. Warring. 1976. "Social Perception of the Victim's Casual Role in Rape: An Exploratory Examination of Four Factors." *Human Relations* 29 (6): 517–26.

Cammisa, Rebecca, dir. 2009. *Which Way Home*. Mr. Mudd Production in association with Documentress Films.

Canizales, Stephanie L. 2014. "Exploitation, Poverty, and Marginality among Unaccompanied Migrant Youth." *Center for Poverty Research Policy Brief* 2 (12). http://poverty.ucdavis.edu.

———. 2015. "American Individualism and the Social Incorporation of Unaccompanied Guatemalan Maya Young Adults in Los Angeles." *Ethnic and Racial Studies* 38 (10): 1831–47.

Cantú, Lionel Jr., Eithne Luibhéid, and Alexandra Minna Stern. 2005. "Well-Founded Fear: Political Asylum and the Boundaries of Sexual Identity in the US/Mexican Borderlands." In *Queer Migrations: Sexuality, US Citizenship, and Border Crossings*, edited by E. Luibhéid and L. Cantú Jr., 61–74. Minneapolis: University of Minnesota Press.

Carling, Jørgen, Cecilia Menjívar, and Leah Schmalzbauer. 2012. "Central Themes in the Study of Transnational Parenthood." *Journal of Ethnic and Migration Studies* 38 (2): 181–217.

Carlson, Elizabeth, and Anne Marie Gallagher. 2015. "Humanitarian Protection for Children Fleeing Gang-Based Violence in the Americas." *Journal on Migration and Human Security* 3 (2): 129–58.

Carroll, Sean T., Robert H. Riffenburgh, Timothy A. Roberts, and Elizabeth B. Myhre. 2002. "Tattoos and Body Piercings as Indicators of Adolescent Risk-Taking Behaviors." *Pediatrics* 109: 1021–27.

Carter, Shannon K., and Amanda Koontz Anthony. 2015. "Good, Bad, and Extraordinary Mothers: Infant Feeding and Mothering in African American Mothers' Breastfeeding Narratives." *American Sociological Association* 1 (4): 517–31.

Castillo, Jennifer. 2014. "Tolerance in Schools for Latino Students: Dismantling the School-to-Prison Pipeline." *Harvard Journal of Hispanic Policy* 26: 43–58.

Caswell, Lina M. 2016. "The Role of Volunteer Child Advocates for Unaccompanied Immigrant Children in the US: Considering the Best Interest of Children." Master's thesis, Department of Sociology and Social Justice, Kean University.

Caumont, Andrea. 2013. "12 Trends Shaping Digital News." Pew Research Center. October 16. www.pewresearch.org.

Cerbino, Mauro. 2011. "Jóvenes víctimas de violencias, caras tatuadas y borramientos." *Perfiles Latinoamericanos*, Julio/Diciembre, 9–38.

Chan, Jennifer, and Katharina Obser. 2015. "The Complex History and Tragic Return of Family Detention." National Immigrant Justice Center. July 9. https://immigrantjustice.org/staff/blog/complex-history-and-tragic-return-family-detention.

Chang, Heewon. 2007. "Autoethnography: Raising Cultural Consciousness of Self and Others." *Studies in Educational Ethnography* 12: 207–21.

Chavez, Leo R. 2008. *The Latino Threat: Constructing Immigrants, Citizens, and the Nation*. Stanford, CA: Stanford University Press.

Chavez, Lilian, and Cecilia Menjívar. 2010. "Children without Borders: A Mapping of the Literature on Unaccompanied Migrant Children to the United States." *Migraciones Internacionales* 5 (3): 71–111.

Chen, Annie, and Jennifer Gill. 2015. "Unaccompanied Children and the US Immigration System: Challenges and Reforms." *International Affairs* 68 (2): 115–33.

Chen, Pan, Dexter R. Voisin, and Kristen C. Jacobson. 2013. "Community Violence Exposure and Adolescent Delinquency: Examining a Spectrum of Promotive Factors." *Youth and Society* 48 (1): 33–57.

Chu, Ann T., and Anne P. DePrince. 2013. "Perceptions of Trauma Research with a Sample of at-Risk Youth." *Journal of Empirical Research on Human Research Ethics: An International Journal* 8 (4): 67–76.

Chu, Ann T., Anne P. DePrince, and Kristin M. Weinzierl. 2008. "Children's Perception of Research Participation: Examining Trauma Exposure and Distress." *Journal of Empirical Research on Human Research Ethics: An International Journal* 3 (1): 49–58.

Clark, Rob. 2011. "Child Labor in the World Polity: Decline and Persistence, 1980–2000." *Social Forces* 89 (3): 1033–55.

Clark-Ibáñez, Marisol. 2015. *Undocumented Latino Youth: Navigating Their Worlds.* Boulder, CO: Lynne Rienner.

Clarno, Andy. 2009. "Does It Explode? Collecting Shells in Gaza." *Social Psychology Quarterly* 72 (2): 95–98.

Coe, Anna-Britt, and Darcie Vandegrift. 2015. "Youth Politics and Culture in Contemporary Latin America: A Review." *Latin American Politics and Society* 57 (2): 132–53.

Collins, Patricia Hill. 1998. *Fighting Words: Black Women and the Search for Justice.* Minneapolis: University of Minnesota Press.

———. 2000. *Black Feminist Thought: Knowledge, Consciousness, and the Politics of Empowerment.* New York: Routledge.

———. 2017. "On Violence, Intersectionality, and Transversal Politics." *Ethnic and Racial Studies* 40 (9): 1460–73.

Colmant, Stephen, Lahoma Schultz, Rockey Robbins, Peter Ciali, and Yvette Rivera-Colmant. 2004. "Constructing Meaning to the Indian Boarding School Experience." *Journal of American Indian Education* 43 (3): 22–40.

Coltrane, Scott, Ross D. Parke, and Michele Adams. 2004. "Complexity of Father Involvement in Low-Income Mexican American Families." *Family Relations* 53 (2): 179–89.

Combahee River Collective. 1981. "A Black Feminist Statement." In *This Bridge Called My Back: Writings by Radical Women of Color,* edited by C. Moraga and G. Anzaldúa, 210–18. New York: Kitchen Table Press.

Connell, R. W., and James W. Messerschmidt. 2005. "Hegemonic Masculinity: Rethinking the Concept." *Gender & Society* 19 (6): 829–59.

Cook, Maria Lorena. 2011. "Humanitarian Aid Is Never a Crime: Humanitarianism and Illegality in Migrant Advocacy." *Law & Society Review* 45 (3): 561–91.

Correa, Jennifer G. 2013. "'After 9/11 Everything Changed': Re-formations of State Violence in Everyday Life on the US-Mexico Border." *Cultural Dynamics* 25: 99–199.

Cotera, María Eugenia. 2008. *Native Speakers: Ella Deloria, Zora Neale Hurston, Jovita González, and the Poetics of Culture.* Austin: University of Texas Press.

Cradock, Gerald. 2007. "The Responsibility Dance: Creating Neoliberal Children." *Childhood* 14 (2): 153–72.

Crenshaw, Kimberle. 1991. "Mapping the Margins: Intersectionality, Identity Politics, and Violence against Women of Color." *Stanford Law Review* 43 (6): 1241–99.

Daniels, C. Wess. 2010. "Convergent Friends: The Emergence of Postmodern Quakerism." *Quaker Studies* 14 (2): article 16.

Davies, Michelle, Kerry Austen, and Paul Rogers. 2011. "Sexual Preference, Gender, and Blame Attributions in Adolescent Sexual Assault." *Journal of Social Psychology* 151 (5): 592–607.

Davis, Nanette J. 1999. *Youth Crisis: Growing Up in the High-Risk Society*. Westport, CT: Praeger.

Dawsey, Josh. 2018. "Trump Derides Protections for Immigrants from 'Shithole' Countries." *Washington Post*, January 12. www.washingtonpost.com.

De Keijzer, Benno, and Gabriela Rodríguez. 2003. "Jóvenes Rurales: Género y Generación en un Mundo Cambiante." In *Varones Adolescentes: Género, Identidades, y Sexulidades en América Latina*, edited by José Olavarría. Santiago, Chile: FNUAP.

Delgado Bernal, Dolores, Rebeca Burciaga, and Judith Flores Carmona. 2012. "Chicana/Latina Testimonios: Mapping the Methodological, Pedagogical, and Political." *Equity & Excellence in Education* 45 (3): 363–67.

Department of Homeland Security. 2014. "Southwest Border Unaccompanied Alien Children FY 2014." United States Customs and Border Protection. Accessed April 19, 2021. www.cbp.gov.

———. 2017. "DHS Announces Launch of New Office for Victims of Illegal Immigrant Crime." Office of the Press Secretary Department of Homeland Security. April 26. www.dhs.gov.

———. 2018. "Unaccompanied Alien Children and Family Units Are Flooding the Border Because of Catch and Release Loopholes." Department of Homeland Security press release. February 15. www.dhs.gov.

———. 2019a. "Asylum Eligibility and Procedural Modifications." Interim final rule. *Federal Register: The Daily Journal of the United States Government* 84, no. 136 (Tuesday, July 16): 33829–45. www.federalregister.gov.

———. 2019b. "Assessment of the Migrant Protection Protocols (MPP)." Department of Homeland Security. October 28. www.dhs.gov.

———. 2019c. Victims of Immigration Crime Engagement (VOICE) Office, United States Immigration and Customs Enforcement. Updated December 19. www.ice.gov.

Diallo, Yacouba, Alex Etienne, and Farhad Mehran. 2013. *Global Child Labour Trends, 2008 to 2012*. Geneva: International Labour Office. www.ilo.org.

Diaz, Evelyn. 2019. "Where We Stand on Immigration." Heartland Alliance. June 28. www.heartlandalliance.org.

DiMaggio, Paul J., and Walter W. Powell. 1983. "The Iron Cage Revisited: Institutional Isomorphism and Collective Rationality in Organizational Fields." *American Sociological Review* 48 (2): 147–60.

Doty, Roxanne Lynne, and Elizabeth Shannon Wheatley. 2013. "Private Detention and the Immigration Industrial Complex." *International Political Sociology* 7: 426–43.

Dreby, Joanna. 2007. "Children and Power in Mexican Transnational Families." *Journal of Marriage and Family* 69: 1050–64.

———. 2009. "Honor and Virtue: Mexican Parenting in the Transnational Context." *Gender and Society* 20 (1): 32–59.

———. 2010. *Divided by Borders: Mexican Migrants and Their Children*. Los Angeles: University of California Press.

———. 2015. *Everyday Illegal: When Policies Undermine Immigrant Families*. Oakland: University of California Press.

Dreby, Joanna, and Lindsay Stutz. 2012. "Making Something of the Sacrifice: Gender, Migration, and Mexican Children's Educational Aspirations." *Global Networks* 12 (1): 71–90.

Dreier, Hannah. 2018. "I've Been Reporting on MS-13 for a Year: Here Are the 5 Things Trump Gets Most Wrong." ProPublica. June 25. www.propublica.org.

Dukes, Richard L. 2016. "Deviant Ink: A Meta-Analysis of Tattoos and Drug Use in General Populations." *Deviant Behavior* 37 (6): 665–78.

Duncan, Garett Albert. 2000. "Urban Pedagogies and the Celling of Adolescents of Color." *Social Justice: A Journal of Crime, Conflict, and World Order* 27 (3): 29–42.

Dunn, Timothy J. 1996. *The Militarization of the US-Mexico Border, 1978–1992: Low Intensity Conflict Doctrine Comes Home*. Austin: Center for Mexican American Studies, University of Texas at Austin.

Edwards, Frank. 2016. "Saving Children, Controlling Families: Punishment, Redistribution, and Child Protection." *American Sociological Review* 81, no. 3 (June): 575–95. https://doi.org/10.1177/0003122416638652.

Ehrenreich, Rosa. 1997. *Slipping through the Cracks: Unaccompanied Children Detained by the US Immigration and Naturalization Service*. New York: Human Rights Watch.

Enchautegui, María E., and Cecilia Menjívar. 2015. "Paradoxes of Family Immigration Policy: Separation, Reorganization, and Reunification of Families under Current Immigration Laws." *Law & Policy* 37 (1/2): 32–60.

Exec. Order No. 13768, 82 Fed. Reg. 8799 (January 25, 2017).

FAIR Proceedings Act, S.2389, 116th Congress (2019). www.congress.gov.

Faries, Olivia. 2010. "Difficult Pathways through Federal Custodial System." *International Migration* 49 (5): 14–16.

Fassin, Didier. 2010. "*Noli me tangere*: The Moral Untouchability of Humanitarianism." In *Forces of Compassion: Humanitarianism between Ethics and Politics*, edited by E. Bornstein and P. Redfield, 35–52. Santa Fe, NM: School for Advanced Research Press.

———. 2012. *Humanitarian Reason: A Moral History of the Present*. Los Angeles: University of California Press.

Fassin, Didier, and Richard Rechtman. 2009. *The Empire of Trauma: An Inquiry into the Condition of Victimhood*. Princeton, NJ: Princeton University Press.

Feld, Barry C. 2017. *The Evolution of the Juvenile Court: Race, Politics, and the Criminalizing of Juvenile Justice*. New York: NYU Press.

Flores v. Reno, 507 US 292 (1993).

Flores-Gonzáles, Nilda. 2010. "Immigrants, Citizens, or Both? The Second Generation in the Immigrant Rights Marches." In *Marcha: Latino Chicago and the Immigrant Rights Movement*, edited by A. Pallares and N. Flores-González, 198–214. Urbana: University of Illinois Press.

Foster, Carly Hayden. 2017. "Anchor Babies and Welfare Queens: An Essay on Political Rhetoric, Gendered Racism, and Marginalization." *Women, Gender, and Families of Color* 5 (1): 50–72.

Fresnoza-Flot, Asuncion. 2015. "The Bumpy Landscape of Family Reunification: Experiences of First- and 1.5-Generation Filipinos in France." *Journal of Ethnic and Migration Studies* 41 (7): 1152–71.

Friedland, Roger, and Robert R. Alford. 1991. "Bringing Society Back In: Symbols, Practices, and Institutional Contradictions." In *The New Institutionalism in Organizational Analysis*, edited by W. W. Powell and P. J. DiMaggio, 232–66. Chicago: University of Chicago Press.

Frydman, Lisa, Elizabeth Dallam, Blaine Bookey, Megan McKenna, and Wendy Ramirez. 2014. *A Treacherous Journey: Child Migrants Navigating the US Immigration System*. San Francisco: Center for Gender & Refugee Studies and Kids in Need of Defense. www.supportkind.org.

Fulgini, Andrew J., and Christina Hardway. 2004. "Preparing Diverse Adolescents for the Transition to Adulthood." *Future of Children* 14 (2): 98–119.

Galbraith, Jim. 2008. "A Squatter on the Fourth Estate: Google News." *Journal of Library Administration* 46 (3/4): 191–206.

Galli, Chiara. 2018. "No Country for Immigrant Children: From Obama's 'Humanitarian Crisis' to Trump's Criminalization of Central American Unaccompanied Minors." California Immigration Research Initiative (CIRI) Research Brief Series 6, Spring. https://ccis.ucsd.edu.

Garcia, Lorena. 2009. "'Now Why Do You Want to Know about That?': Heteronormativity, Sexism, and Racism in the Sexual (Mis)education of Latina Youth." *Gender & Society* 23 (4): 520–41.

———. 2012. *Respect Yourself, Protect Yourself: Latina Girls and Sexual Identity*. New York: NYU Press.

Gatrell, Peter. 2013. *The Making of the Modern Refugee*. Oxford, UK: Oxford University Press.

Gee, Jennifer. 2003. "Housewives, Men's Villages, and Sexual Respectability: Gender and the Interrogation of Asian Women at the Angel Island Immigration Station." In *Asian/Pacific Islander American Women: A Historical Anthology*, edited by S. Hune and G. Nomura, 90–105. New York: NYU Press.

Gingling, T. H., and Sara Poggio. 2012. "Family Separation and Reunification as a Factor in the Educational Success of Immigrant Children." *Journal of Ethnic and Migration Studies* 38 (7): 1155–73.

Glass, Ira. 2019. "The Out Crowd." Episode 688 in *This American Life* (online audio recording). Produced in collaboration with WBEZ Chicago. November 15. www.thisamericanlife.org.

Glenn, Evelyn Nakano. 2002. *Unequal Freedom: How Race and Gender Shaped American Citizenship and Labor*. Cambridge, MA: Harvard University Press.

Goffman, Alice. 2014. *On the Run: Fugitive Life in an American City*. Chicago: University of Chicago Press.

Goffman, Erving. 1956. *The Presentation of Self in Everyday Life*. New York: Bantam Doubleday Dell.

Golash-Boza, Tanya, and Pierrette Hondagneu-Sotelo. 2013. "Latino Immigrant Men and the Deportation Crisis: A Gendered Racial Removal Program." *Latino Studies* 11: 271–92.

Gomberg-Muñoz, Ruth. 2011. *Labor and Legality: An Ethnography of a Mexican Immigrant Network*. New York: Oxford University Press.

Gonzalez, Juan. 2011. *Harvest of Empire: A History of Latinos in America*. New York: Penguin.

Gonzales, Roberto G. 2010. "On the Wrong Side of the Tracks: Understanding the Effects of School Structure and Social Capital in the Educational Pursuits of Undocumented Immigrant Students." *Peabody Journal of Education* 85 (4): 469–85.

———. 2011. "Learning to Be Illegal: Undocumented Youth and Shifting Legal Contexts in the Transition to Adulthood." *American Sociological Review* 76 (4): 602–19.

———. 2016. *Lives in Limbo: Undocumented and Coming of Age in America*. Oakland: University of California Press.

Gonzales, Roberto G., and Leo R. Chavez. 2012. "Awakening to a Nightmare: Abjectivity and Illegality in the Lives of Undocumented 1.5-Generation Latino Immigrants in the United States." *Current Anthropology* 53 (3): 255–81.

Gonzalez-Barrera, Jens, Manuel Krogstad, and Mark Hugo Lopez. 2014. "Many Mexican Children Migrants Caught Multiple Times at Border." Pew Research Center. www.pewresearch.org.

González-López, Gloria. 2004. "Fathering Latina Sexualities: Mexican Men and the Virginity of Their Daughters." *Journal of Marriage and Family* 66: 1118–30.

Goode, William J. 1960. "A Theory of Role Strain." *American Sociological Review* 25 (4): 483–96.

Gordon, Linda. 2001. *The Great Arizona Orphan Abduction*. Cambridge, MA: Harvard University Press.

Graff, E. J. 2008. "The Lie We Love." *Foreign Policy* 169 (November/December): 58–66.

Guerette, Rob T., and Ronald V. Clark. 2005. "Border Enforcement, Organized Crime, and Deaths of Smuggled Migrants on the United States–Mexico Border." *European Journal on Criminal Policy and Research* 11 (2): 159–74.

Gumbel, Andrew. 2018. "'They Were Laughing at Us': Immigrants Tell of Cruelty, Illness, and Filth in US Detention." *Guardian*, September 12. www.theguardian.com.

Gunadi, Christian. 2019. "On the Association between Undocumented Immigration and Crime in the United States." *Oxford Economic Papers* 73 (1): 200–224. https://doi.org/10.1093/oep/gpz057.

Gutierrez, Elena R. 2008. *Fertile Matters: The Politics of Mexican-Origin Women's Reproduction*. Austin: University of Texas Press.

Gutmann, Matthew C. 1997. "Trafficking in Men: The Anthropology of Masculinity." *Annual Review of Anthropology* 26: 385–409.

———. 2007. *The Meanings of Macho: Being a Man in Mexico City.* 10th anniversary ed. Los Angeles: University of California Press.

Guy, Mary Ellen, and Meredith A. Newman. 2004. "Women's Jobs, Men's Jobs: Sex Segregation and Emotional Labor." *Public Administration Review* 64 (3): 289–98.

Hagedorn, John M., and Bradley A. MacLean. 2012. "Breaking the Frame: Responding to Gang Stereotyping in Capital Cases." *University of Memphis Law Review* 42: 1–33.

Hagopian, Amy, and Kathy Barker. 2011. "Should We End Military Recruiting in High Schools as a Matter of Child Protection and Public Health?" *American Journal of Public Health* 101 (1): 19–23.

Halstead, Mark J., and Monica J. Taylor. 1996. *Values in Education and Education in Values.* London: Falmer Press.

Hamilton, Erin R., and Maryann Bylander. 2016. "Life Course, Autonomy, and the Migration of Children from Mexico to the United States." Presentation at the 111th American Sociological Association, Seattle, WA.

Harris, Marian S., and Mark E. Courtney. 2003. "The Interaction of Race, Ethnicity, and Family Structure with Respect to the Timing of Family Reunification." *Children and Youth Services Review* 25 (5/6): 409–29.

Hart, Roger A. 1997. *Children's Participation: The Theory and Practice of Involving Young Citizens in Community Development and Environmental Care.* New York: UNICEF.

Harvey, David. 2005. *A Brief History of Neoliberalism.* New York: Oxford University Press.

Hays, Sharon. 1996. *The Cultural Contradictions of Motherhood.* New Haven, CT: Yale University Press.

Heger Boyle, Elizabeth, Trina Smith, and Katja M. Guenther. 2007. "The Rise of the Child as an Individual in Global Society." In *Youth, Globalization, and the Law,* edited by Suhir Alladi Venkatesh and Ronald Kassimir, 255–83. Redwood City, CA: Stanford University Press.

Heidbrink, Lauren. 2014. *Migrant Youth, Transnational Families, and the State: Care and Contested Interests.* Philadelphia: University of Pennsylvania Press.

———. 2017. "Assessing Parental Fitness and Care for Unaccompanied Children." *RSF: The Russell Sage Foundation Journal of the Social Sciences* 3 (4): 37–52.

———. 2020. *Migranthood: Youth in a New Era of Deportation.* Stanford, CA: Stanford University Press.

Heidbrink, Lauren, and Michele Statz. 2017. "Parents of Global Youth: Contesting Debt and Belonging." *Children's Geographies* 15 (5): 1–13.

Hemming, Peter J. 2007. "Mixing Qualitative Research Methods in Children's Geographies." *Area* 40 (2): 152–62.

Hennessy-Fiske, Molly. 2019. "The New Family Separation: Migrant Parents Stranded on Border Send Kids across Alone." *Los Angeles Times,* November 27. www.latimes.com.

Hernández, David. M. 2015. "Unaccompanied Child Migrants in 'Crisis': New Surge or a Case of Arrested Development?" *Harvard Journal of Hispanic Policy* 27: 13–17.

Hernández Hernández, Oscar Misael. 2012. "Migración, Masculinidad, y Menores Repatriados por la Frontera Matamoros-Brownsville." *Trayectorias* 33/34: 76–94.

Hesford, Wendy S., and Wendy Kozol. 2005. "Introduction." In *Just Advocacy? Women's Human Rights, Transnational Feminisms, and the Politics of Representation*, edited by W. S. Hesford and W. Kozol, 1–29. New Brunswick, NJ: Rutgers University Press.

Hines, Alice M., Kathy Lemon, Paige Wyatt, and Joan Merdinger. 2004. "Factors Related to the Disproportionate Involvement of Children of Color in the Child Welfare System: A Review and Emerging Themes." *Children and Youth Services Review* 26 (6): 507–27.

Hlass, Laila L., and Rachel Prandini. 2018. "Deportation by Any Means Necessary: How Immigration Officials Are Labeling Immigrant Youth as Gang Members." Immigrant Legal Resource Center. www.ilrc.org.

Hoang, Kimberly. 2013. "Performing Third World Poverty: Racialized Femininities in Sex Work." In *The Kaleidoscope of Gender*, edited by Joan Spade and Catherine Valentine, 1–29. 4th ed. Thousand Oaks, CA: Sage.

Hochschild, Arlie R. 1983. *The Managed Heart: Commercialization of Human Feeling*. Berkeley: University of California Press.

Hoffman, Peter J., and Thomas G. Weiss. 2008. "Humanitarianism and Practitioners: Social Science Matters." In *Humanitarianism in Question: Politics, Power, Ethics*, edited by Michael Barnett and Thomas G. Weiss, 264–87. Ithaca, NY: Cornell University Press.

Hogan, P. T., and S. F. Siu. 1988. "Minority Children and the Welfare System: An Historical Perspective." *Social Work* 33 (6): 493–98. https://doi.org/10.1093/sw/33.6.493.

Holt, M. 1992. *The Orphan Trains: Placing Out in America*. Lincoln: University of Nebraska Press.

Hondagneu-Sotelo, Pierrette. 1994. *Gendered Transitions: Mexican Experiences of Immigration*. Berkeley: University of California Press.

———. 2003. "Gender and Immigration: A Retrospective and Introduction." In *Gender and US Immigration: Contemporary Trends*, edited by P. Hondagneu-Sotelo, 14–30. Berkeley: University of California Press. https://ebookcentral.proquest.com.

Hondagneu-Sotelo, Pierrette, and Ernestine Avila. 1997. "'I'm Here, but I'm There': The Meanings of Latina Transnational Motherhood." *Gender and Society* 11 (5): 548–71.

Huacuz Elías, María Guadalupe, and Anabella Barragán Solís. 2008. "Cruzar la Frontera: la Migración Internacional como Rito de Construcción de la Masculinidad en Jóvenes de Guanajuato." *La Manzana: Revista Internacional de Estudios sobre Masculinidades* 3 (5): 21–62.

"HuffPost: Immigration and Gang Violence." 2018. Huffington Post/YouGov survey. July 5–6. https://big.assets.huffingtonpost.com. Accessed August 10, 2021.

Hughes, Anwen. 2009. *Denial and Delay: The Impact of the Immigration Law's "Terrorism Bars" on Asylum Seekers and Refugees in the United States*. New York: Human Rights First. www.humanrightsfirst.org.

Human Rights Watch. 2010. *Deportation by Default: Mental Disability, Unfair Hearings, and Indefinite Detention in the US Immigration System.* New York: Human Rights Watch. www.hrw.org.

———. 2019a. "US: Family Separation Harming Children, Families" (online news release). Human Rights Watch. July 11. www.hrw.org.

———. 2019b. "US Move Puts More Asylum Seekers at Risk" (online news release). Human Rights Watch. September 25. www.hrw.org.

Hunt, Nancy Rose. 1997. "Condoms, Confessors, Conferences: Among AIDS Derivatives in Africa." *Journal of the International Institute* 4 (3): 1, 15–17.

Immigrant Legal Resource Center, National Immigrant Justice Center, and National Immigration Law Center. 2019. "Funding for ICE Homeland Security Investigations (HIS) Is Funding for Trump's Anti-Immigrant Agenda." National Immigrant Justice Center. April 29. www.immigrantjustice.org.

Isacson, Adam, Maureen Meyer, and Gabriela Morales. 2014. *Mexico's Other Border: Security, Migration, and the Humanitarian Crisis at the Line with Central America.* Washington, DC: Washington Office on Latin America. www.wola.org.

Jackson, Chris. 2019. "More Americans Have Tattoos Today Than Seven Years Ago." *Ipsos*, August 29. www.ipsos.com.

James, Erica Caple. 2010a. *Democratic Insecurities: Violence, Trauma, and Intervention in Haiti.* Berkeley: University of California Press.

———. 2010b. "Ruptures, Rights, and Repair: The Political Economy of Trauma in Haiti." *Social Science & Medicine* 70: 106–13.

Jennings, Wesley G., Bryanna Hahn Fox, and David P. Farrington. 2014. "Inked into Crime? An Examination of the Causal Relationship between Tattoos and Life-Course Offending among Males from the Cambridge Study in Delinquent Development." *Journal of Criminal Justice* 42 (1): 77–84.

Johnson, Monica Kirkpatrick, Justin Allen Berg, and Toni Sirotzki. 2007. "Differentiation in Self-Perceived Adulthood: Extending the Confluence Model of Subjective Age Identity." *Social Psychology Quarterly* 70 (3): 243–61.

Jonas, Susanne. 1991. *Battle for Guatemala: Rebels, Death Squads, and US Power.* Boulder, CO: Westview.

Jordan-Zachery, Julia S. 2007. "Policy Interaction: The Mixing of Fatherhood, Crime, and Urban Policies." *Journal of Social Policy* 37 (1): 81–102.

Joyce, Kathryn. 2013. *The Child Catchers: Rescue, Trafficking, and the New Gospel of Adoption.* New York: Public Affairs.

Kaminer, Debra, and Gillian Eagle. 2010. "Trauma and Children." In *Traumatic Stress in South Africa,* 122–45. Johannesburg, South Africa: Wits University Press.

Kandel, William A. 2016. "Unaccompanied Alien Children: An Overview." Congressional Research Service. Updated October 9, 2019. http://fas.org.

Kang, Miliann, and Katherine Jones. 2007. "Why Do People Get Tattoos?" *Contexts* 6 (1): 42–47.

Kanno-Youngs, Zolan, and Elisabeth Malkin. 2019. "US Agreement with El Salvador Seeks to Divert Asylum Seekers." *New York Times,* September 20. www.nytimes.com.

Kantor, Glenda Kaufman, and Liza Little. 2003. "Defining the Boundaries of Child Neglect: When Does Domestic Violence Equate with Parental Failure to Protect?" *Journal of Interpersonal Violence* 18: 338–55.

Keller, Allen S., Barry Rosenfeld, Chau Trinh-Shevrin, Chris Meserve, Emily Sachs, Jonathan A. Leviss, Elizabeth Singer, et al. 2003. "Mental Health of Detained Asylum Seekers." *Lancet* 362 (9397): 1721–23.

Kelly, John. 2017. "Memorandum: Implementing the President's Border Security and Immigration Enforcement Improvements Policies." Department of Homeland Security. February 20. www.dhs.gov.

Kelly, Liz, and Jill Radford. 1990. "'Nothing Really Happened': The Invalidation of Women's Experience of Sexual Violence." *Critical Social Policy* 10 (30): 39–53.

Khalili, Laleh. 2013. *Time in the Shadows: Confinement in Counterinsurgencies.* Stanford, CA: Stanford University Press.

Kids in Need of Defense. 2015. "Special Immigrant Juvenile Status." In *Representing Unaccompanied Children: Training Manual for KIND Pro Bono Attorneys* (online resource). April 12. https://supportkind.org.

Kim, Eleana. 2009. "The Origins of Korean Adoption: Cold War Geopolitics and Intimate Diplomacy." US-Korea Institute at SAIS. Washington DC. https://escholarship.org.

Kolb, Kenneth H. 2011. "Claiming Competence: Biographical Work among Victim-Advocates and Counselors." *Symbolic Interaction* 34 (1): 86–107.

Krause, E. L. 2010. "The Challenge of Giving Voice." *International Migration* 49 (5): 19–21.

Kraut, Alan M. 1994. *Silent Travelers: Germs, Genes, and the "Immigrant Menace."* New York: Basic Books.

Kruckewitt, Joan. 2005. "US Militarization of Honduras in the 1980s and the Creation of CIA-Backed Death Squads" In *When States Kill: Latin America, the US, and Technologies of Terror*, edited by C. Menjívar and N. Rodríguez, 170–98. Austin: University of Texas Press.

Lam, Amy Mong Chow, Ting Sam Chan, and Kon Wah Tsoi. 2011. "Meaning of Family Reunification as Interpreted by Young Chinese Immigrants." *International Journal of Adolescent Medicine and Health* 17 (2): 105–22.

Lancey, David F. 2008. *The Anthropology of Childhood: Cherubs, Chattel, Changelings.* Cambridge, UK: Cambridge University Press.

Landgrave, Michelangelo, and Alex Nowrasteh. 2017. *Criminal Immigrants: Their Numbers, Demographics, and Countries of Origin.* Immigration Research and Policy Brief No. 1. March 15. Washington, DC: Cato Institute. www.cato.org.

Lapierre, Simon. 2010. "Striving to be 'Good' Mothers: Abused Women's Experiences of Mothering." *Child Abuse Review* 19: 342–57.

Latina Feminist Group. 2001. *Telling to Live: Latina Feminist Testimonios.* Durham, NC: Duke University Press.

Laufer, Peter. 2004. *Wetback Nation: The Case for Opening the Mexican-American Border.* Chicago: Ivan R. Dee.

Lee, Ena. 2015. "Doing Culture, Doing Race: Everyday Discourses of 'Culture' and 'Cultural Difference' in the English as a Second Language Classroom." *Journal of Multilingual and Multicultural Development* 36 (1): 80–93.

Lee, Jolie. 2014. "Now Hiring: School Consultant for Unaccompanied Immigrant Students." *USA Today*, August 23. www.usatoday.com.

Levitt, Peggy. 2001. *The Transnational Villagers*. Berkeley: University of California Press.

Li, Nan, Ashley A. Anderson, Dominique Brossard, and Dietram A. Scheufele. 2013. "Channeling Science Information Seekers' Attention? A Content Analysis of Top-Ranked vs. Lower-Ranked Sites in Google." *Journal of Computer-Mediated Communication* 19 (3): 562–75.

Liao, Pei-An, and Hung-Hao Chang. 2014. "Is Tattooing a Risk Factor for Adolescents' Criminal Behavior? Empirical Evidence from an Administrative Data Set of Juvenile Detainees in Taiwan." *Risk Analysis* 34 (12): 2080–88.

Light, Michael T., and Ty Miller. 2017. "Does Undocumented Immigration Increase Violent Crime?" *Criminology* 56, no. 2 (May): 370–401.

Lindo, Jason M., Jessamyn Schaller, and Benjamin Hansen. 2013. "Caution! Men Not at Work: Gender-Specific Labor Market Conditions and Child Maltreatment." National Bureau of Economic Research. www.nber.org.

Linton, Julie M., Marsha Griffin, and Alan J. Shapiro. 2017. "Detention of Immigrant Children." *Pediatrics* 139 (5).

Liu, Dongyang, Ziaobo Yu, Yuncai Wang, Haigin Zhang, and Guofang Ren. 2014. "The Impact of Perception of Discrimination and Sense of Belonging on the Loneliness of the Children of Chinese Migrant Workers: A Structural Equation Modeling Analysis." *International Journal of Mental Health Systems* 8 (1): 52–58.

Lofland, John, David A. Snow, Leon Anderson, and Lyn H. Lofland. 2006. *Analyzing Social Settings: A Guide to Qualitative Observation and Analysis*. Belmont, CA: Wadsworth/Thomson Learning.

Longazel, Jamie G., and Benjamin Fleury-Steiner. 2013. "Beware of *Notarios*: Neoliberal Governance of Immigrants as Crime Victims." *Theoretical Criminology* 17 (3): 359–76.

Loyd, Jenna M., and Alison Mountz. 2018. *Boats, Borders, and Bases: Race, the Cold War, and the Rise of Migration Detention in the United States*. Oakland: University of California Press.

Lozano Verduzco, Ignacio, Mauro A. Vargas Urías, and Alma J. Beltrán Cruz. 2012. "Diferencias de género en el trayecto migratorio de niños, niñas y adolescentes mexicanos/as." *La Manzana: Revista Internacional de Estudios sobre Masculinidades* 6 (10).

Lucal, Betsy. 1999. "What It Means to Be Gendered Me: Life on the Boundaries of a Dichotomous Gender System." *Gender & Society* 13 (6): 781–97.

Luque, John S., Angel Bowers, Ahmed Kabore, and Ric Stewart. 2011. "Who Will Pick Georgia's Vidalia Onions? A Text-Driven Content Analysis of Newspaper Coverage on Georgia's 2011 Immigration Law." *Human Organizations* 72 (1): 31–43.

Lyda, Clark, and Jesse Lyda, dirs. 2009. *The Least of These: Family Detention in America*. Documentary film. Indiepix.

Macias-Rojas, Patrisia. 2016. *From Deportation to Prison: The Politics of Immigration Enforcement in Post–Civil Rights America*. New York: NYU Press.

Maira, Sunaina, and Elisabeth Soep. 2004. "United States of Adolescence? Reconsidering US Youth Culture Studies." *Research on Youth and Youth Cultures* 12 (3): 245–69.

Malkki, Liisa. 2010. "Children, Humanity, and the Infantilization of Peace." In *In the Name of Humanity*, edited by I. Feldman and M. Ticktin, 58–85. Durham, NC: Duke University Press.

Markus, Hazel Rose, and Paula M. L. Moya, eds. 2010. *Doing Race: 21 Essays for the 21st Century*. New York: Norton.

Martin, Karin A. 1998. "Becoming a Gendered Body: Practices of Preschools." *American Sociological Review* 63 (4): 494–511.

Martínez, Isabel. 2009. "What's Age Gotta Do with It? Understanding the Age-Identities and School-Going Practices of Mexican Immigrant Youth in New York City." *High School Journal* 29 (4): 34–48.

Mason, R. Chuck. 2013. *Securing America's Borders: The Role of the Military*. CRS Report No. R41286. Washington, DC: Congressional Research Service. https://fas.org.

Massey, Douglas, Rafael Alarcón, Jorge Durand, and Humberto González. 1987. *Return to Aztlan: The Social Process of International Migration from Western Mexico*. Berkeley: University of California Press.

Massey, Douglas S., Jorge Durand, and Nolan J. Malone. 2002. *Beyond Smoke and Mirrors: Mexican Immigration in an Era of Economic Integration*. New York: Russell Sage Foundation.

Mauss, Marcel. 1970 (1923–24). *The Gift: Forms and Functions of Exchange in Archaic Societies*. London: Cohen and West.

McDuffie, Eric S. 2011. *Sojourning for Freedom: Black Women, American Communism, and the Making of Black Left Feminism*. Durham, NC: Duke University Press.

McGowan, B. G. 2010. "An Historical Perspective on Child Welfare." In *From Child Welfare to Child Well-Being: An International Perspective on Knowledge in the Service of Policy Making*, edited by S. Kamerman, S. Phipps, and A. Ben-Arieh, 25–47. New York: Springer.

McMillion, Rhonda. 2015. "Against Family Immigration Detention: The ABA Cites Health and Well-Being of Asylum-Seeking Mothers and Children." *ABA Journal* 101 (8): 70.

Menjívar, Cecilia. 2000. *Fragmented Ties: Salvadoran Immigrant Networks in America*. Berkeley: University of California Press.

Menjívar, Cecilia, and Leisy Abrego. 2012. "Legal Violence: Immigration Law and the Lives of Central American Immigrants." *American Journal of Sociology* 117 (5): 1380–1421.

Menjívar, Cecilia, Leisy J. Abrego, and Leah C. Schmalzbauer. 2016. *Immigrant Families*. Malden, MA: Polity.

Menjívar, Cecilia, Andrea Gómez Cervantes, and Daniel Alvord. 2018. "The Expansion of 'Crimmigration,' Mass Detention, and Deportation." *Sociology Compass* 12 (4): 1–15.

Miranda, Jeanne, and Rupinder Legha. 2019. "The Consequences of Family Separation at the Border and Beyond." *Journal of the American Academy of Child and Adolescent Psychiatry* 58, no. 1 (January): 139–40.

Mirandé, Alfredo. 1979. "A Reinterpretation of Male Dominance in the Chicano Family." *Family Coordinator* 28: 473–79.

Miroff, Nick. 2019. "US Announces Asylum Deal with Honduras, Could Send Migrants to One of World's Most Violent Nations." *Washington Post*, September 25. www.washingtonpost.com.

Mohanty, Chandra Talpade. 2003. *Feminism without Borders: Decolonizing Theory, Practicing Solidarity*. Durham, NC: Duke University Press.

Moore, Robert. 2019. "Here's What You Should Know about the Agency in Charge of Unaccompanied Immigrant Children." *Texas Monthly*, January 16. www.texasmonthly.com.

Mora, Richard. 2012. "'Do It for All Your Pubic Hairs!': Latino Boys, Masculinity, and Puberty." *Gender and Society* 26 (3): 433–60.

Morris, Edward W. 2005. "'Tuck In That Shirt!': Race, Class, Gender, and Discipline in an Urban School." *Sociological Perspectives* 48 (1): 25–48.

Morse, Janice M., Linda Niehaus, Stanley Varnhagen, Wendy Austin, and Michele McIntosh. 2008. "Qualitative Researchers' Conceptualizations of Risks Inherent in Qualitative Interviews!" *International Review of Qualitative Research* 1 (2): 195–215.

Myers, John E. B. 2008. "A Short History of Child Protection in America." *Family Law Quarterly* 42 (3): 449–63.

Naber, Nadine. 2012. *Arab America: Gender, Cultural Politics, and Activism*. New York: NYU Press.

National Immigrant Justice Center. 2020a. *A Legacy of Injustice: The US Criminalization of Migration*. July. www.immigrantjustice.org.

———. 2020b. *Practice Advisory: Applying for Asylum after Matter of A-B-*. August 31. www.immigrantjustice.org.

Nazario, Sonia. 2006. *Enrique's Journey: The Story of a Boy's Dangerous Odyssey to Reunite with His Mother*. New York: Random House.

Nevins, Joseph. 2000. "The Remaking of the California-Mexico Boundary in the Age of NAFTA." In *The Wall around the West: State Borders and Immigration Control in North America and Europe*, edited by P. Andreas and T. Snyder, 99–114. Lanham, MD: Rowman & Littlefield.

Ngai, Mae. 2004. *Impossible Subjects: Illegal Aliens and the Making of Modern America*. Princeton, NJ: Princeton University Press.

Nguyen, Vinh-Kim. 2010. *The Republic of Therapy: Triage and Sovereignty in West Africa's Time of AIDS*. Durham, NC: Duke University Press.

Noah, Timothy. 2012. *The Great Divergence: America's Growing Inequality Crisis and What We Can Do about It*. New York: Bloomsbury.

Noguera, Pedro A. 2003. "Schools, Prisons, and Social Implications of Punishment: Rethinking Disciplinary Practices." *Theory into Practice* 42 (4): 341–50.

Norget, Kristin. 2005. "Caught in the Crossfire: Militarization, Paramilitarization, and State Violence in Oaxaca, Mexico." In *When States Kill: Latin America, the US, and Technologies of Terror*, edited by C. Menjívar and N. Rodríguez, 115–42. Austin: University of Texas Press.

Noroña, Carmen Rosa, and Marcy Safyer. 2018. "Trauma-Based Approaches to Working with Immigrant Children." Training material, Young Center for Immigrant Children's Rights.

Nugent, Christopher. 2006. "Whose Children Are These? Towards Ensuring the Best Interests and Empowerment of Unaccompanied Alien Children." *Boston University Public Interest Law Journal* 15 (Spring): 219–35.

O'Conner, Kate Eliza. 2006. "'You Choose to Care': Teachers, Emotions, and Professional Identity." *Teaching and Teacher Education* 24: 117–26.

Office of the Attorney General. 2018. "Matter of A- B-, Respondent." Interim decision 3929. United States Department of Justice, Executive Office for Immigration Review. www.justice.gov.

Office of the Governor Rick Perry. 2005. "Gov. Perry Awards $6 Million to Border Counties for Border Security." News release. Accessed May 30, 2014. http://governor.state.tx.us (news release page no longer available).

———. 2006. "Operation Rio Grande." News release. Accessed May 30, 2014. http://governor.state.tx.us (news release page no longer available).

Office of the Press Secretary. 2014. "Presidential Memorandum: Response to the Influx of Unaccompanied Alien Children across the Southwest Border." The White House, Office of the Press Secretary. June 2. https://obamawhitehouse.archives.gov.

Office of Refugee Resettlement, United States Immigration and Customs Enforcement, and United States Customs and Border Protection. 2018. "Memorandum of Agreement Regarding Consultation and Information Sharing in Unaccompanied Alien Children Matters." Accessed January 26, 2021. www.texasmonthly.com.

Oliva, Sonia. 2010. "Permission to March? High School Youth Participation in the Immigrant Rights Movement." In *Marcha: Latino Chicago and the Immigrant Rights Movement*, edited by A. Pallares and N. Flores-Gonzalez, 163–78. Champaign: University of Illinois Press.

Ong, Aihwa. 1995. "Making the Biopolitical Subject: Cambodian Immigrants, Refugee Medicine, and Cultural Citizenship in California." *Social Science & Medicine* 40 (9): 1243–57.

———. 2007. "Neoliberalism as a Mobile Technology." *Transactions of the Institute of British Geographers* 32 (1): 3–8.

Orellana, Marjorie Faulstich. 2009. *Translating Childhoods: Immigrant Youth, Language, and Culture*. New Brunswick, NJ: Rutgers University Press.

Orr, Jackie. 2006. *The Panic Diaries: A Genealogy of Panic Disorder*. Durham, NC: Duke University Press.

Osofsky, Joy D., and Betsy McAlister Groves. 2018. *Violence and Trauma in the Lives of Children*. Vol. 2. Santa Barbara, CA: ABC-CLIO.

Osterling, Kathy Lemon, and Meekyung Han. 2011. "Reunification Outcomes among Mexican Immigrant Families in the Child Welfare System." *Children and Youth Services Review* 33 (9): 1658–66.

Overseas Security Advisory Council. 2018. "Honduras 2018 Crime and Safety Report." United States Department of State Bureau of Diplomatic Security. www.osac.gov.

Pache, Anne-Claire, and Filipe Santos. 2013. "Embedded in Hybrid Contexts: How Individuals in Organizations Respond to Competing Institutional Logics." *Research in the Sociology of Organizations* 39 (B): 3–35.

Parsons, Talcott. 1959. "The School Class as a Social System: Some of Its Functions in American Society." *Harvard Educational Review* 29 (4): 298–318.

Payan, Tony. 2006. *The Three US-Mexico Border Wars: Drugs, Immigration, and Homeland Security*. Westport, CT: Praeger Security International.

Peña, Laura. 2019. *The Real National Emergency: Zero Tolerance and the Continuing Horrors of Family Separation at the Border*. Texas Civil Rights Project. www.texascivilrightsproject.org.

Peña, Susana. 2005. "Visibility and Silence: Mariel and Cuban American Gay Male Experience and Representation." In *Queer Migrations: Sexuality, US Citizenship, and Border Crossings*, edited by E. Luibhéid and L. Cantú Jr., 125–45. Minneapolis: University of Minnesota Press.

Pérez, Sonia D. 2019. "Mexican Police Detain Hundreds of Central American Migrants." Associated Press. April 22. www.apnews.com.

Perreira, Kirsta M., Katleen Mullan Harris, and Dohoon Lee. 2007. "Immigrant Youth in the Labor Market." *Work and Organizations* 34 (1): 5–34.

Pesonen, Anu-Katriina, and Katri Räikkönen. 2012. "The Lifespan Consequences of Early Life Stress." *Physiology and Behavior* 106, no. 5 (16 July): 722–27.

Petryna, Adriana. 2002. *Life Exposed: Biological Citizens after Chernobyl*. Princeton, NJ: Princeton University Press.

Pew Research Center. 2014. "More Prioritize Border Security in Immigration Debate." September 3. pewresearch.org.

Phillips, Kristine. 2019. "They Left Food and Water for Migrants in the Desert: Now They Might Go to Prison." *Washington Post*, January 20. www.washingtonpost.com.

Phillips, Susan A. 2011. "Tattoo Removal: Three Snapshots." *Visual Anthropology Review* 27 (2): 117–18.

Pierce, Jennifer L. 1995. *Gender Trials: Emotional Lives in Contemporary Law Firms*. Berkeley: University of California Press.

Pisaro Clark, Barbara. 2017. Letter to the Chairman of the Committee on Homeland Security and Governmental Affairs. Department of Health and Human Services. June 21. www.hsgac.senate.gov.

Platt, Anthony M. 2009. *The Child Savers: The Invention of Delinquency*. 40th anniversary edition. New Brunswick, NJ: Rutgers University Press.

Plyler v. Doe, 457 US 202 (1982).

Polczyk, Patrycja. 2012. "Autoethnography as an Accessible Method of Research." *Forum Oswiatowe* 2 (47): 175–82.

Polletta, Francesca. 2006. *It Was like a Fever: Storytelling in Protest and Politics*. Chicago: University of Chicago Press.

Portes, Alejandro, and Alejandro Rivas. 2011. "The Adaptation of Migrant Children." *Future of Children* 21 (1): 219–46.

Potter, Mark W. 2011. "Solidarity as Spiritual Exercise: Accompanying Migrants at the US/Mexico Border." *Political Theology* 12 (6): 830–42.

Public Law 104–208, 104th Congress, September 30, 1996.

Raff, Jeremy. 2019. "How Family Separations Brought Down a Migrant Mogul." *Atlantic*, August 16. www.theatlantic.com.

Ramirez, Hernan. 2011. "Masculinity in the Workplace: The Case of Mexican Immigrant Gardeners." *Men and Masculinities* 14 (1): 97–116.

Rana, Junaid. 2011. "The Language of Terror: Panic, Peril, Racism." In *State of White Supremacy: Racism, Governance, and the United States*, edited by M. K. Jung, J. H. Costa Vargas, and E. Bonilla-Silva, 211–28. Stanford, CA: Stanford University Press.

Ray, Ranita. 2018. *The Making of a Teenage Service Class: Poverty and Mobility in an American City*. Oakland: University of California Press.

Redfield, Peter, and Erica Bornstein. 2010. "An Introduction to the Anthropology of Humanitarianism." In *Forces of Compassion: Humanitarianism between Ethics and Politics*, edited by E. Bornstein and P. Redfield, 3–30. Santa Fe, NM: School for Advanced Research Press.

Reed-Danahay, Deborah F. 1997. *Auto/Ethnography: Rewriting the Self and the Social*. New York: Bloomsbury Academic.

Reich, Jennifer A. 2005. *Fixing Families: Parents, Power, and the Child Welfare System*. New York: Routledge.

Reid, Jason. 2012. "'My Room! Private! Keep Out! This Means You!': A Brief Overview of the Emergence of the Autonomous Teen Bedroom in Post–World War II America." *Journal of the History of Childhood and Youth* 5 (3): 419–43.

Rios, Victor. 2011. *Punished: Policing the Lives of Black and Latino Boys*. New York: NYU Press.

Rizzo, John R., Robert J. House, and Sidney I. Lirtzman. 1970. "Role Conflict and Ambiguity in Complex Organizations." *Administrative Science Quarterly* 15 (2): 150–63.

Robbins, Liz. 2018. "A Rule Is Changed for Young Immigrants, and Green Card Hopes Fade." *New York Times*, April 18. www.nytimes.com.

Roberts, David J., and Minelle Mahtani. 2010. "Neoliberalizing Race, Racing Neoliberalism: Placing 'Race' in Neoliberal Discourses." *Antipode* 42 (2): 248–57.

Roberts, Timothy A., and Sheryl A. Ryan. 2002. "Tattooing and High-Risk Behavior in Adolescents." *Pediatrics* 110: 1058–63.

Rodriguez, Naomi Glenn-Levin. 2016. "Translating 'Best Interest': Child Welfare Decisions at the US-México Border." *Political and Legal Anthropology Review* 39 (S1): 154–68.

Roethlisberger, F. J., and William J. Dickson. 1939. *Management and the Worker: An Account of a Research Program Conducted by the Western Electric Company, Hawthorne Works, Chicago.* Cambridge, MA: Harvard University Press.

Romagnoli, Amy, and Glenda Wall. 2012. "'I Know I'm a Good Mom': Young, Low-Income Mothers' Experiences with Risk Perception, Intensive Parenting Ideology, and Parenting Education Programmes." *Health, Risk & Society* 14 (3): 273–89.

Romero, Elena Vilaboa. 2006. *Caracterización de la Niñez Migrante en la Frontera Norte de México.* Tijuana, Mexico: Save the Children Suecia Corredor Bilateral.

Rosas, Gilberto. 2012. *Barrio Libre: Criminalizing States and Delinquent Refusals of the New Frontier.* Durham, NC: Duke University Press.

Rose, Joel, and Laura Smitherman. 2019. "Fear, Confusion, and Separation as Trump Administration Sends Migrants Back to Mexico." NPR (website). July 1. www.npr.org.

Rose, Nikolas. 1990. *Governing the Soul: The Shaping of the Private Self.* London: Routledge.

Rose, Nikolas, and Carlos Novas. 2005. "Biological Citizenship." In *Global Assemblages: Technology, Politics, and Ethics as Anthropological Problems*, edited by A. Ong and S. J. Collier, 439–63. Malden, MA: Blackwell.

Rosie, Anthony. 1993. "'He's a Liar, I'm Afraid': Truth and Lies in a Narrative Account." *Sociology* 27 (1): 144–52.

Ruehs, Emily. 2016. "Adventures in *El Norte*: The Identities and Immigration of Unaccompanied Youth." *Men and Masculinities* 20 (3): 364–84.

———. 2018. "Front Door, Backdoor, No Door? An Exploration of Formal and Informal Means for Recruiting Unaccompanied Immigrant Youth for Research." *SAGE Research Methods Cases.* https://www.doi.org/10.4135/9781526428011.

Rumbaut, Rubén G. 2004. "Ages, Life Stages, and Generational Cohorts: Decomposing the Immigrant First and Second Generations in the United States." *International Migration Review* 38 (3): 1160–1205.

Ruppel-Schlichting, Katharina, Sonia Human, and Oliver C. Ruppel, eds. 2013. "Climate Change and Children's Rights: An International Law Perspective." In *Climate Change: International Law and Global Governance.* Vol. 1, *Legal Responses and Global Responsibility*, 349–77. Baden-Baden, Germany: Nomos.

Salazar Parreñas, Rhacel. 2005. *Children of Global Migration: Transnational Families and Gendered Woes.* Stanford, CA: Stanford University Press.

Sanchez, Melissa. 2020. "Inside the Lives of Immigrant Teens Working Dangerous Night Shifts in Suburban Factories." ProPublica. November 19. www.propublica.org.

Scanlan, Stephen J. 2014. "'Mined' for Its Citizens? Poverty, Opportunity Structure, and Appalachian Soldier Deaths in the Iraq War." *Journal of Appalachian Studies* 20 (1): 43–67.

Schäfer, Nadine. 2012 "Finding Ways to Do Research on, with, and for Children and Young People." *Geography* 97 (3): 147–54.

Schilt, Kristen, and Laurel Westbrook. 2009. "Doing Gender, Doing Heteronormativity: 'Gender Normals,' Transgender People, and the Social Maintenance of Heterosexuality." *Gender and Society* 23 (4): 440–64.

Schmidt, Leigh Anne, and Stephanie Buechler. 2017. "'I Risk Everything Because I Have Already Lost Everything': Central American Migrants Speak Out on the Migrant Trail in Oaxaca, Mexico." *Journal of Latin American Geography* 16 (1): 139–64.

Schrock, Douglas, and Michael Schwalbe. 2009. "Men, Masculinity, and Manhood Acts." *Annual Review of Sociology* 35: 277–95.

Secure Fence Act of 2006, Pub. L. No. 109–367, H.R. 6061, 109th Cong.

Senehi, Jessica. 2002. "Constructive Storytelling: A Peace Process." *Peace and Conflict Studies* 9 (2): 41–63.

Shdaimah, Corey. 2010. "'The Law Cannot Terminate Bloodlines': Families and Child Welfare Decisions." *Children and Youth Services Review* 32: 704–10.

Silva, Andrea. 2016. "Neoliberalism Confronts Latinos: Paradigmatic Shifts in Immigration Practices." *Latino Studies* 14 (1): 59–79.

Slack, Jeremy, and Scott Whiteford. 2011. "Violence and Migration on the Arizona-Sonora Border." *Human Organization* 70 (1): 11.

Smith, Andrea. 2006. "Heteropatriarchy and the Three Pillars of White Supremacy: Rethinking Women of Color Organizing." In *Color of Violence: The INCITE! Anthology*, edited by Incite! Women of Color Against Violence, 66–73. Cambridge, MA: South End Press.

Solórzano, Daniel G., Amanda Datnow, Vicki Park, and Tara Watford. 2013. *Pathways to Postsecondary Success: Student Success; Maximizing Access for Youth in Poverty*. Los Angeles: UC/ACCORD. https://pathways.gseis.ucla.edu.

Solórzano, Daniel G., Octavio Villalpando, and Leticia Oseguera. 2005. "Educational Inequities and Latina/o Undergraduate Students in the United States: A Critical Race Analysis of Their Educational Progress." *Journal of Hispanic Higher Education* 4 (3): 272–94.

Somers, Aryah. 2010. "Voice, Agency, and Vulnerability: The Immigration of Children through Systems of Protection and Enforcement." *International Migration* 49 (5): 3–14.

Soto, Lilia. 2018. *Girlhood in the Borderlands: Mexican Teens Caught in the Crossroads of Migration*. New York: NYU Press.

Southern Poverty Law Center. 2020. "Family Separation under the Trump Administration: A Timeline." June 17. www.splcenter.org.

Speakman, Sue, and Mick Marchington. 1999. "Ambivalent Patriarchs: Shiftworkers, 'Breadwinners,' and Housework." *Work, Employment & Society* 13 (1): 83–105.

Spener, David. 2004. "Mexican Migrant-Smuggling: A Cross-Border Cottage Industry." *Journal of International Migration and Integration* 5 (3): 295–320.

Squire, Vicki. 2014. "Desert 'Trash': Posthumanism, Border Struggles, and Humanitarian Politics." *Political Geography* 39: 11–21.

Staiano, Fulvia. 2013. "Good Mothers, Bad Mothers: Transnational Mothering in the European Court of Human Rights' Case Law." *European Journal of Migration & Law* 15 (2): 155–82.

Steger, Manfred B., and Ravi K. Roy. 2010. *Neoliberalism: A Very Short Introduction*. New York: Oxford University Press.

Stephen, Lynn. 2018. "Fleeing Rural Violence: Mam Women Seeking Gendered Justice in Guatemala and the US." *Journal of Peasant Studies* 46 (2): 229–57.

Stephens, Doug. 2019. "Why I Quit My Job Carrying Out Trump's Immigration Policies." *New York Times*, November 20. www.nytimes.com.

Stewart, Emily. 2018. "The Multi-Billion-Dollar Business of Sheltering Immigrant Children, Explained." *Vox*, June 25. www.vox.com.

Still, Ashlyn, and Mica Rosenberg. 2019. "Shrinking Projections." Reuters Graphics. https://graphics.reuters.com.

Suárez-Orozco, Carola, Hee Jin Bang, and Ha Yeon Kim. 2010. "I Felt like My Heart Was Staying Behind: Psychological Implications of Family Separations and Reunifications for Immigrant Youth." *Journal of Adolescent Research* 26 (2): 222–57.

Suárez-Orozco, Carola, Marie Onaga, and Cécile de Lardemelle. 2010. "Promoting Academic Engagement among Immigrant Adolescents through School-Family-Community Collaboration." *Professional School Counseling* 14 (1): 15–26.

Suárez-Orozco, Carola, and Marcelo M. Suárez-Orozco. 2001. *Children of Immigration*. Cambridge, MA: Harvard University Press.

Suárez-Orozco, Carola, Irina L. G. Todorova, and Josephine Louis. 2002. "Making Up for Lost Time: The Experience of Separation and Reunification among Immigrant Families." *Family Process* 41 (4): 625–43.

Sutter, Megan, and Paul B. Perrin. 2016. "Discrimination, Mental Health, and Suicidal Ideation among LGBTQ People of Color." *Journal of Counseling Psychology* 63 (1): 98–105.

Swain, Jon. 2003. "How Young Schoolboys Become Somebody: The Role of the Body in the Construction of Masculinity." *British Journal of Sociology of Education* 24 (3): 299–314.

Swanson, Kate, and Rebecca Maria Torres. 2016. "Child Migration and Transnationalized Violence in Central and North America." *Journal of Latin American Geography* 15 (3): 23–48.

Sweet, Paige L. 2015. "Chronic Victims, Risky Women: Domestic Violence Advocacy and the Medicalization of Abuse." *Signs: Journal of Women in Culture and Society* 41 (1): 81–106.

Swerts, Thomas. 2015. "Gaining a Voice: Storytelling and Undocumented Youth Activism in Chicago." *Mobilization* 20 (3): 345.

Sylomovic, Susan. 2005. *The Performance of Human Rights in Morocco*. Philadelphia: University of Pennsylvania Press.

Taft, Jessica K. 2010. *Rebel Girls: Youth Activism and Social Change across the Americas*. New York: NYU Press.

———. 2020. "Hopeful, Harmless, and Heroic: Figuring the Girl Activist as Global Savior." *Girlhood Studies* 13 (2): 1–17.

Tardy, Rebecca W. 2000. "'But I Am a Good Mom': The Social Construction of Motherhood through Health-Care Conversations." *Journal of Contemporary Ethnography* 29 (4): 433–73.

Taxin, Amy. 2016. "Children's Asylum Approvals Vary by US Region." Associated Press, June 1. https://apnews.com.

Terrio, Susan J. 2015. *Whose Child Am I? Unaccompanied, Undocumented Children in US Immigration Custody*. Oakland: University of California Press.

Thomas, Mark. 2014. "Neoliberalism, Racialization, and the Regulation of Employment Standards." In *Neoliberalism and Everyday Life*, edited by Susan Braedley and Meg Luxton, 68–90. Montreal, Canada: McGill-Queen's University Press.

Thompson, Amy. 2008. *A Child Alone and without Papers: A Report on the Return and Repatriation of Unaccompanied Undocumented Children by the United States*. Austin, TX: Center for Public Policy Priorities. www.cppp.org.

Ticktin, Miriam. 2010. "From Redundancy to Recognition: Transnational Humanitarianism and the Production of Nonmoderns." In *Forces of Compassion: Humanitarianism between Ethics and Politics*, edited by E. Bornstein and P. Redfield, 174–201. Santa Fe, NM: School for Advanced Research Press.

———. 2011. *Casualties of Care: Immigration and the Politics of Humanitarianism in France*. Berkeley: University of California Press.

Todrys, Katherine Wiltenburg, and Joseph Amon. 2009. *Discrimination, Denial, and Deportation: Human Rights Abuses Affecting Migrants Living with HIV*. New York: Human Rights Watch.

Torres, Mara de los Angeles. 2004. *The Lost Apple: Operation Pedro Pan, Cuban Children in the US, and the Promise of a Better Future*. Boston, MA: Beacon Press.

TRAC Immigration. 2014. "New Data on Unaccompanied Children in Immigration Court." Report date July 15. https://trac.syr.edu.

———. 2020. "Judge-by-Judge Asylum Decisions in Immigration Courts FY 2015–2020." https://trac.syr.edu.

Trinch, Shonna L., and Susan Berk-Seligson. 2002. "Narrating in Protective Order Interviews: A Source of Interactional Trouble." *Language in Society* 31 (3): 383–418.

Trotta, Daniel. 2019. "US Says Guatemala Must Agree to Asylum Pact to Get Development Aid." Reuters, October 15. www.reuters.com.

Trump, Donald J. (@realdonaldtrump). 2017. "Departing for Long Island now. An area under siege from #MS13 gang members. We will not rest until #MS13 is eradicated. #LESM." Twitter, July 28, 9:24 a.m. https://twitter.com/realDonaldTrump/status/890971233159962624.

———. 2019a. "Four people in Nevada viciously robbed and killed by an illegal immigrant who should not have been in our Country . . ." Twitter, January 21, 3:37 p.m. https://twitter.com/realDonaldTrump/status/1087494416347074561.

———. 2019b. "Most of the MS-13 Gang members indicted & arrested in L.A. were illegal aliens, 19 of 22. They are said to have killed many people in the most brutal fashion . . ." Twitter, July 18, 8:10 a.m. https://twitter.com/realdonaldtrump/status/115187183556432691 8?lang=en.

Trump, Pence: Make America Great Again. 2016. "Immigration: Donald J. Trump's Vision." Accessed October 26, 2016. www.donaldjtrump.com.

Tucker, Christine M., Pilar Torres-Pereda, Alexandra M. Minnis, and Sergio A. Bautista-Arredondo. 2012. "Migration Decision-Making among Mexican Youth:

Individual, Family, and Community Influences." *Hispanic Journal of Behavioral Sciences* 35 (1): 61–84.

Tuhiwai Smith, Linda. 1999. *Decolonizing Methodologies: Research and Indigenous People.* New York: Zed Books.

Tushman, Michael L. 1977. "Special Boundary Roles in the Innovation Process." *Administrative Science Quarterly* 22 (4): 587–605.

Tyler, Imogen, Nick Gill, Deirdre Conlon, and Ceri Oeppen. 2014. "The Business of Child Detention: Charitable Co-option, Migrant Advocacy, and Activist Outrage." *Race & Class* 56 (1): 3–21.

Uehling, Greta Lynn. 2008. "The International Smuggling of Children: Coyotes, Snakeheads, and the Politics of Compassion." *Anthropological Quarterly* 81 (4): 833–71.

United Nations Development Programme. 2013. *Citizen Security with a Human Face: Evidence and Proposals for Latin America.* www.latinamerica.undp.org.

United Nations Educational, Scientific, and Cultural Organization. 2013–2014. *Teaching and Learning: Achieving Quality for All Honduras; Fact Sheet.* EFA Global Monitoring Report. www.unesco.org.

United Nations General Assembly. 1989. Convention on the Rights of the Child. November 20. United Nations Treaty Series 1577: 3.

United Nations High Commissioner of Refugees. 2015. *Children on the Run: Unaccompanied Children Leaving Central America and Mexico and the Need for International Protection.* Washington, DC: United Nations High Commissioner of Refugees Regional Office for the United States and the Caribbean. www.unhcrwashington.org.

United Nations World Food Programme. 2017. *Food Security and Emigration: Why People Flee and the Impact on Family Members Left Behind in El Salvador, Guatemala, and Honduras.* www.wfp.org

United States Bureau of Labor Statistics. 2017. "High School Graduates Who Work Full Time Had Median Weekly Earnings of $718 in Second Quarter." TED: Economics Daily. July 21. www.bls.gov.

United States Citizenship and Immigration Services. 2011. "Eligibility Status for SIJ." www.uscis.gov.

United States Customs and Border Protection. 2012. "Border Safety Initiative Kicks Off in El Paso, Texas." Media release. Last modified February 9, 2017. www.cbp.gov.

———. 2014. "Border Patrol History." Last modified October 5, 2018. www.cbp.gov.

———. 2016. "United States Border Patrol Southwest Family Unit Subject and Unaccompanied Alien Children Apprehensions Fiscal Year 2016." Statement by Secretary Johnson on Southwest Border Security. www.cbp.gov.

———. 2020. "US Border Patrol Southwest Border Apprehensions by Sector Fiscal Year 2020." Last modified January 4. www.cbp.gov.

———. 2021. "Nationwide Enforcement Encounters: Title 8 Enforcement Actions and Title 42 Expulsions." Last modified January 7. www.cbp.gov.

United States Department of Education. 2018. "Annual Earnings of Young Adults." National Center for Education Statistics. Last updated February 2019. https://nces.ed.gov.

United States Department of Health and Human Services. 2014. "Legal Resource Guide." Office of Refugee Resettlement. July 8. www.acf.hhs.gov.

———. 2015. "Children Entering the United States Unaccompanied." Office of Refugee Resettlement. January 30. www.acf.hhs.gov.

———. 2016. "Unaccompanied Children's Services." Office of Refugee Resettlement. www.acf.hhs.gov.

———. 2017. "Facts and Data." Office of Refugee Resettlement. Last reviewed January 8, 2020. www.acf.hhs.gov.

———. 2018. "Testimony from Steven Wagner on TVPRA and Exploited Loopholes Affecting Unaccompanied Alien Children before Committee on the Judiciary." Assistant Secretary for Legislation. Reviewed May 30. www.hhs.gov.

United States Department of Justice. 2018. "Another Defendant Pleads Guilty in Connection with Labor Trafficking of Minors at Ohio Egg Farm." US Attorney's Office, Northern District of Ohio. September 18. www.justice.gov.

United States Department of Labor. N.d. "Youth and Labor." Accessed January 25, 2021. www.dol.gov.

Varsanyi, Monica W. 2008. "Rescaling the 'Alien,' Rescaling Personhood: Neoliberalism, Immigration, and the State." *Annals of the Association of American Geographers* 98 (4): 877–96.

Vásquez, William F., and Alok K. Bohara. 2010. "Household Shocks, Child Labor, and Child Schooling: Evidence from Guatemala." *Latin American Research Review* 45 (2): 165–86.

Verma, Saunjuhi, Patricia Maloney, and Duke W. Austin. 2017. "The School to Deportation Pipeline: The Perspectives of Immigrant Students and Their Teachers on Profiling and Surveillance within the School System." *Annals of the American Academy of Political and Social Science* 673: 209–29.

Waldram, James B. 2014. "Healing History? Aboriginal Healing, Historical Trauma, and Personal Responsibility." *Transcultural Psychiatry* 51 (3): 370–86.

Walkerdine, Valerie, and Helen Lucey. 1989. *Democracy in the Kitchen: Regulating Mothers and Socialising Daughters.* London: Virago.

Walters, William. 2011. "Foucault and Frontiers: Notes on the Birth of the Humanitarian Border." In *Governmentality: Current Issues and Future Challenge,* edited by U. Bröckling, S. Krasmann, and T. Lemke, 138–64. New York: Routledge.

Warin, Jo, Yvette Solomon, Charlie Lewis, and Wendy Langford. 1999. *Fathers, Work, and Family Life.* London: Family Policy Studies Centre for Joseph Rowntree Foundation.

Waters, Tony. 1999. *Crime and Immigrant Youth.* Thousand Oaks, CA: Sage.

Way, Niobe, and Helena Stauber. 1996. "Are 'Absent Fathers' Really Absent? Urban Adolescent Girls Speak Out about Their Fathers." In *Urban Girls: Resisting Stereotypes, Creating Identities,* edited by B. J. Ross Leadbeater and N. Way, 132–48. New York: NYU Press.

Weaver, David. A., and Bruce Bimber. 2008. "Finding News Stories: A Comparison of Searches Using LexisNexis and Google News." *Journalism and Mass Communications Quarterly* 85 (3): 515–30.

Weiss, Thomas G., and Michael Barnett. 2008. "Humanitarianism: A Brief History of the Present." In *Humanitarianism in Question: Politics, Power, Ethics*, edited by M. Barnett and T. G. Weiss, 1–48. Ithaca, NY: Cornell University Press.

Weizman, Eyal. 2011. *The Least of All Possible Evils: Humanitarian Violence from Arendt to Gaza*. New York: Verso.

Wessler, Seth Freed. 2011. *Shattered Families: The Perilous Intersection of Immigration Enforcement and the Child Welfare System*. Race Forward: Center for Racial Justice Innovation. www.raceforward.org.

West, Candace, and Don H. Zimmerman. 1987. "Doing Gender." *Gender and Society* 1 (2): 125–51.

Whitaker, Julie. 2009. "Mexican Deaths in the Arizona Desert: The Culpability of Migrants, Humanitarian Workers, Governments, and Businesses." *Journal of Business Ethics* 88: 365–76.

The White House. 2017. "Remarks by President Trump to Law Enforcement Officials on MS-13." July 28. www.whitehouse.gov. Transcript available *Newsday*, July 28, 2017.

———. 2018. "Remarks by President Trump on the United States-Mexico-Canada Agreement." October 1. www.whitehouse.gov. Video version available on YouTube, October 2, 2018, https://www.youtube.com/watch?v=E4VxNdD9dUQ. Accessed April 20, 2021.

———. 2019a. "Press Briefing by USCIS Acting Director Ken Cuccinelli." August 12. www.whitehouse.gov. Transcript available at the American Presidency Project, University of California–Santa Barbara. Accessed April 20, 2021. presidency.ucsb.edu.

———. 2019b. "Remarks by President Trump on the Humanitarian Crisis on our Southern Border and the Shutdown." January 19. www.whitehouse.gov. Transcript available at Trump White House Archives. Accessed April 20, 2021. trumpwhitehouse.archives.org.

Williams, Jill M. 2015. "From Humanitarian Exceptionalism to Contingent Care: Care and Enforcement at the Humanitarian Border." *Political Geography* 47: 11–20.

———. 2016. "The Safety/Security Nexus and the Humanitarianisation of Border Enforcement." *Geographical Journal* 182 (1): 27–37.

Wilson, John Paul, Kurt Hugenberg, and Nicholas O. Rule. 2017. "Racial Bias in Judgements of Physical Size and Formidability: From Size to Threat." *Journal of Personality and Social Psychology* 11 (3): 59–80.

Wilson, Lloyd Lee. 2014. *Radical Hospitality*. Wallingford, PA: Pendle Hill.

Wilson, Tamar Diana. 2014. "Introduction: Violence against Women in Latin America." *Latin American Perspectives* 41 (1): 3–18.

Wiltfang, Gregory L., and Doug McAdam. 1991. "The Costs and Risks of Social Activism: A Study of Sanctuary Movement Activism." *Social Forces* 69 (4): 987–1010.

Wise, Raúl Delgado, and Mariana Ortega Breña. 2006. "Migration and Imperialism: The Mexican Workforce in the Context of NAFTA." *Latin American Perspectives* 33 (2): 33–45.

Wolkomir, Michelle, and Jennifer Powers. 2007. "Helping Women and Protecting the Self: The Challenge of Emotional Labor in an Abortion Clinic." *Qualitative Sociology* 30 (2): 153–69.

World Bank. 2021. "Intentional Homicides (per 100,000 people)—El Salvador." UN Office on Drugs and Crime's International Homicide Statistics Database. Accessed January 26. https://data.worldbank.org.

Yee, Vivian, and Kirk Semple. 2017. "Policy under Trump Bars Obama-Era Path to US for Central American Youths." *New York Times*, August 15. www.nytimes.com.

The Young Center for Immigrant Children's Rights. 2011. "Best Interests of the Child Visa." Last updated June 2013. www.theyoungcenter.org.

———. 2016. "History." About the Young Center. http://theyoungcenter.org.

Zelizer, Viviana A. 1994. *Pricing the Priceless Child: The Changing Social Value of Children*. Princeton, NJ: Princeton University Press.

Zietsma, Charlene, and Thomas B. Lawrence. 2010. "Institutional Work in the Transformation of an Organizational Field: The Interplay of Boundary Work and Practice Work." *Administrative Science Quarterly* 55: 189–221.

Zilberg, Elana. 2007. "Refugee Gang Youth: Zero Tolerance and the Security State in Contemporary US-Salvadoran Relations." In *Youth, Globalization, and the Law*, edited by S. Venkatesh and R. Kassimir, 61–89. Stanford, CA: Stanford University Press.

INDEX

abandonment, 69

abuse, 53, 72; child, 12, 75–76, 141–42; family, 40; by guardians, 47; human rights, 158; ORR and, 60; in relationships, 55, 146; in schools, 13; sexual, 12; trauma and, 74–75, 77

activism, 29, 188n136; meeting for, 155; radical hospitality, 144, 195n15

adolescence, 85–89

adoptions: international, 14; transracial, 14

adulthood, transition to, 22

adult school program, 96

advocate organizations, 159

age, migration and, 23–24

agency, 104; sexual, 189n18

age-out policy, 158–59

aid, for immigrant youth, 2–7; histories and logics of, 8–11

alienation, feeling of, 59

American Bar Association, 135

analysis, document, 32

Anderson, Bridget, 195n1

Andres (immigrant youth), 99–101

Angelica (immigrant youth), 37–40, 41, 54–55, 101, 163

anti-immigration, 104, 157, 176

Anzaldúa, Gloria, 6–7, 11, 187n108

Aries, Phillipe, 20

Arzú, Alvaro, 39

Ashley (social worker), 114, 142–43

assault, sexual, 130

asylum, 5–6, 78, 150; attacks on, 184n24; denial for, 163

attacks, September 11, 8

attendance, school, 85–86, 120

attorneys, 27, 71, 72–73, 77, 80–81, 113; Funding Attorneys for Indigent Removal Proceedings Act, 159; pro bono, 137, 138, 163; role strain and, 135, 138; therapist and, 139; trauma and, 151; women, 136–37; for youth, 5

Aurora (advocate), 108–9, 115–16

autoethnography, 32–33; in secret spaces, 174–75

background checks, for sponsors, 46–47

ban, research, 26

barriers: government, 169; structural, 123

bedroom sharing, 49

behavior issues, 120–21, 146

belonging, 6–7, 11

"Best Interest Visa," 159

Beth (education advocate), 96

biases: cultural, 49; gender, 135

Biden, Joe, 163

birth certificates, 48

Black children, 12

Black men, 10

Black women, 187n108

blended families, 59, 60

bodies, innocence and, 113–18

border, US-Mexico, 4, 7, 68. *See also specific topics*

border crossing, 2–3, 82

border enforcement, 8–11

borderland legends, 65–71

Border Safety Initiative (1998), 19

border security, 9–10

funding, 161

Funding Attorneys for Indigent Removal Proceedings Act, 159

gangs, 6, 43, 78, 108, 123, 126; in El Salvador, 37–38; MS-13, 103–4, 116, 192n18; ORR and, 192n7; recruitment, 71–72; tattoos and, 116–17

gang violence, 37–38, 43, 192n18

gender, 136–37, 146; behavior and, 121–22; deportation and, 10; intersection of, 23; parents and, 25

gender bias, 135

gendered violence, 70

geography, 189n138

girls, 3, 19; behavior and, 121–22; trauma and, 31

global inequality, 29–30

goal changing, 144–46

Goode, William, 134

Gordon, Linda, 13

government barriers, 169

government support, for youth, 5

Grace (attorney), 79

graduates, high school, 83–84

The Great Arizona Orphan Abduction (Gordon), 13

green card, 123

guardians, 100–101; abusive, 47; legal, 89, 120, 146

Guatemala, 2, 23, 39, 82, 83, 183n5

guilt, 69; parents and, 51–52

harassment, in school, 98

healer (curandero), 1

healing, 130

health: emotional, 127; mental, 74, 128

health insurance, 96

Heidbrink, Lauren, 175

La Hielera (Ice Box), 106

high school, 55, 88; graduates of, 83–84; socializing and, 85

history, right side of, 150–53

holistic assistance, for youth, 161–62

homelessness, 91–92, 101–2, 145

Honduras, 2, 42–44, 128, 183n5

households, precarious, 89–92

housing, 146; renting, 145

humanitarianism, 2, 130, 131; neoliberal, 16–20; politics of, 18, 19; as warfare, 19–20; women and, 18

human rights abuses, 158

human smuggling, 4, 20, 23, 41, 69–70, 160

human trafficking, 15–16, 23; red flags for, 46–47

hunger, chronic, 126

hyperfertility, stereotypes of, 23

ICE. See Immigration and Customs Enforcement

identity, 140

ideologies, 7

"Imagining a World without Borders" (Anderson), 195n1

Immigration Act of February 20, 1907, 14

Immigration and Customs Enforcement (ICE), 9

Immigration and Naturalization Service (INS), 15, 158, 177

immigration policies, 3; family-separation policy, 155, 157; "Remain in Mexico" policy, 157–58

immigration politics, 8–9, 11

immigration professionals, 132–33; role strain and, 134–40; women as, 135–36

immigration reform, 65

Immigration Reform and Control Act (1986), 8

immigration system: broken, 150–51; change of, 156

incarceration, mass, 10

independence, 40, 93, 131

indigeneity, 23

indigenous community, 39, 40

protesters, anti-immigration, 176
PTSD, 75

Q'eqchi language, 41, 67

race, 22–23
racialized child welfare, 11–16
racial profiling, 109–10
racial stereotypes, 118
racism: color-blind, 64; Trump and, 104
radical hospitality activism, 144, 195n15
raids, 10–11
rape, 130; statutory, 55
Ray, Ranita, 190n19
Reagan, Ronald, 16
Rebel Girls (Taft), 25
recruitment, gang, 71–72
"red flags," sponsor, 46–47, 49
reform, immigration, 65
refugees, Southeast Asian, 74
refugee status, 6
relationships: abusive, 146; romantic, 55,
    190n19
religious-based organizations, 13
"Remain in Mexico" policy, 157–58, 189n10
rent, housing, 145
rescue, child, 12–13
research ban, ORR, 26, 27, 172, 175–77
resilience, mentorship and, 99–102
resistance, 144–46; disappearance as,
    146–50
responsibility, personal, 122–25
reunification. *See* family reunification
Ricki (social worker), 74, 124–25, 194n47
rights, of children, 12
role strain, 134–40
romantic relationships, 55, 190n19
Rosa (reunification worker), 130–31

safety, of migrants, 41
Salma (reunification worker), 107–8, 150
Salvadoran men, 106
Samantha (attorney), 135–36

Sanctuary Movement, 144
school, 85–89, 100–101, 161, 173; abuse in,
    13; adult school program, 96; atten-
    dance in, 85–86, 120; bureaucracy in,
    89, 95–98; to deportation pipeline,
    109–10; discrimination in, 95–96, 98;
    exclusion in, 96–98; legal status and,
    95; mandate for, 94; as problem, 93–99.
    See also high school
school attendance, 85–86, 120
school culture, 141
school system, 60, 84
school-to-prison pipeline, 84
security, border, 9–10
self-concept, 140
self-regulation, 17
"separated child," 24, 152
separation: of children and parents, 13,
    152–53, 189n10; of families, 10, 92, 102,
    159–60
September 11 attacks, 8
Sessions, Jeff, 184n24
sexual abuse, 12
sexual agency, 190n18
sexual assault, 130
sexual violence, 121–22, 126
shelters, 26, 68, 119–20, 144–45; age-out
    policy for, 158–59; criminalization and,
    107–8, 195n17; detainment, 4–5, 46;
    ORR, 32, 151, 184n14; release from, 51;
    volunteer work at, 174
siblings, abandonment of, 69
SIJS. *See* Special Immigrant Juvenile
    Status
smuggling, human, 4, 20, 23, 41, 69–70,
    160
snowball sampling method, 27
social inequality, 83
socializing, high school and, 85
social media, 149, 195n12
social workers, 46, 95–96, 136, 137, 156
Southeast Asian Mental Health, 74
Southeast Asian refugees, 74

ABOUT THE AUTHOR

EMILY RUEHS-NAVARRO is Assistant Professor of Sociology at Elmhurst University, where she teaches a wide range of courses on race, gender, youth, and globalization. Her research interests include youth, migration, and humanitarianism.